# Re-imagining the Bible for Today

# Re-imagining the Bible for Today

Sigrid Coenradie, Bert Dicou and
Anna-Claar Thomasson-Rosingh

scm press

© Sigrid Coenradie, Bert Dicou and
Anna-Claar Thomasson-Rosingh, 2017

First published in 2017 by SCM Press
Editorial office
3rd Floor, Invicta House,
108–114 Golden Lane,
London EC1Y 0TG

SCM Press is an imprint of Hymns Ancient & Modern Ltd
(a registered charity)

Hymns Ancient & Modern® is a registered trademark of
Hymns Ancient & Modern Ltd
13A Hellesdon Park Road, Norwich,
Norfolk, NR6 5DR, UK

www.scmpress.co.uk

Translation: Textcase, Deventer, The Netherlands
Translation made possible by a grant from the
Vera Gottschalk-Frank Foundation

Translated quotes from Dutch language books: Authors' translation.

British Library Cataloguing in Publication data

A catalogue record for this book is available
from the British Library

978 0 334 05544 0

Printed and bound in Great Britain by
CPI Group (UK) Ltd

# Contents

# I

# Re-imagining the Bible

## SIGRID COENRADIE, BERT DICOU, ANNA-CLAAR THOMASSON-ROSINGH

## Why Read the Bible

All three authors of this book are enthusiastic about the Bible; understandably, you would say, because all three are theologians and all three are ministers. However, this is not *completely* obvious. One of them works in Salisbury, the other two in the Netherlands. What unites them is that all three share a background with a Dutch denomination that is not particularly known for its enthusiasm about the Bible: the Remonstrants. Emerged from the debate on tolerance in the seventeenth century, this denomination is really more philosophical and socio-culturally oriented than purely biblical-theological. It is the kind of group that is known to be reluctant in accepting religious views purely because they have been passed down for generations. In 2016, the Remonstrants were advertising themselves with the slogan 'Faith starts with you.' If faith starts 'with you', what is the relevance of intensively reading a book, although the source and starting point for the Christian faith for centuries, which clearly has a strong archaic character? The youngest parts of the Bible are almost 2,000 years old, the oldest nearly 3,000.

And yet ministers still try to explain the Bible to churchgoers on a weekly basis. That too, is less obvious than you might think. In many sermons and church services the Bible is read but soon forgotten. The sermon becomes a 'thought for the day' which more often refers to Facebook than to the Bible. Moreover, the question whether the Bible is still an authoritative document is also asked within the churches. In liberal corners this has been going on for a while now. A century ago, there was a minister in a village in secular and quirky West Friesland, who removed the Bible from the pulpit one Sunday morning. 'We do not need this book any longer,' was his explanation. Insights from philosophy, the general culture and, last but not least, one's own thoughts and feelings were more than enough to show believers the way (or to discover it for themselves). You can also compare it with the Quakers. For them, silence is a much more obvious way to God than reading Bible stories and hearing a preacher interpreting Bible stories.

A more concise version of the book *Re-imagining the Bible* was published in the Netherlands in 2017. The Dutch title of the book is *Weg met de Bijbel*, which means 'Away with the Bible'. The title refers to the anti-religious tendencies in the Netherlands (and perhaps also in the UK), characteristic of a society that is trying to free itself from the oppressive authority of religious institutions. Values derived from Christian faith determine less and less the values of society. The book Christians derive their values from, the Bible, is perceived by some as an obstacle in the way to achieving a freer society. The consequences are unmistakable: the number of people familiar with Bible stories is declining sharply. Schools still tell the story of David and Goliath and the birth of Jesus, but that's usually where it ends.

For a while now, there has been unrest among both 'modern believers' as well as cultural critical thinkers regarding the many wonderful stories in the Bible, including a creation in seven days and many miracle stories – healing by laying on of hands, raising people from the dead, inexplicable natural phenomena such as walking on water (Jesus) or the dry passage through the Red Sea (the Israelites, after their escape from Egypt). In addition, people thought, influenced by the insights of the Enlightenment, that the moral of biblical scriptures was not always as convincing and uplifting. What can we still benefit from this book and do we still have use for it?

While we were working on this book, a comprehensive Dutch edition of *The Jefferson Bible* was published.[1] This 'Bible' is the work of Thomas Jefferson, the third president of the United States and author of the Declaration of Independence. It is a version of the Bible that he compiled purely for himself. He completed it in 1820, but never informed anyone about it. After rediscovering the manuscript at the end of the nineteenth century, it became widely known. In 1904, 9,000 copies were printed, a considerable amount. Each new senator in Congress received a copy of the book. Incidentally, Jefferson titled his book *The Life and Morals of Jesus of Nazareth*.

The work is not *written* in the strict sense of the word, but rather cut and pasted. Jefferson bought two Bibles, so he could use the front and back side of the pages, then selected Bible passages he liked and cut them out with a knife. He disregarded the Old Testament and he despised Paul, therefore he limited himself to the four Gospels. Now he could put it nicely together into one chronologically continuous story. Inspired by the ideas of the Enlightenment, he omitted everything that to him seemed dated, secondary or lacked credibility. Miracle stories and healings were left out, but he also omitted implicit references to the divinity of Jesus and even the resurrection. What remained was a new gospel in which Jesus emerges as someone who imparts deep wisdom to the world and, in particular, an innovative system of ethics: the ethics of charity. Jesus' Sermon on the Mount was a highlight of the gospel for Jefferson. Might this be a good solution?

The authors of this book do not think so; they have a different opinion than the West Frisian minister or Thomas Jefferson. We believe that it is useful and good to take the Bible – as it is – seriously and especially to keep reading it. Or to *start* reading it. And to help others to read it. In our opinion, reading the Bible is an interesting and exciting endeavour, not only for experienced churchgoers but for everyone. It is not easy to just start reading the Bible and this book is meant as a tool. We hope this book offers ways of reading the Bible, taking the many complaints against it seriously. We want to help people read the Bible in a completely honest way and without hypocrisy. We want to open up the text, also, for people who are more sceptical about religion. Thus we offer different methods and approaches that can help the reader with personal study but also to introduce Scripture to others. We hope this book offers plenty of ideas on how we can bring the Bible to life for people who think critically.

Between all the different reading methods we research, present and adopt, there are two ways we use most: imagination and conversation. Not only do we discuss our own imagination, but also the imagination of writers, poets, film makers and artists of our time and throughout history. We enter into dialogue, not only with each other but also with others who we think can shed light on how and what we read in the Bible. It is re-imagining the Bible in conversation.

## Anna-Claar Thomasson-Rosingh

*Anna-Claar, you teach biblical studies at Sarum College, Salisbury. Some of your students will become priests or ministers in different denominations and congregations across England. Some of these churches will be liberal, others are conservative. With the students you will explore without doubt the question: Why do we read the Bible? For some it may be self-evident to read the Scriptures, for others you might have to convince them that this is worthwhile. The same will count for the readers of this book.*

Reading the Bible with fresh imagination and through different eyes is not only necessary but also very satisfying and fruitful. I agree with Sherwood (2012, p. 3): 'Our modern sense of the Bible is so limited, so closed, so pious, that it will inevitably be blasphemed against from within the Bible itself.'

This book wants to invite its readers to read anew and afresh the ancient texts of the Christian Bible. This invitation is made in the acute awareness of how strange an invitation this is; ultimately it is an invitation to step outside our own safe cultural boundaries and encounter otherness in its bewildering variety. It is an invitation to go where we do not know, to walk in the dark.[2] This invitation might be seen as dangerous, irrelevant and rather difficult.

*Surely there are already more than enough people who take the Bible rather too seriously. Would it be better for many problems and issues in this world if people would read this diverse collection of books less rather than more?*

4

Certainly homophobia, misogyny, slavery and even apartheid are being defended or have been defended with the Bible. That is not to mention many of the larger-scale evils that are immediate in our time such as climate change and ever-increasing economic inequalities. Issues that many argue convincingly find their source and lifeblood from texts like the sacred Scriptures of Christianity and Judaism. And this is only the beginning of a long list of reasons for not bothering to even open the Bible.

My invitation to read the Bible is not rooted in the conviction that the biblical texts are moral, beautiful or historically interesting. Even though some of the biblical text might be all of those things, other biblical texts are clearly neither moral nor beautiful and definitely pose more historical questions than they are answering. One thing clearly and historically undisputed is that the Bible comprises religious texts from a time when both the context and the religious institutions were so different from our context and religious institutions that they are hardly comparable. How can they ever be relevant?

My invitation to read the Bible also does not presume that this is an easy task, one which just requires literacy skills. Most people who have seriously tried to read Christian Scriptures will have had a hard time interpreting the texts. Even with internet tools and intelligent commentaries to help us on the way, many passages remain baffling. Specialist religious leaders (such as priests and ministers) who preach weekly in churches sometimes circumvent saying anything at all about the ceremonially read Scriptures. When scholars who have devoted their lives to studying the Bible are not always agreed on what they mean, how can other people stand a chance? Reading a text that was written in a time and a culture long gone: is that not impossible without specialist knowledge? I would like to invite you to join all those who do read the Christian Scriptures in spite of these difficulties and take the risk of maybe not always understanding everything.

Finally my invitation to read the Scriptures is not motivated by a wish to convert. If you want to become a believing Christian you might do well to shun some of the texts of the Bible rather than read them, since they are utterly bewildering, violent and sometimes outright offensive. Large parts are definitely 18-rated and evoke embarrassment and disgust. This book argues that, in spite of all these issues, the Bible is still worth reading, whether you count yourself a Christian or not. It aims to help you do just that in ways that take all these problems into account.

After these warnings ... four reasons to start reading the Bible:

### 1. It is delightful

The first and most important (and maybe most compelling) reason to read the Bible is that it is enjoyable. The danger, irreverence and complexity that is inherent in opening a book that many try to keep closed is in itself a thrilling experience. Looking in the forbidden cupboard and finding it filled with absolutely fascinating twists on well-worn platitudes is a delight in and of itself. Finding that this religious text is sometimes laugh-out-loud funny and meant to entertain might come as a surprise. Just as with all good comedy it also makes you think. At other times there is suspension and tension built into the text that is worthy of any modern whodunnit. The text is never outright pornographic, but even so there is plenty of interesting sexual detail to be enjoyed (excellent to re-engage teenage boys, if only we would dare). Then there is the gorgeously crafted poetry. And around the next corner you find prophets entertaining us with strange behaviour and controversial social ideas. For those of us who are into genealogies and identity-searching in lineage there are also plenty of ancestry puzzles to be done on the pages of the Christian Scriptures. For history geeks the Bible is the ultimate treasure trove, no other ancient text is so accessible. For all different tastes there is something to be found within Scripture that is just simply pleasurable. If you read for the fun of it, it is not a problem that the Bible is so diverse. The parts that you do not like you can just skip – although, if you do that, you never know what you are missing.

### 2. The Bible was and is a defining factor in our culture

Our culture in Western Europe is saturated with language, imagery and thought patterns that originate in the Scriptures. Our culture is in constant dialogue with stories, poems, images and ideas from the Scriptures. All the adaptations drive us back to the original where we get a sense of the hidden energy that drives the formation of new ideas in society. In this book, we bring out this dialogue between culture and Bible in how we structure our suggestions for reading the scriptural text anew: with associations and examples from films, books and music that resonate with the Scriptures explored. We read the Bible because it enhances the imagination and understanding of our cultural life. We read Scripture because it fertilizes our cultural imagination and makes sense of sometimes hidden structures or norms and values in society. Of course, if you read the Bible to understand our culture you will only want to read those parts that have had an influence on it, although it will be hard to decide which parts have not.

3. The Bible redefines 'the sacred'
The Bible claims to be a holy book. Even if you do not regard it as such, you cannot get away from the presence of God as an important character in most of it, nor can you get away from fellow readers who doggedly keep reading it as if it is sacred. This might be a reason not to read the book; I argue this is a reason *to* read it. If Scripture is read without censoring, it invites us to reassess what is holy and what is not. It invites us to rethink the divide between sacred and secular, also where it pertains to Scripture itself. The reading of Scripture provides us with a critical insight into the religious practices of our time. Moreover the weaving and reweaving of the sacred and the secular, of the holy and the mundane, into different patterns is a worthwhile formative experience for both believers and unbelievers. So we do not want to read Scripture because it is holy, but we do want to read Scripture because it changes our sense of what might be holy. The Bible surprises us with finding holiness in the most unlikely places. Those who like Jefferson pick out certain parts of the Bible that are deemed 'holy' and only read a selection of 'worthy' passages, miss the essence of what the Bible offers us.

4. The Bible invites questions
Our secular culture shows a (surprisingly) high regard and respect for the Bible (Sherwood, 2012). This is partly given by the 'rules' of a tolerant democracy that state you are not allowed to be rude

about another's Scriptures. It is also rooted in a sense that 'our' Judeo-Christian heritage is somehow superior to the sacred texts of others. The sense of regard and superiority are both firmly anchored in a non-reading of the text. The invitation to open this closed book and read endangers the respect we have for the text and our smug sense of superiority. The awareness of these dangers is another first sign of resonance with our motives. We do not invite you to read the Bible because we think it is superior to other Scriptures. In reading the Bible you will find out that it is not. We do not invite you to read the Bible because we think you will respect it more. When the Scriptures are opened, it might be more difficult to be respectfully tolerant because some of it is intolerable. The loss of superiority is in itself something that is worthwhile to pursue. The loss of some of the respect or tolerance might make space to become resistant and involved readers. We claim that wrestling with these texts proves to be a worthwhile formative experience. It is not so much a text to uncritically adhere to; it is more a text that helps us sharpen our critical ability. Why do I not like this? What do I really think? Which presuppositions are at play here? Who wins? Who loses out? These are questions to which the biblical text inherently invites us.

This means you do not always have to agree with what you read. Many believers assume that you have to approve of everything you encounter in the biblical text. This is not the case at all. The Bible is not a book that wants to be embraced unthinkingly. The Bible is a book that invites us to reconsider, reconsider what is holy, reconsider what is normative, and reconsider our own position. To be able to do this we have to read the entire biblical witness, not just the popular parts. In particular, the sections which are normally avoided and estrange readers provide material for a fruitful critical conversation.

*Anna-Claar, you compare the reading of the Bible with encountering a stranger...*

Yes, all these reasons to entice you to open the Scriptures: enjoyment, cultural enrichment, sacred fluidity, critical ability, all include a sense of the unexpected and of disturbance. Reading the

Bible is like meeting a stranger. The best way to meet a stranger is wholeheartedly and with compassion. There are many who (as when meeting the stranger) only want to deal with what is understandable, agreeable and shared. This is not only dangerous (if you miss, for example, the complete disillusionment of the stranger you will not be able to relate to the following violence), but also misses the point of the gift of the presence of the stranger. When the stranger becomes 'one of us' she cannot teach and challenge us any more. Whether it is *The Jefferson Bible* or a lectionary that keeps leaving out the same things: it is misguided. It is imperative that when we read the Bible we are open to all of it.

Of course, this does not mean that we agree with all of it (we do not have to become the stranger, especially not a violent stranger), or that we read all of it in the same way or with the same tools. It is evident than poetry is different from letters, that parables are different from genealogies. It is evident that the meaning or nonsense, the questions or challenges that we get from them will be very different. It is evident that from some passages the real inspiration might be the opposite of what the text claims. It also doesn't mean we do not sometimes have to make choices. It does mean we need to be aware that we are, for example, skipping that text about bashing the heads of little ones (Psalm 137.9). It also means we need patience both with ourselves and with the text.

Being wholeheartedly open to all of the Bible does not mean there are no other places where we can find what we find there. Many books, movies and music are enjoyable, enrich our cultural understanding, help us find our way around the sacred (or find God, should you wish to) and sharpen our critical ability. When we read the Bible, we do not stop engaging with these media and using them. That befits Scripture. But none of the other cultural treasures are so widely read and so ancient as the Bible. Ultimately, I believe that the Bible is the cultural expression that is most like a Celtic 'thin place'. It is the one that is easiest to use by the Spirit for our enjoyment, growth in wisdom, challenge and spiritual maturity.

# Bert Dicou

*Bert, just like Anna-Claar, you teach Bible courses at a seminary, in your case at the Arminius Institute at the VU University in Amsterdam. You train ministers who go to work with the Remonstrants. You are also a part-time Remonstrant minister. Do you recognize yourself in Anna-Claar's argument?*

Yes, I certainly recognize myself in it. To me the Bible is a fascinating but not always easily accessible religious book and many texts feel 'strange' instead of familiar. My interest in the subject of theology was actually aroused by the story of Easter, the resurrection of Jesus from the dead. Jefferson leaves this utterly incomprehensible story out of his book. But in all the Gospels, this is the finale they are working towards. For Paul, the other personality of the New Testament, the resurrection is the cornerstone in everything he writes. Moreover, it has become the religious subject of choice. Why is this? What type of book is this? I wanted to know more about it. Later I grasped the enormous wealth and diversity of the Old Testament. Just as the New Testament, it consists of a large number of different 'books', many of which have a completely unique style and philosophy. It is certainly not exceptional that they contradict each other. Many of those books have fascinating historical origins. They were not written in one go, from the first to the last page. It took decades and sometimes centuries to mould and shape them. Passages were added, modified, and probably also deleted. A book of the Bible often reflects an ongoing conversation – with itself, with the texts and beliefs of previous generations. It is wonderful that we can add our own conversation to it. As Anna-Claar also indicates, it would be pretty boring to regard the Bible as a static item, as a monument from a distant past, which should be especially respected. That respect is in place, but the Bible is not a museum piece, not an object you admiringly may look at but certainly cannot touch.

Recently I visited York Minster, an impressive old English cathedral. Daily, thousands of visitors come to admire the imposing building and all the treasures which have been collected since the Middle Ages. They are warmly welcomed. But they also see a banner with a message: 'Encounter. Experience York Minster's true significance and join us in one of our daily services'. The real significance of this building reveals itself in the encounter with tradition that is handed down here. Visitors are invited to *participate*. Part of the experience that this encounter provides is amazing – suddenly you are listening to a choir performing a perfect polyphonic hymn by Tomkins. The other part is almost boring – you are joining a tiny group of elderly people in a chapel for a short standard Eucharist. Both are part of the experience. Likewise the Bible unlocks itself to those who really want to participate.

Just as at the Minster, you don't need to be a believer to participate in it. A non-believer can surrender to the Bible just as they indulge in another book. Any reader knows that the best books are not those in which you feel perfectly at ease because the hero is so much like you and experiences only nice things. Such books tire easily. The best books are those that mislead you, that surprise you, even sometimes unpleasantly surprise you, because they make you think about aspects of yourself that you are not so happy with or embarrassed about. A good book stirs you, lets you sympathize, makes you think, annoys you, consoles you, but can also disturb you. I believe the Bible has all these characteristics.

For the reader who believes – or the reader who wonders whether they could be a believer – there is a significant plus: the knowledge that Christians do not just believe in 'God' or 'a God', but in *the God of the Bible*. In other words, the Bible is the book that gives access to knowledge about God; as the Qur'an does for Muslims, and the Upanishads do for Hindus. For believers, this is the main reason to take up the Bible. It is also the reason why I teach soon-to-be preachers to read the Bible and I read from the Bible in every service in my town of Hoorn (as do the more than 2 billion Christians in towns all over the globe). However, it is more difficult for Christians than Muslims and Hindus, because they acknowledge that all these biblical books are indeed inspired, but also written by fallible humans. Christians relativize the importance of the Bible even further by saying that God did not speak his key word in a book, but through a person: Jesus Christ. And of course, not to forget, through creation and in the liberation of his people from slavery in Egypt. But as far as the Bible tells us about it, this book is a means of communication between God and humankind. Fortunately not the only one – for why would God not continue to talk to us today? Indeed, why not also in today's cultural expressions? The Bible is an important source, a solid touchstone which has by now proven its durability.

## Sigrid Coenradie

*Sigrid, you are a minister of a congregation of two denominations: Mennonites and Remonstrants. You also have extensive experience in religious education in secondary schools. And considering you just completed a dissertation on vicarious substitution in the work of writer Shūsaku Endō, who writes about Christ figures in a Japanese context, you like to look beyond the boundaries of religion, philosophy and culture. Why do you advocate to keep honouring the Bible? And how should we do that?*

When I was still teaching philosophy at a high school, a Muslim girl approached me after class and asked: 'Madam, do you believe?' When I answered affirmatively, she said, 'But then why are the Bibles over there.' She pointed at the crates with Bibles on the ground in a corner of the classroom. In her eyes the Qur'an, and therefore the Bible, was a holy book. You are supposed to treat it with respect. Obviously, I didn't show her what her fellow students wrote and drew in those piles of Bibles.

Her response made me think about my dealings with the Bible. Like my colleagues Bert Dicou and Anna-Claar Thomasson-Rosingh, I absolutely love the Bible. I think it is a wonderful book that keeps surprising me. But do I consider it holy? My own copy is thumbed due to using it all the time; there are marked sections of text; there is water damage from carrying it around in my bicycle bag. At a training course for ministers, the teacher once put a Bible on a chair. The group of ministers was asked to take a place in the room to suit their relationship to the Bible. My first inclination was to sit on the chair with the book on my lap. To me, the Bible is primarily a tool.

The Bible is the foundation of the experience of people with God. Thus, it is not God who speaks in the Bible, but humans. It is far from clear how God is spoken about in the Bible. Sometimes he is acting and speaking front and centre; sometimes he is marginally present. Some stories only have God's absence as a theme. There is some fear, desire, hope and cursing. The Bible is a library of all kinds of literature: records, rules and stories. The stories form the core. There is a reason why they have been written in the form of a story. Not as cultural heritage, but as a story, with the intention that it would appeal to us. We have to get something out of it. They must contain truth.

It is often said that the Bible should be read metaphorically. It did not all really happen, you have to look at the symbols. I personally think that Bible stories are true. And whether they are true, does indeed matter. But 'true' to me does not mean 'true' in the sense of 'it really happened'. The philosopher Jürgen Habermas makes a threefold split which can be enlightening here. In his theory of communicative action, Habermas distinguishes constative, regulative and expressive speech acts. He states that speakers can either raise the following claims to validity, respectively: the *truth* about the objective state of affairs in reality, the *rightness* of the social relations of the communicating persons and the *truthfulness or authenticity* of the subjective intentions of those who communicate. The basis of truth is what is happening or has happened in the objective reality. For example: 'Today you have a new attractive colleague.' You can check the truth of this statement by walking to her department, to find that she is indeed attractive, and get acquainted. The basis of accuracy is the social reality, what we consider normal. When you introduce yourself to the new colleague, you shake her hand. In other cultures, correct and appropriate experiences can differ. A Muslim man does not shake his female colleague's hand; after all, perhaps she is the wife of another. And that other person needs to be respected. In the Muslim context it is not right to shake hands with a female colleague. Truthfulness is one's personal reality. It is about authenticity; can you live with yourself if you get your married colleague drunk on her first day at work and kiss her?

Applied to Bible stories: they are not true or false in the sense of 'it really happened'. You cannot step into a time machine and see if the blind man could indeed see again, if the lame walked again, or how it went with the woman who was caught in adultery, but was not stoned, because we all sometimes overstep the boundaries. Interpretations of Bible stories are right or wrong, that is, socially correct or incorrect. Statements where slaves, (lesbian) women, bisexuals, transgenders and gay men are excluded are perceived as not fitting our times. On the other hand, the ten commandments are reflected almost verbatim in the Declaration of Human Rights, thus still highly topical. But that does not mean we can read selectively. You can also interpret the story differently, in line with your own situation. Also genealogy can be surprisingly revealing, as shown by Ingeborg Löwisch (2013), whose research saw a parallel with a documentary.

In my opinion however, the truth and the value of Bible stories lies especially in the *truthfulness*. They are written with a view to a better world, aimed at people getting along better with each other. They are written with the best intentions, to comfort and encourage people. The biblical authors wanted to show: look how we have struggled with life, we found support in a relationship with God and each other. Those authors and those special people who were inspired by the stories, have lived for us and challenged us. Moses, Elijah, Jesus, but also half-hearted types like Jonah and Peter. They were an example for us. Hopefully they are also an example for you. But your situation is different, and therefore we did not write a recipe book, but a storybook. Intended as inspiration. Use it as you please.

What interests me is the relationship between theology and literature. The Bible consists largely of stories. In the New Testament, Jesus shows himself a master storyteller. Stories are ambiguous, unlike doctrines. In the last decades, theologians increasingly used modern literature in their discourses. Literature is not a picture or ornament on the truths of theology and philosophy, but it is valuable because it can create new meanings. Theology is challenged to stay in motion because meanings are never fixed.

As mentioned earlier, the Bible was not written by God, but by people. So the human experience is the starting point for living and interpreting the Bible. Therefore, this book focuses on themes such as having little (or not enough) money, conflict and reconciliation, sacrifice of something (or someone), vulnerability, dealing with the environment, and (lack of) confidence in the future. It involves basic human categories and not a theological triad such as creation, sin and redemption, sometimes followed by gratitude. There is a reason why the slogan for the Remonstrant membership recruitment action reads 'Faith starts with you'. The question is not whether you believe in miracles or believe in the afterlife, or accept a particular set of belief statements as true. The question is whether YOU find it useful. And you are the only person who can answer the question 'Is this useful to me?'

In this book we try to establish a link between our culture and the Bible. Through stories of our time, compacted in novels and films, we want to show where the biblical stories connect to our own daily lives. However, rather than one approach to the stories from a cultural, literary or spiritual perspective, we want to show the relevance of the Bible for the reader.

---

## Questions for Reflection

How do the three authors differ in their view of the Bible?

How are they similar?

Which author appeals most to you? Why is that?

How do you disagree with the authors?

---

## Ways of Reading

Throughout the centuries, the Bible has been read in very different ways: as a text to meditate upon, sentence by sentence or even word for word; as a puzzle, each text indicating a higher hidden truth (in early Christianity and the Middle Ages a very popular allegorical method of reading); as a literary work of art; as musical, sacred text (the ordinary faithful heard the text in songs, in a language they did not know and which was accessible only to the clergy); as a book on the history of humanity and even the history of the universe (this peculiar way of reading was popular in the nineteenth century, and today still lives on in the way some fundamentalist groups read the Bible); as a textbook on 'contemporary Christian morality'; as a political manifesto, either for conservation or for overthrowing the existing social order; as a collection of images and stories for depth psychology.

These ways of reading will not be considered here. We restrict ourselves to the way of reading which was the most common in the twentieth and early twenty-first centuries, in different variants: the context-oriented reading method. The main characteristic is the first question when we start the reading process: *Who* is reading this text? The text is no longer expected to produce its objective truth. Meaning arises, truth arises in the interaction between text and reader, so the reader is very relevant. This includes questions such as: from which perspective is this individual or this group reading the Bible? What is their background? What does this person or group hope and expect from reading the Bible? Depending on the answers, other aspects from the text will be highlighted. And possibly a text may even be fiercely contradicted.

We selected our own choice from a number of reading methods which are all the rage at the moment. Anna-Claar Thomasson-Rosingh discusses 'feminist reading' and 'Godly play'. Bert Dicou examines eco-biblical theology and a method for contextual Bible study developed in Brazil, among others. Sigrid Coenradie introduces 'queer reading of the Bible'.


## Contextual study: actively connecting the Bible with everyday reality

'Contextual Bible Study' is a Bible study method developed in South Africa and Brazil. The main starting point is that the Bible only comes into its own when one actively looks for connecting lines between the biblical story and the specific social context people find themselves in. This method is currently also being used in various European countries. In Scotland for example, there is an active group that uses this method in urban priority areas and prisons, but also in typical congregations. They described their work in the booklet *What is Contextual Bible Study?* (Riches, 2010).

In the Netherlands, the method is used by the Protestant organization Kerk in Actie, which deals with international cooperation. More can be found on their website (www.kerkinactie.nl) under 'Reading the Bible through other eyes'. They write:

> In church we often first read a text or story, and then we ask what that passage means to us. But what if we turn this around? We start with our reality: the context of everyday life. A reverse way of studying the Bible.

In 2015, four Dutch theologians were sent to Latin America to study the methodology more closely and to learn to work with it. Below is an interview with Sietske Blok, one of the four theologians, who was stationed at the CEBI (Ecumenical Center for Biblical Studies) in Brazil. CEBI has a large nationwide network including 80,000 trained volunteers who lead local groups. In September 2015 I asked her about her experiences. Sietske Block explained:

> In recent months I have had the opportunity to learn much about CEBI and work with them. CEBI studies the Bible with the purpose of transformation and liberation in mind. The Bible is seen as a 'medium' to talk about the important things in life and society. The Bible can offer a different perspective, can stimulate us to take action. This way of reading the Bible is called *leitura popular*, and in the Netherlands we have translated this into 'Contextual Bible Study'. My mission is to master this method of Bible study, to help each other, to think together, and to see how we might use this method in the Netherlands. Interesting work!
>
> I live in Salvador, an enormous city (3 million inhabitants!) and quite chaotic. It is a city of contrasts, like most cities in Brazil. There are favelas, poor neighbourhoods with makeshift homes, but there are also expensive and upscale condominiums with security personnel by the front door. Compared to the Netherlands, where I come from, poverty is much more visible

here. There are significantly more homeless people. On the way to my regular restaurant I invariably see people who are sleeping on the streets. Although the country has had an economic catch-up and social welfare has improved significantly under President Lula, the differences between rich and poor are still very big.

From an ecclesiastical point of view there is still a lot of intolerance in Brazil. Churches compete with each other. It is quite common for a minister to say during the sermon why that other church is wrong. It is therefore not obvious that CEBI works well as an ecumenical organization. They are proud of it. In practice, you see that the vast majority of participants are Catholic. However, Protestants are also involved.

The organization works on two levels. On the academic level their theology advocates a more open approach in dealing with the Bible and focuses especially on the political significance of the Bible. The Old Testament shows much interest in the prophets. After all, prophetic literature often involves identifying and denouncing abuse. The other side of the organization is that it is a movement at the base of society. As the term *leitura popular* suggests, they intend for people to have their say. Their motto is 'Anyone can practice theology.'

According to CEBI, mainstream academic biblical science has arrived at a dead end, and that is because it has lost the connection with ordinary life. They see opportunities to rediscover well-known, but also lesser-known biblical stories by connecting them with experiences. Their meetings always start by sharing experiences. Recently I was in Ubatã for a weekend retreat, and they were talking about young people and the Bible. So first we discussed what it is like to be 'a young person' in this region.

Then the conversation is looked at more closely by studying the Bible story. The facilitator, a theologically trained group leader, will then provide a broader perspective and will ask exciting questions to continue the conversation.

The meetings start and end in prayer, which is also intended to strengthen the community feeling of this way of study. For CEBI it is important to form a community together that can actually change things. That community feeling is also essential for the study process as such. From a 'we' point of view one will ask different questions and different things will be noted as compared to when you read on your own.

From what I have seen so far, it works, but there are some obstacles as well. A table in a lovely little space is more suitable for in-depth group discussions than a corner somewhere in a noisy church hall, but for financial reasons, such church halls are often used.

From a methodical point of view and in terms of reaching its objective, this movement is under development. You could say that the *leitura popular* emerged from the liberation theology of the 1960s. Back then, strong emphasis was also placed on a theology with room for ordinary life. The theologians of that time showed that the Bible mentions remarkably often the marginalized people of society, poverty and wealth and the injustice of a skewed distribution. The church had to choose the side of the oppressed, and be a place of resistance. People thought of it as very dualistic, and highly political: it was a socialist movement.

Although older theologians involved in contextual study often still think along these lines, the method develops in a more pluralistic direction. For the younger generation, the situation is more complex than that of oppressed versus oppressor. And although liberation and transformation remain core concepts, it is no longer obvious that it should necessarily be the socialist way.

This development also means that the method may be of interest to the European situation. In Scotland, many are already using the contextual Bible study method and the method is translated to the situation at hand. I certainly see possibilities for it in our part of the world, although most people here (including church members) do not feel as connected to the Bible as the average Brazilian. It seems to me a fruitful method to keep making the connection between faith and daily life. Both at a personal level – the discovery of similarities between your own life and something from the Bible – as on a social level. Although it is not so easy to determine what prophetic speech of the church should consist of, it is certainly true that the biblical message is about the whole of society and this can not be ignored. As we ask ourselves before starting a theme: 'What can be said at the moment about life in Northeast Brazil?', we can also ask ourselves this question in a Dutch context (or in any other context).

Anyway, I think it worthwhile to make an effort to boost Bible study in the Netherlands. The largest Protestant church in the country is currently focusing on promoting faith conversation. However, this often proves uncomfortable. Conversations based on the method that I am learning here would make more sense: linking everyday experiences with biblical stories. In the end, the Bible is the source of choice for our faith. It also offers a different, more participatory and community-building way of celebrating. I tried it once in the Netherlands. We started with a simple liturgical moment (lighting a candle, joint prayers), and sharing experiences and Bible study were immediately framed differently. People thought it was a bit uncomfortable, but appreciated this method afterwards.

One of the goals of my mission (and that of my colleagues) is that we want to create a follow-up at the end of the two-year mission. We are thinking of a manual or training sessions for churches, a conference, or setting up a network of interested people who want to get to work.

## Questions for Reflection

What is the context in which you might be reading the Bible?

How does that influence what you read?

How would you critique this method?

## Feminist reading of the Bible

If we start studying the Bible with the question, 'who is doing the study?', then about 50 per cent of the time the answer will be, 'a woman'. In our time and in our world the equality between men and women is naturally assumed. This is very different in the Bible. The Bible is written at a time when a woman was considered part of her husband's or father's property, it is historically read in a situation that is politically, economically and academically dominated by men. The voice and perspective of women in the Bible is hard to find. How can modern girls and women still read these texts? Sometimes women are simply ignored; often there is profound discrimination or even abuse.

To investigate these questions, I spoke with Lesley Edwards, a colleague I met because we both are interested in feminist theology. Lesley Edwards is a freelance celebrant (www.choiceceremonies. co.uk/). She has a violent history: abused by her grandfather, abandoned by her husband, mistreated in the church. She finds the strength to walk her own way in Scripture. I asked her how she can still read the Bible, which is so dominated by men.

## Interview with Lesley Edwards

*Lesley, as a woman and as a feminist, why do you read the Bible?*

I read the Bible to draw comfort in difficult times. I greatly enjoy studying the texts to find out what is behind them. I want to understand them. I started reading the Bible when I was eight, first with diaries from the 'Scripture Union'. When I was eleven I started asking questions.

I was raised by my grandfather who preached hell and damnation: a great speaker and a paedophile. He was my 'god'. So you see, there were a lot of tough times. Through the entire trauma I kept turning to the Bible. And I have never been disappointed, there is always comfort, liberation and all of life is embraced.

Of course the text is patriarchal, it was written in patriarchal times. You should look at the text as a tool, you can use it to build something or break something down. I am very aware of both. But context is everything. When you begin to understand the original context, when you ask questions and when you discuss it and argue with it, something beautiful always comes out of it. Sometimes you need to dig deep. It is very important to feel free not to agree with the Bible; this is part of a feminist way of reading.

What I repeatedly 'hear' in Scripture is that God is on my side. Just as I question everything, the Bible questions everything too. And when you try to dig up sense and meaning, you will encounter inspiration and hope.

I'm very inspired by the lesbian theologian Isabel Carter Heyward and her book *The Redemption of God* (1982). In that book, Carter Heyward explores the concepts of 'power' and 'reciprocity' in the Gospel of Mark. Reading the Bible in a feminist way undermines the patriarchal tendencies of the Bible.

I read as if I were a child, I try to pull the text towards me, I bring it to my own level. If we do good things in the world then we *are* Christ. Therefore, Christ is both male and female. If you ask enough questions and if you go looking for the text, you will find that the Bible is very inspiring for women. If you search long enough you will always find liberation. That gives me strength to stand up for others.

## Feminists and the Bible

Not all feminists are so positive about the possibility of still reading the Bible. Along with throwing out patriarchal and paternalistic religion, many also discarded patriarchal religious texts.

Take Mary Daly for example. In her book *Beyond God the Father* (1973) there is no room for a reformation and critically rereading of the Bible. The language is too masculine and too dangerous. She suggests that we need to speak of a 'Goddess'. For someone like Daphne Hampson, the Bible is part of an irreversible oppressive religion. In her book *After Christianity* (1997) she argues that women cannot be Christians and that the Bible as a source of spirituality disappears completely from view. It is a shame that we are losing these most critical voices when we do reopen the Bible.

Fortunately, there have been many women who did want to reread, read differently and read between the lines. During the first feminist wave that began just after 1870 and focused mainly on the legal rights of women, such as voting rights, Elizabeth Cady Stanton wrote *The Woman's Bible* (1895–98).[3] She comments on selected texts. Her explanation is still very readable and can be found on the internet. Yet it was not until the second wave of feminism, which began in the 1960s, that feminist theology really began to develop. In this development we see a growth of feminist ways of reading the Bible, both direct interpretations of texts by and for women (exegesis) as well as a more philosophical explanation of the ways in which we can read the biblical texts (hermeneutics). For example, in her book *In Memory of Her* (1984) Elisabeth Schussler-Fiorenza stimulates a feminist hermeneutics.

Feminist theologians point out that, although the Bible has much more masculine than feminine images and stories, we do find maternal characteristics for God in the Bible. In Isaiah 66.13 we read: 'As a mother comforts her child, so will I comfort you', and in Job 38 we read about the womb of God. In Deuteronomy 32.18, the Lord 'gave birth' to the people. The wisdom of God is personified as Lady Wisdom (Prov. 9) and the Spirit of God in the Old Testament is often grammatically feminine. Not everybody thinks this is helpful for women but it does mean God is not only spoken of in male terms.[4] The book *Searching for the Holy Spirit* (Thomasson-Rosingh, 2015) explores the role of the female Spirit both in Scripture and in theology.

Although women play a much less important role in Scripture than men, still, they are not entirely absent, and it is interesting and exciting to look up these women and give them a voice. We hear of Hagar and Dinah, Rahab and Ruth, Deborah and Hannah, not to forget the Marys from the New Testament of course, or Junias, the female apostle whom Paul greets in Romans 16. Who was she? A good example of someone who listens to the voices of women in Scripture in a wonderful way is Phyllis Trible. In her *Texts of Terror* (1984) we see the stories through the eyes of the female protagonist.[5]

There are also many female readers who, like Lesley Edwards, read in the tradition of liberation theology. They believe that time and time again the Bible stands up for the small, the poor and the oppressed and the common thread that runs through the entire Scripture is one of liberation. For feminist readers this will be interpreted as liberation from patriarchal oppression. Thus, the entire Bible is transformed into a feminist manifesto. The voice of liberation theology is often strongest in the voices of women who are not from the wealthy Western hemisphere. Kwok Pui-lan, for example, approaches the Bible as a Chinese feminist in *Discovering the Bible in the Non-Biblical World* (2003). There are many different feminist commentaries, some in one volume for the whole Bible, see for example, Schottroff, Wacker and Rumscheidt (2012), and Newsom, Ringe and Lapsley, eds (2012).

Other commentaries come in series like the Feminist Companion of Bloomsbury[6] and the Wisdom Commentary.[7] Examples of those series are Bourland Huizenga's commentary on *1-2 Timothy, Titus* (2016) and Levine and Robbins (eds) *A Feminist Companion to the New Testament Apocrypha* (2006).

Books which focus on feminist interpretation include: Schussler Fiorenza, *Wisdom Ways: Introducing Feminist Biblical Interpretation* (2001) and Trible and Russell (eds), *Hagar, Sarah, and Their Children: Jewish, Christian, and Muslim Perspectives* (2006).

---

### Questions for Reflection

How can men and women profit from feminist insight in the Bible?

How can we read a book (like the Bible) that has in this area different values from many of us?

What are the dangers of this way of reading the Bible?

---

## It is not what it seems. Queer reading of the Bible

At a small symposium on religion and sexual diversity one of the participants was handing out pink cards with the text *What did Jesus say about homosexuality?* On unfolding the card it turned out to be completely blank on the inside. Blank. Nada. Jesus says nothing about homosexuality. But of course homosexuality was present in the time of Jesus as well. Sexual diversity is timeless. The card suggests that the reader probably thinks that the Bible speaks disapprovingly about homosexuality. But is that actually the case? Would Jesus, whose life was marked by standing up for – and doing justice to – those who are excluded by others, not defend homosexuals? And maybe he was a homosexual himself, who knows?

We studied the Bible the queer way during three evening sessions at Het Penninckshuis, a religious community in the Dutch city of Deventer. Just as women in feminist theology and the poor in liberation theology, we can study the Bible from a specific LGBTI point of view. We then read Bible stories from the perspective of sexual diversity. This provides surprising insights, which are just as important for heterosexuals, because it can expose the domination and hierarchy in sexual relationships. As an example, we could think of the idea in the New Testament that the Church is the bride of Christ. This image confirms the ideal of a monogamous, heterosexual marriage as the only form of sexual desire. A queer reading of this biblical metaphor asks questions, such as the exclusive masculinity of Christ, or by pointing to the fact that the Church is a community of people who are diverse in terms of gender and sexuality, among others. This method of reading challenges the hetero-normativity.

The local newspaper ran advertisements for these evening sessions. The first night, there were participants from the local advocacy group for gays and lesbians (COC), congregants with sexually diverse families, and curious people, both parishioners and outsiders. After a short introduction we read the story of Emmaus. It is the Easter story of Luke (Luke 24.13–35). Two men are walking to the village of Emmaus. Nothing special about that. What is interesting is where they come from. They come from Jerusalem, where Jesus had been crucified as a criminal. They are talking about what happened. The dream of the future of these men lies in tatters. Then a stranger joins them, he walks alongside them for a while and they tell him their story. When it gets dark, the men insist that the stranger (Jesus) stays with them. Jesus accepts the invitation and they share bread and wine. Only then do the two men recognize Jesus.

From a queer perspective, a number of things stand out in the story: the relationship between these men who do not belong to the inner circle of the disciples of Jesus, but who hold a central role in the Gospel of Luke. Cleopas and the man without a name are called 'friends'. Perhaps they were lovers? Jesus walks with them on purpose; in the wrong direction. They invite him to spend the night with them. After he leaves, they realize what they are feeling for him: 'Were not our hearts burning within us?' It is obvious that they are fascinated by Jesus. It could just be that not only the words but also the man himself was appealing to them.

On the second night, coincidentally 8 March, International Women's Day, we looked at a story about women. In the Bible, women are often anonymous, as are the women in Mark 5: a 12-year-old girl and a woman who had been bleeding for 12 years. In Jewish tradition blood means uncleanliness. That means that the bleeding woman has no social life and is excluded from the community. She comes up behind Jesus and tries to touch Jesus' clothes. But he turns around and asks who touched him. An outstanding question, because in the crowd around him it would be almost impossible that he not be touched constantly, similar to a cyclist during the Tour de France. Jesus calls the woman forward and literally places her in the middle of the crowd. Visible in the middle of the community. Remarkably, the touch of the woman does stop her bleeding. A person feels recognized and loved when touched. Rowan Williams (1996) states that the body can be a source of joy when it is received, accepted and cared for by another. One of the participants with a strict orthodox background told how his parents were advised to pray for healing of his homosexuality and that he was accepted as a human being, but not as a homosexual: he was allowed to be homosexual, but not practise it. He experienced the queer point of view as liberating: by lovingly touching each other your existence is confirmed.

During the final session a participant chose his own text to discuss. There is no 'Jew or Greek, slave nor free man, male or female – you are all one in Christ Jesus.' A text from Paul's letter to the Galatians (3.28). We soon agreed: in Jesus' movement women were assigned an important role. And even now women generally perform most of the work in the church and church life. Your identity is not determined by your nationality, social status or because you feel like a man or a woman, or both. What is materially important in your life may not be identified. Maybe you can shape it yourself in solidarity with one another within the religious community?

The conversations will be continued. Next to a queer reading of biblical texts, we want to master the Bible through an open and broad way of study. Therefore, we also engage in the questioning of our own position, interests and concerns. Through which glasses do we read the Bible? And what does a fresh look at the Bible offer us?[8]

---

## Questions for Reflection

How does difference (in sexuality, but also in gender, ethnicity and culture) enhance our understanding of the Bible?

What could you learn from queer readings?

Do you experience resistance against some of the readings that have been proposed? How will you respond to that resistance?

---

## Ecotheology and the Bible

Ecotheology is a form of theology which has increased in popularity in recent decades. Not many people seemed to be concerned with caring for the environment in the past. But since the 1980s and 1990s environmental concerns have become an issue that is widely perceived as one of the most important issues of our time. The destruction of natural areas and large-scale pollution of the oceans, the increasingly visible effects of global warming due to $CO_2$ emissions, not only raise practical political questions, but also raise more fundamental ones. Is there also something in the origins of our culture and our religion which causes this attitude? If so, is it not urgently required that we re-examine our origins and develop a theology that allows for a different attitude? That 'different attitude' will be determined by how we are experiencing our existence as human beings – as part of the cosmos and the earth's ecosystem.

Gradually and in increasingly broader circles people become

aware of what one might call a 'post-Darwin/post-Einstein' consciousness: the realization that to the depths of their DNA profile
the species of 'humans' is linked to the rest of the living beings and
the realization that life itself is a beautiful, but also very small,
part of the history of an unimaginably vast universe the workings
of which we barely understand.

## *The* Earth Bible *Project*

Many an ecotheology approaches these issues on a philosophical-
theological level, but even the field of biblical research contributes
to it. The so-called *Earth Bible Project* propagated and developed
a new method of reading the Bible. The basic principle is that
the Bible is questioned critically on the ecological implications of
texts which feature nature (prose and poetry).

As in other postmodern, contextual approaches, the perspective
of the 'underlying other' is chosen. What clear or hidden mechan-
isms are visible in biblical texts that deprive the other person from
their space? How can the text be deconstructed so that this is
made clear, and the other regains their space? In short, the *Earth
Bible Project* is aimed at giving *Earth* (with a capital letter) and the
plant and animal kingdoms their rightful place back. Well-known
and lesser-known biblical texts are examined from the questions,
'Where can the voice of Earth be heard in the text?', or 'How can
that voice be made more audible by reading the relevant text from
Earth's point of view?' On the one hand, the postmodern principle of 'suspicion' is important – which interests are being swept
under the carpet in this text? – and on the other, the principle of
the 'other' which is made to speak.

The starting point is a number of ecojustice principles. On their
website (www.webofcreation.org/earth-bible) we read:

The project explores text and tradition from the perspective
of Earth, employing a set of ecojustice principles developed in
consultation with ecologists, suspecting that the text and/or its
interpreters may be anthropocentric and not geocentric, but
searching to retrieve alternate traditions that hear the voice of
Earth and value Earth as more than a human instrument.

and

> Ecojustice principles are used as guidelines as they ask questions
> of the text: Does a given text value or de-value Earth? Is the voice
> of Earth heard or suppressed? Are humans portrayed as 'rulers'
> over Earth or kin with Earth? Does Earth suffer unjustly?

The project was originally developed at the University of Adelaide
(Australia). Later, biblical scholars from other parts of the world
became involved. It was introduced in a first collection, *Read-
ings from the Perspective of Earth* (Habel, 2000). Then came four
books in the Earth Bible series focusing on the 'Earth Story' in
Genesis (Habel and Wurst, 2000), Wisdom Literature (Habel and
Wurst, 2001), the Psalms and the Prophets (Habel 2001) and the
New Testament (Balabanski and Habel, 2002).

A good example of this alternative and often very creative
approach is the article by William Urbrock from the Psalms/
Prophets bundle, 'The Earth Song in Psalms 90–92' (Urbrock
2001). In what he calls a 'terracentric reading', he imagines that
the *Earth* is the 'you' in Psalm 91 who is promised God's protection and he interprets the psalm from that perspective.

For example:

> A thousand may fall at your side,
> ten thousand at your right hand,
> but it will not come near you. (Ps. 91.7)

Many living things have become extinct, from dinosaurs to species
threatened with extinction today, but the earth itself will survive
this. Those who 'do evil' and 'are punished' in the next verse, are
perhaps, ourselves, humanity – at least insofar as we do not want
to face the ecological damage we cause today and refuse to change
our lifestyle.

We will be speaking with one of the theologians who were
involved in the project and contributed to the Earth Bible bundles
in a later chapter.

The researchers from the Earth Bible Project were not the first
ones to find that the new ecological consciousness cast a fresh
light on what is being said in the Bible about the role of humans

on earth. Anne Primavesi is a well-known name. In 1991 she published a book *From Apocalypse to Genesis: Ecology, Feminism and Christianity*. It was the first in a series of books she wrote on ecology and religion. The title of the first book takes the normal reading order of the Bible and turns it around: the apocalypse, the subject of the book of Revelation, now comes first and Genesis, the first book of the Bible, comes last. With this reversal she wants to give shape to a new, optimistic religious view of our relationship with nature. From an ecological viewpoint, she says, there is every reason to speak of an apocalyptic mood. The mass extinction of species, climate change and global environmental pollution have led to a dramatic deterioration in the condition of our planet, and it will only get worse. But a new orientation of the creation stories in Genesis, now explicitly seen from an ecological perspective, can give a positive impulse to a more constructive way of dealing with nature. In her book, she designs a new biblical–ecological paradigm. She sees this contribution as 'a theological act of faith in the future' (p. 3).[9]

A more recent book in which biblical material is mapped out in this way is Richard Bauckham's *Bible and Ecology. Rediscovering the Community of Creation* (2010), an adaptation of the *Sarum Theological Lectures* which he held in Salisbury Cathedral in 2006. In 2008, Harper Bibles published the *Green Bible*. It is the New Revised Standard Version of the Bible that focuses on ecological issues.

Not only are all texts on nature highlighted in green, the edition is also made of recycled paper, namely old Bibles. In addition, the *Green Bible* also contains articles on ecology and religion, and profiles of famous people for whom reading the Bible offers a stimulus for a green lifestyle.

---

### Questions for Reflection

In what contexts is a 'green' reading of the Bible appropriate?

How can this method surprise you with fresh interpretations?

Which of these three methods: feminist, queer and green do you prefer? Why?

---

## Play with the text (Godly Play)

Besides women, LGBTI and eco-activists there are many other groups and individuals that read the Bible. One last group I would like to mention here is children. They might not read the text themselves but even so the text is presented to them in a variety of ways. How does age affect the way we read the Bible? There is one specific method of presenting the Bible to children that has inspired some of the chapters in this book. This method stands out from all the Children's Bibles and Bible stories because it has questions at its heart; it is called 'Godly Play'. The questions are playful rather than serious and the name of the method acknowledges that play is a child's way of study or work. Revd Dr Jerome Berryman, theologian and educator, based this curriculum of religious education on the ideas of Sofia Cavaletti and Maria Montessori. Godly Play is introduced on its website with the following words:

- Godly Play is a creative, imaginative approach to Christian formation and spiritual guidance.
- Godly Play has a Montessori foundation with 40+ years of research and practice.
- Godly Play values process, openness, discovery, community and relationships.
- Godly Play models the worship life, stories, symbols and rituals of Christian congregations.
- Godly Play allows practitioners to make relevant and personal theological meaning.
- Godly Play nurtures participants to larger dimensions of belief and faith through wondering and play.[10]

For our purposes it is especially the creative and imaginative approach to Christian stories and the values of openness and discovery and the goal of trying to find within those stories relevant meaning and a larger dimension of faith, that are inspiring.

What is relevant about the Godly Play way of reading the Bible, in this book on reading the Bible afresh, is that it is done with a deep respect for the text and that it asks interesting questions. Typical basic Godly Play questions include:

1. I wonder which part of the story you like best?
2. I wonder which part of the story is the most important?
3. I wonder which part of the story you like the least?
4. I wonder if there's a part of the story we could leave out and still have all of the story?
5. I wonder which part of the story is most about you? / I wonder where you are in the story?

Of these questions especially 1 and 5 seem relevant to me. Question 4 I would like to formulate rather differently: 'Why are these things in Scripture?' What does it mean that this part of the story that seems uncomfortable, irrelevant or unimportant is included in Scripture? Other questions that are suitable to ask after sharing Scripture are:

1. What is your reaction to this story?
2. What questions would you like to ask about the story?
3. I wonder what in the story makes you feel uncomfortable.

In Godly Play specific questions may be added for specific stories, for example, Genesis 6. 'I wonder what it felt like for Noah and his family to be shut inside the ark for so long?' Or John 10: 'I wonder who the sheep could really be?'[11]

It belongs to the values of the method that everyone's thoughts and contributions are equally valued and valid, and must be treated as such. Therefore the interpretation in community becomes important. You do not read and interpret on your own; you listen as a community to the Bible and you respond together to the stories of the Bible.

As a method of introducing children to Bible stories Godly Play also has disadvantages. You need expensive materials, trained leaders and a designated space to do it. As an inspiration for biblical study Godly Play is amazing. Certain aspects of the ideas of Berryman and Godly Play are translatable to the reading of the Bible in many different contexts, including academic contexts. I am aware that within Godly Play it is especially the experience of God and spirituality that is important rather than the opening-up of the Bible. Interestingly it seems that opening up the Bible becomes a side effect of seeking a spiritual experience. It is this side effect that is of interest. It seems to be borne out by the values (such as openness and community), the attitude (of respect) and the questions (see above). These make Godly Play into a sound and unique interpretative approach to the biblical text that could enhance and enrich other approaches, including those of scholars.

Especially fruitful for biblical studies is the open and wondering approach to the text. For example, the question, 'What could be left out?' undermines a possessive and prejudiced hold on the text that can dominate in churchy (or ecclesial) readings which think the text *must* be read in a certain way and *must* mean a certain thing. This question also begs the follow-up question which is, 'What could be added?' This is the question that the arts have been answering for centuries and which give us a multilayered impact history of rather more than just the biblical text.

With this reflection, we have firmly left Godly Play behind but used its ideas in trying to find reinvigorated ways of reading the Bible.[12]

---

### Questions for Reflection

Is Godly Play a form of contextual study or not? How is it different from all the other methods we have discussed?

What questions would you like to ask after reading a biblical text?

Are there questions that are inappropriate to ask? Which questions are those?

---

## Notes

1 *The Jefferson Bible*, translation and introduction by Sadije Bunjaku and Thomas Heij (2016). English copy at http://uuhouston.org/files/The_Jefferson_Bible.pdf or www.angelfire.com/co/JeffersonBible/

2 Reference to the title of a book by Barbara Brown Taylor (2014).

3 www.sacred-texts.com/wmn/wb/ accessed 20 December 2016.

4 www.jhsonline.org/cocoon/JHS/a066.html accessed 20 December 2016.

5 www.religion-online.org/showarticle.asp?title=1281, accessed 20 December 2016.

6 www.bloomsbury.com/us/series/feminist-companion-to-the-bible-second-series/, accessed 20 December 2016.

7  www.wisdomcommentary.org/, accessed 20 December 2016.

8  For more on this way of reading, see *The Queer Bible Commentary*, edited by Deryn Guest, Robert Goss and Mona West, SCM Press, 2006.

9  Another theologian who stands for such a paradigm shift is Sallie McFague, author of a series of books about a biblically founded advocacy of religious-environmental awareness. She uses the image of 'the body of God' for nature. More about her vision in Chapter 4, The Planet.

10  www.godlyplayfoundation.org/starting-a-godly-play-program/ accessed 10 July 2016.

11  From: http://southwell.anglican.org/wp-content/uploads/2014/02/Quick-Guide-Godly-Play-and-Reflective-Storytelling.pdf accessed 10 June 2016.

12  If you want to know more about Godly Play there is a Complete Godly Play Guide in 8 parts and some other books by John Berryman: Berryman, Jerome, 1995, *Godly Play: An Imaginative Approach to Religious Education*, Minneapolis: Augsburg Books; Berryman, Jerome, 2009, *Teaching Godly Play: How to Mentor the Spiritual Development of Children*, Denver: Morehouse Education Resources.

# Topics

After this more general, reflective part of the book, in the following chapters we will discuss in detail where we started out: reading the Bible! We selected a number of topics which in our opinion connect subjects that receive much attention in the Bible on the one hand and resonate with major social issues of our time on the other. These topics are:

- Sacrifice: the sacrifice of yourself and/or others for the greater good. In our world we find this currently in an extreme form: suicide bombings and other forms of terrorism.
- Vulnerability: this includes, for example, current interest in elderly care.
- The planet: here we look at biblical views of nature and today's ecological problems. The climate crisis invites us to link this to how we think about the future.
- Economy: this includes thinking about the distribution of resources, debt and the possibility of a new beginning. Linked to these ideas is also guilt and forgiveness.

A striking text from stories, poetry or prophetic literature from the Bible is always the starting point. Then we look at the comparison of patterns and images in recent cultural expressions.

# 2

# Sacrifice

## Introduction

ANNA-CLAAR THOMASSON-ROSINGH

Sacrifice might seem a strange subject in a book that tries to relate the Bible to current areas of interest. Is sacrifice an area of current interest? A quick look at MTV shows that sacrifice is not only something of ancient times and neither is it always religious. Looking at a 'heroes mashup' from recent movies (www.mtv.com/news/2815193/movie-heroes-mashup/) all the stories are about sacrifice. Of course many of these stories are set in a context of war and are about comradeship and the sacrifice soldiers make in war; in these clips they often offer their own life. It is not only in film but also in the remembering of our history that we honour those soldiers who gave their life for our freedom. There might also be other contexts of sacrifice that we recognize, for example when a boy who saves his brother, but is himself drowned in the act, makes the newspaper headlines.

All these examples might still feel a world away from most people's lives; but we might add that there is a daily sacrifice of living together. There are the sacrifices people offer for the sake of their children or the sacrifices they bring to care for elderly family members. The sacrifices people make for their career or the career of a spouse. The sacrifices that are necessary to follow a passion, to become good at sport or music. The early mornings needed for birdwatching, or the lack of food needed to fit into the wedding dress.

In recent times the world has been shaken by suicide bombers. Onlookers wonder whether this is sacrifice or despair. The newspapers always speak of terrorists, understandably demonizing perpetrators. But the real motivations behind the destruction often remain vague; an organization claiming responsibility for the sake of publicity. While the true causes of the act are not always clear-cut: can it be real passion for the cause and a willingness to give all, or is it just mental health problems and an unbalanced mind? It seems as if the lure of heroism in giving yourself so totally to a movement is huge, especially for young people seeking for meaning.

Sacrifice also plays a major role in the Bible and in Christianity. It is one of the interpretations of Jesus' death that he gave himself as a sacrifice. This interpretation is especially strong in the letter to the Hebrews, but is not the only interpretation of Jesus' death.

I wonder whether a look at some of the biblical texts about sacrifice can help us to make sense both of the daily humdrum of giving and receiving but also of the passionate forces that are willing to give even unto death?

# The Forbidden Sacrifice

ANNA-CLAAR THOMASSON-ROSINGH

## What to sacrifice and what not to sacrifice

The book of Leviticus is about how to and what to sacrifice in the religion of old Israel. In a certain way, it seems the most out-of-date book in the Bible. Since the destruction of the Jewish temple in AD 70 in Jerusalem no sacrifice has been offered in this way. What is striking is not only what (animal or grain, oil or frankincense) you sacrifice in what circumstance but also what you are under no circumstance allowed to sacrifice. In this religious view there are not only sacrifices you have to make: '… you shall bring a female goat without blemish as your offering, for the sin that you have committed' (Lev. 4.28). There are sacrifices you are not allowed to make, even animals that are 'unclean' which might even make you unclean when you touch them: 'Every animal that has divided hoofs but it is not cloven-footed or does not chew the cud is unclean for you' (Lev. 11.26).

If looked at from the animal's point of view, being 'unclean' is about the best protection you can get. The whole set of rules on how to deal with dead animals and what is 'clean' and what is 'unclean' could in modern parlance be translated into ecological laws of nature preservation. Important for the reflections in this chapter is the idea that not everything is suitable for sacrifice. There are things you are not allowed to offer. The most note-worthy of the sacrifices that you are not allowed to make are children. Under no condition are you allowed to sacrifice your children. This is repeated again and again in various different strands of biblical literature but we also find it in Leviticus: 'You shall not give any of your offspring to sacrifice them to Molech' (Lev. 18.21). There is a discussion about what 'Molech' might mean. It could be the name of a certain god; it could also denote the practice of child-sacrifice itself. In either case it is clear through-out the Bible that you do not sacrifice your children.

Slightly at odds with this clear command is the idea that the firstborn belongs to God: 'the firstborn of your sons you shall give to me' (Ex. 22.29). Not an idea we find in Leviticus but again an idea that does pervade different kinds of biblical literature. The firstborn belongs to God as a sign and a memory of the deliverance from Egypt when the firstborn males of all Egyptians and their animals were killed. The question that immediately surfaces is whether that awful bloody exit from Egypt was like a sacrifice. It could also just be a punishment for the evil Egyptians or collateral damage in war. The last option is more palatable but makes the link with the sacrifice of the first fruit more tenuous. The narrative is ambiguous and a lot less squeamish than modern sensibilities.

Israelites had to offer their firstborn but were not allowed to offer their offspring. So then there are the rules about how this can be done. How can the firstborn belong to God but not be killed at the same time? This is called redemption and there are different stories and laws around how to deal with it. The firstborn are redeemed by the Levites (a full clan that is especially consecrated for God and duty in the Temple as a substitute for the firstborn Num. 3.11–13) or by money (Num. 18.15–18) or probably by both. Although these rules are not in Leviticus we do find them in Numbers, the other book that is also written by priests.

There are some notable stories about the sacrificing or otherwise of children. The most haunting and by far the most discussed is the story where Abraham tries to sacrifice his son. The binding of Isaac, or the *akedah* as it is called in Jewish circles, is the most mysterious and ambiguous tale about sacrifice and therefore helps us ponder sacrifice very effectively.

## Abraham and his son: the unlikely beginning

The story has the most unlikely of beginnings:

> After these things God tested Abraham ... He said, 'Take your son, your only son Isaac, whom you love, and go to the land of Moriah, and offer him there as a burnt-offering on one of the mountains that I shall show you'. (Gen. 22.1–2)

And against all the odds Abraham gets on to do it. This does not fit. It does not fit the story of Abraham with the promise of blessing, land and offspring. It does not fit his haggling with God over Sodom and Gomorrah. It does not sit well with having just lost his other son in the previous chapter. It also does not fit the story of God. Although so far the image is somewhat capricious what with Adam and Eve, Cain and Abel, the great flood and the tower of Babel. It does not fit with the story of God as it unfolds and the strong repeated curse on sacrificing children. It does not fit with Isaac either; he is not Abraham's only son and his name means laughter: not the kind of name for someone with an early demise. The absence of Sarah, Isaac's mother, Abraham's wife, is also very unfitting. Her role in the conception and birth of Isaac has been central and suddenly she has disappeared from the story. Goodman (2013, p. 5) writes about this beginning: 'I was stunned. It was not at all what I had anticipated ... And what could I do? I was just a reader who thought the story had come out wrong.' Of course many concur with Goodman: the story *has* come out wrong. And this is not the only story that has come out wrong! Why keep reading these stories if they are clearly wrong?

My own first reaction to the start of this story is: Abraham must have misunderstood God. How can it otherwise be? Of course I laugh at my own certainty of knowing both Abraham and God better than the ancient writer and/or editor that let this story be. Is this the moment I have to take leave and decide that after all this is not about a god I would want to have anything to do with? Or are the questions the story raises too important to ignore? Is reading these narratives about learning to ask questions rather than about getting to know answers? Like in Godly Play, the story is an invitation to wonder. The story is there to remind the reader of the questions she needs to ask in her own life, questions she might otherwise not think of.

Why do people think up gods that would want to test them? What do people test themselves with? What did God in the story test anyway? If it was loyalty, how can you be loyal to a god that asks for your child? If it was faith, what did Abraham believe about God that he would want to sacrifice his son for it? If it was obedience, to whom or to what should one be obedient? Clearly the God of Genesis 22 was not yet omniscient, why otherwise test Abraham? An omniscient god knows the outcome of the test. Why do people test anyway? What kind of things are tested and for what purpose? Surely if a sacrifice is offered it is for some purpose? What was the purpose of this sacrifice?

The other barrage of questions that comes with the opening of this story is: If Abraham did misunderstand God, do I not do the same? Which voices convince me of the sacrifices that are needed in my life? And what or who do I sacrifice to? Is it economic laws that are to be followed and need obedience? Or is it the laws of a healthy lifestyle? Is compassion a good motive for sacrifice or is it ambition that is the voice that tests us to put all else (including children) aside? Linking in with the topic 'Economy' in this book, what sacrifices are being made for a 'healthy economy'? Who pays the price? Why them?

Reading against the immediate grain of the story, maybe the test that God gives Abraham in the story is a test of fatherly love and protection of his son. Maybe God wanted Abraham to contest God's command. Maybe God was disappointed that Abraham immediately did as asked. Or asking the same question on a different level: What does the writer of the story want his readers to think? Are the readers meant to say, 'Oh, no, no, no, don't do that, Abraham!' Or are the readers meant to piously revere Abraham for his extraordinary obedience? The fact that this is not immediately clear captures our attention at a deeper level. There is a freedom of response that is unexpected and gives the reader a greater responsibility. This is not a tale with only one possible meaning. This is not a story that captures the reader and convinces the reader against the reader's better judgement. This is a tale that gives the responsibility for meaning back to the reader: as in a mirror different readers will find different images and different meanings.

## To the place that God will show him

The story continues; once again Abraham travels to a place that God shows him. This happened in chapter 12 before, now it happens again. Three days they travel: Abraham, Isaac and two 'young men'. Three days to ponder God's word. Three days to change his mind. These three days reverberate down the corridors of history and biblical story. They echo in the story of Jonah and they echo in the story of Jesus. Both Jonah and Jesus have three days being dead. Abraham has three days to deal with death. Only after three days Abraham starts speaking. It is the first thing he says since the 'Here I am' of verse 1. He did not even respond to God with 'Yes' or 'OK'. Now after three days he speaks with the young men that have come along: 'Stay here with the donkey; the boy and I will go over there; we will worship, and then we will come back to you' (Gen. 22.5).

All the time I have been wondering, how has Abraham explained this expedition to people? Does Sarah know he is gone? Is there nobody that thinks what is going on is a bit odd? Is there not a community of people that are responsible to keep Isaac safe from the religious madness of his father? All the questions communities over the world are asking when one of their young ones turns to fanatical and terrorist religion. How can this be prevented?

The text remains odd. So sparse with words, it allows Abraham to say, 'we will come back to you'. As a reader I thought that one of them would not be coming back. Why does Abraham say this if it is in the story so untrue? Has Abraham now also become a liar? Does the god who asks him to sacrifice his son allow him to lie? Or do we have a marker here from the ancient writer or redactor that Abraham is on the wrong path? Is this the moment when the reader is asked not to sympathize with Abraham any longer? Is this the clear sign that he has taken the wrong turn? If one cannot be truthful and transparent about worship, something must be wrong. And what is there to see in the mirror? What sacrifices have I lied about? How often have I said: 'Oh, it is nothing'? How often does a sacrifice go unnoticed by the community? Is it still called a sacrifice if it is done in secret? Are not the legitimate sacrifices that one is asked to make (as in Leviticus in the Temple) sacrifices that are made in public? Which sacrifices have I made hidden from view? Was that a good thing or a bad thing? What about the right hand not knowing what the left hand is giving (Matt. 6.3)?

On the other hand Abraham is right in what he says, although he cannot know it at this point in the story. Maybe this makes Abraham a prophet rather than a liar. Maybe it is Abraham's longing that speaks. Does the reader hear in Abraham's 'we will come back' his resistance to God's command? Is it the defiance of a faithful believer who knows that whatever is offered to God will be received back manyfold (Mark 10.29–30)? Can Abraham himself even after three days not believe what is going to happen? These questions have still not lost their currency. The question remains whether sacrifice is like sowing. The seed is given up in the hope of a plentiful harvest. The purpose of the sacrifice is receiving back more than has been given. In love this might work. What goes around comes around. The real loss of what is to be sacrificed is not anticipated. In war sons might be sent to a battlefield in the expectation that they will return in one piece. How honest is a sacrifice like this?

## We've got the wood, but where is the lamb?

The story continues. The image drawn is heartbreaking. Abraham carrying the fire and the knife and Isaac carrying the wood:

So the two of them walked on together. Isaac said to his father Abraham: 'The fire and the wood are here, but where is the lamb for a burnt-offering?' Abraham said: 'God himself will provide the lamb for a burnt-offering, my son.' So the two of them walked on together. (Gen. 22.7–8)

The intimacy that is implied by the repeated 'the two of them walked together' is palpable. In this intimacy Isaac finally dares to ask the crucial question: 'Where is the lamb?' Again inadvertently Abraham tells the truth. A truth he does not know, although of course Isaac was the son given by God. In that sense God has provided Isaac as he later provides a ram. It is here that Isaac's role becomes pressing. Who is he? What is his part in this tale? What does Isaac know? What does he suspect? Are there stories of child-sacrifice around in his culture? Is it something that children know might happen to them? Is it an honour? In the biblical narrative these are the first ever words that Isaac utters. The story so far has only told of his birth and his playing with Ishmael. And now he asks this question. What thoughts does it hide? What voice does he use? Are Abraham and Isaac close? How heavy is the silence between them? Is it a relationship between a perpetrator and a victim? Goodman (2013, p. 5) writes that he is just 'a son like Isaac, who had to try to make sense of and peace with a difficult father'. Is that what Isaac is doing?

Of course, these questions hang partly on the issue of Isaac's age. He is old enough to carry the wood, no younger than eight or nine, I would say, but possibly older. The fact that his father lets him carry the wood might indicate that he is stronger than his father. Josephus thinks that Isaac is 25 (Goodman, p. 40). Rabbis who link this scene at Moriah with Sarah's death in chapter 23 say that Isaac is 37 (Goodman, p. 89). These traditions do not prevent interpretations both in art and otherwise to see Isaac still as the innocent, wide-eyed, small boy, who really doesn't know.

Often, though, those sacrificed in the rituals of others do know or at least have a suspicion. How many people today suspect they are being sacrificed for a greater good (a higher god)? What is the response? With whom do I walk? Do I ever wonder whether I am somebody else's sacrifice? How do I react? Am I a willing victim or not? The story is completely open. The reader can make of it what is wanted or needed. Except for the inevitable relationship described between Abraham and Isaac. Do not underestimate how much a common sacrifice binds people together. Even if there is disagreement over what is sacrificed and who pays the price. Still 'walking together' happens against expectation. At the point of sacrifice the togetherness is then ripped apart: 'He bound his son Isaac, and laid him on the altar, on top of the wood. Then Abraham reached out his hand and took the knife to slaughter his son' (Gen. 22.9–10).

The story needs a silence here: a moment's pause. Can one ever sacrifice another human being? Does not every human person already belong so totally and unconditionally to God that trying to sacrifice them is the ultimate blasphemy? Do parents own children in this way that they can give them away? Who would really sacrifice a son? Or is this common among all humanity? Are children sacrificed on the altars of their parent's ambitions, dreams and expectations? Are employees sacrificed on the altars of the survival needs of the business? Are troublemakers sacrificed to keep the equilibrium of the status quo? Are the vulnerable sacrificed for the aggrandizement of the powerful?

## (Not) the end

But this is not the end, it is a new beginning: 'Abraham, Abraham', this time it is not 'God' calling but 'the angel of the Lord'. Abraham answers for the third time in the story with, 'Here am I.' The first time was when God tested him in verse 1; the second time was in response to Isaac in verse 7 and now: 'Here am I.' 'Do not lay your hand on the boy or do anything to him; for now I know that you fear God, since you have not withheld your son, your only son, from me' (Gen. 22.12). Why go all this way? Why fear God? John knows that the perfect love drives out fear (1 John 4.18) but the fear of the Lord (Ps. 19.9) is still a main theme throughout the Bible. Is it out of that fear that we sacrifice? Is sacrifice often based on fear? Is that what drives the young suicide bombers? Is that what drives sacrifices which people in the modern world make?

The God of Abraham, Isaac and Jacob is also called the 'fear of Isaac' (Gen. 31.42). Does that refer to this passage?

This story is the binding of Isaac rather than the sacrifice of Isaac. Abraham was so convinced that he needed to sacrifice Isaac, but he did not. When big decisions about big sacrifices are made it is important that there is openness for a substitute. Even if people think this really needs to happen then at the eleventh hour there might be a different solution. There might be a substitute. Abraham finds a 'ram caught in a thicket by his horns' which he sacrifices instead of his son. 'So Abraham called that place "the Lord will provide"; as it is said to this day, "On the mount of the Lord it shall be provided"' (Gen. 22.14). All's well that ends well. A sigh of relief is heaved. Alas this is not the end of an eventful journey of questions about sacrifice. It seems somebody else wanted to say something else about it again. And the angel calls a second time to repeat the promise of offspring and blessing to Abraham. For me this is a real disappointment. The story was finished in verse 14. Why add anything? This promise of God to Abraham that we also find in chapters 12, 15 and 17 was God's initiative. Now it almost has become God's response to Abraham's obedience rather than the other way around. God in his choice of Abraham suddenly has a reason to choose Abraham. Maybe it is easier to understand God now, but it is such a shame to link God's choice with human endeavour. Even so, it hammers home the lesson that Jesus picks up generations later, that it is only in giving up that one can receive (Matt. 10.39). Abraham has given Isaac away: totally. The last verse of our story makes this clearer: 'Abraham returned to his young men … and Abraham lived at Beer-Sheba' (Gen. 22.19). Isaac is not mentioned again. He does not come down with his father. The next thing that happens in the story is that Sarah dies, but again Isaac is not mentioned. Isaac's own story starts in chapter 24 when a wife is found for him who comforts him after his mother's death. The break between Abraham and Isaac seems complete. The only conversation they ever have on the pages of the Bible is in this story of sacrifice.

## Interpretations

Goodman (2013, p. 5) writes that he is 'a father, another difficult father, who had to figure out' what biblical stories he 'wanted to try to pass on to my sons'. This raises the question whether this story is a story to treasure and to pass on. Clearly I think it is, otherwise I would not have written about it. I think Goodman also wants to pass it on. He writes 260 pages about the story of Abraham and Isaac and the forbidden sacrifice. The story does not only afford us innumerable questions about what sacrifice is and how people go about it and what it might mean in our own lives, ultimately it shows that real sacrifice is not about destruction but about 'letting go'. Sacrifice might be about the altar on which each parent is asked to set their children free. It might also be the altar on which each person can set themselves free. The manner and amount of things that will have to go will be different in each context and time. The joy, freedom, satisfaction and real contentment that comes with letting go will be the same.

But this is just one interpretation among many. Lippman Bodoff (2005, p. 28) argues that the story of Abraham is about finding out who God really is. Can he be trusted? According to Bodoff Abraham in Genesis 22 never intended to actually sacrifice his son, and he trusted that God had no intention that he would do so. A just and righteous God would never ask such a sacrifice in the first place. Abraham's prayer during that stop on their way to the mountain was intended to persuade God to intervene. Dalferth (2010, p. 87) goes a bit further and suggests that Abraham's apparent complicity in the sacrifice was actually his way of testing God. Abraham had previously, in Genesis 18, pleaded with God to save lives in Sodom and Gomorrah. By silently complying with God's instructions to sacrifice Isaac, Abraham was challenging God to behave in line with his vows, as a preserver of life. This God then duly does with the giving of the ram.[1]

Arndt, for example, in her reading of this story is especially busy with the 'other'. The 'other' who becomes an ethical imperative: an opportunity to do good. She writes:

... the text has changed me, given me new ways of being in the world. I find myself asking who is the incomprehensible 'other' in my life, and am I attending to her (him, it) with rigor and sensitivity? Am I relating to her as someone existing prior to my own ideas about her and stretching beyond my grasp? Do I grant her a claim on my own life? Do I recognise her 'authority'? (2011, p. 189)

She goes on to notice that both Isaac and the biblical text itself can be seen as 'others':

Suggestive analogies have been drawn between the other and Isaac, and the other and the text itself. An interesting possibility emerges in connecting these two 'others', connecting the status of the beloved son, Isaac, with the status of the biblical text. Loving it, favouring it, recognizing it as 'sacred' (a text loved by us and belonging to God) carries with it the willingness to 'sacrifice' it, 'humiliate' it. Subjecting it to our methods and critical perspectives is the counterpart of allowing the text to emerge in our world with its own value and power. These approaches are our means of travelling to the place that God will show, are our means of performing actions necessary to be in relationship to God and others; they are our donkey, our servants, our knife. (2011, p. 190)

Arndt explains that biblical scholarship and critical theory provide the perspective and language for the contemporary reader to respond to the call of the Akedah: 'Here I am.' But whether this is a call to sacrifice or not to sacrifice remains as ambiguous as in any reading of this story.

---

### Questions for Reflection

What is the role of sacrifice in your context?

How does the story of Abraham and Isaac illuminate sacrificial giving?

What are you not allowed to sacrifice?

---

# Sacrificial redundancy, an interview

## ANNA-CLAAR THOMASSON-ROSINGH

'Peter', a colleague and good friend was made redundant a few years ago. To my surprise he spoke of his redundancy in terms of sacrifice. I asked him if he would be willing to unpack this further in the context of this book.[2]

*Peter, you were made redundant a few years ago. Can you tell us briefly what happened?*

I was working in ministry for two different institutions who had pooled together to employ me: a school and a church. This meant I had two line managers. In the school the leadership and my line management changed, which triggered different developments. In the church I had had for some time grave concerns about the management of human resources and I had voiced some of that concern. In this second institution they clearly wanted to get rid of me.

What followed was a process of review and redundancy. The review was a scam because they reviewed a job that was neither on paper nor in practice a job that I was ever asked to do. The redundancy process was then started by lies and the two institutions pointing to each other as the source of the problem.

*Why do you use the language of sacrifice when you speak of this situation?*

At the time I was really hurt very much by the whole process (both of review and redundancy). I was not a participant in any way in either process and could not make any choices. It was done to me. In ministry people often speak of the sacrifices they have to bring to be able to minister to others. I was losing so much that was not my sacrifice, but somebody else sacrificing me. I was sacrificed so that the lies and the collusion would not come to light.

The church felt it was a mistake to work together with the school. They wanted to come out of that collaboration but maintain the relationship. It had to look as if my post was not

49

functioning well. It was hard for the leadership to explain to the congregation and PCC what was going on. Lies were spread, so people thought the school had pulled out. I had to be sacrificed so that the leadership could save face and maintain certain other relationships. I was sent into the desert for the folly of the decision to collaborate with a school. It was not my life that was sacrificed but it was my work and my vocation.

Because of my prophetic voice different facets of dysfunction of the ministry within the church were beginning to come to light. The leadership could not handle this and slayed the prophet.

*Do you think the language of sacrifice is helpful?*

Church leaders talking of sacrificial giving in ministry can use this language to cover up malpractice in human resource management. What I mean is that the talk of sacrifice allows the church to be less than careful with its workers because they must be willing to make sacrifices to go into ministry. I think we need to be very careful that we do not ask unsuitable sacrifices of each other. That does not only count within the church but also in families and other relationships.

When you are vulnerable and at the mercy of others you should be protected rather than sacrificed. It seems as difficult today (both in society and in personal relationships) not to sacrifice the vulnerable as it was in the days when child sacrifice was a possibility.

## 'He died for our sins'

### SIGRID COENRADIE

During the funeral of Marion's mother her two brothers made a speech in which they thanked her profusely for what she had done for her mother. Their mother became increasingly confused in the last two years of her life. She reacted badly to home care, and Marion had arranged for her mother to come and live in a nursing home in her village. Once there, it seemed her mother could not get used to the new living arrangement. Marion discussed the situation with her husband and they agreed that her mother would spend the last bit of her life in their home. After moving in with her daughter, the mother revived and so she spent nearly two years in Marion's care. Marion quickly became exhausted and gave up her job to care for her mother. Her daughter Sylvia, who always got good grades in school, reproached her that she spent so much time with grandmother. In her graduation year Sylvia received so many bad grades that they didn't know whether she would pass. Marion's relationship with her husband Frank also suffered from the care Marion gave her demented, ill mother.

Yet Marion did not hesitate one moment to take her mother into her home, quit her job and care for her mother until the end, even though towards the end it was almost impossible. During her speech at the cremation ceremony, Marion asked her daughter and husband for forgiveness because she spent so much time with her mother. 'It was harder than I thought,' she said, 'I know my family suffered under it, but I'm glad I was able to do this for my mother.'

Sacrifice sounds a bit old-fashioned. A century ago, it was still quite common for the eldest daughter of a family to renounce marriage in order to care for her elderly parents. Or the daughter of a family would not continue going to school, while her brothers would go to high school. Or a child went to the mission or the monastery, so the rest of the family had more financial elbow room. These are examples of a bygone age. However, Marion's example shows how topical sacrifice is and how far-reaching and dire it can be when someone takes on the care of another. Many informal care-givers hover on the verge of burnout.

This example raises a number of questions. Why is it that we are willing (whether temporarily or not) to sacrifice for someone or something – sports, for example? Why is it that women are generally more willing to undergo such sacrifices? How far does self-sacrifice reach? And, in the context of this book, which example does the sacrifice of Jesus in the New Testament represent? What is the point of it today?

Sacrifice has been emphasized as the very core of the Christian religion. Jesus was thought to have died for our sins. Various Bible texts establish a link between the death of Jesus and the forgiveness of God. For example, Romans 4.25: '[Jesus] who was handed over to death for our trespasses and was raised [by God] for our justification.'

That link has been worked out differently in the course of time: from a theological point of view with an emphasis on reconciliation, from a sociological point of view with the focus on the scapegoat mechanism and from a philosophical point of view with the emphasis on substitution. These approaches are outlined below. Sacrifice in the New Testament is a loaded concept, reminiscent of violence and martyrdom, and suicide terrorism. That is one of the reasons why it is not undisputed. Criticism comes from feminist and gender theology. But also in the hallways of liberal theology there have been objections against the idea of Jesus' death as being a sacrifice. That objection from the liberal angle especially concerns the degree of autonomy of humans. When Jesus dies instead of the people, who actually deserve to die because of their wickedness, what does that say about the freedom of man? And when Jesus dies for the people, what flexibility do people have in their relationship with God? And what does it say about God? The remarks on the sacrifice of Jesus from these different points of view are also discussed below. The reader is invited to take their own position. To conclude, alternative perspectives from literary, musical and cinematographic points of view are put forward.

## 1. Atonement on the cross

The evangelists each provide a different perspective on the life and death of Jesus, but they have in common that they make every effort to show that Jesus was not a criminal when he was crucified by the Romans. They want to demonstrate that his death had a deeper meaning. The idea was that the death of Jesus makes up for what went wrong earlier, from the beginning of time.

The history of humanity has bright beginnings. When God created Adam and Eve, they were perfect in every way and truly lived in paradise, the Garden of Eden (Gen. 2.15). God created humans in his image, meaning that the people had the freedom to take decisions and make choices. There is only one prohibition:

And the Lord God commanded the man, 'You may freely eat of every tree of the garden; but of the tree of the knowledge of good and evil you shall not eat, for in the day that you eat of it you shall die.' (Gen. 2.16–17)

It is very clear that Adam and Eve want to develop, to acquire knowledge and discernment. It is to be expected that they succumb to the temptations of the serpent in Genesis 3. The fatal bite from the apple is seen as the first mistake committed by humankind, and as a result all people – because of the bad nature we apparently inherited from Adam – will not only die a physical death, but also a spiritual one. And if the cards are stacked against you, this death is eternal.

No less than the fate of humankind is therefore at stake. But God is merciful and forgiving. Because of the sacrifice of Jesus, God brings about the resurrection. For this reason Jesus is called the second Adam. Unlike the first Adam, Jesus is obedient and innocent. The association with an innocent lamb being sacrificed is explicitly made by the evangelist John and the apostle Paul. Deliverance happens through the shedding of Jesus' blood. Hebrews 9.22 emphasizes that there was no other way to forgive the trespasses of the people: 'Indeed, under the law almost everything is purified with blood, and without the shedding of blood there is no forgiveness of sins.' Here reference is made to the Law of Moses (Ex. 20.2–17). That law gave people a way to be considered as 'sinless' or 'righteous' in God's eyes by offering animals for the forgiveness of evil caused by people to each other and, through each other, to God. But these sacrifices were only temporary and imperfect compared to the perfect sacrifice of Jesus, which was made once and for all at the cross according to the letter to the Hebrews (Heb. 10.10).

When you read the letters of Paul, the life of Jesus seems almost less important than his death. According to Paul, this is the reason why Jesus lived and especially why he died: to be the ultimate and final sacrifice, the perfect sacrifice for our sins (Col. 1.22; 1 Peter 1.19). If Jesus died for us, then what should people do? According to Paul, the role of humanity is especially faith in the sense of trust (fides), but even that type of faith should be granted to humans.

Through our faith in Christ's blood shed for our sins, we receive eternal life.

> But God, who is rich in mercy, out of the great love with which he loved us even when we were dead through our trespasses, made us alive together with Christ – by grace you have been saved – and raised us up with him and seated us with him in the heavenly places in Christ Jesus, so that in the ages to come he might show the immeasurable riches of his grace in kindness towards us in Christ Jesus. For by grace you have been saved through faith, and this is not your own doing; it is the gift of God – not the result of works, so that no one may boast. For we are what he has made us, created in Christ Jesus for good works, which God prepared beforehand to be our way of life. (Eph. 2.4–9)

## 2. Sacrificial animal

The image of Jesus as the ultimate sacrificial animal (John the evangelist sees Jesus as an innocent lamb that is led to the slaughter table) was interpreted by René Girard (1986) as an example of the scapegoat mechanism. Girard addresses the role of the victim. He explains the death of Jesus as if he were a scapegoat against whom the aggression of the crowd is unloaded, and as such is sacrificed as a substitute. Like a goat, loaded with the sins of all others, sent into the desert, Jesus carries the sins of the world on his shoulders. We also encounter this image in the Bible.

It is to be noted that in the Gospels it is Jesus' accusers who affirm the reconciling value of his death. 'It is expedient that one man should die for the sake of the people,' says the high priest. And Luke 23.12 contains this curious note after Pilate and Herod had shuttled Jesus between them: 'That same day Herod and Pilate became friends with each other; before this they had been enemies.' In this view, Jesus' persecutors intended his death to bring peace; it offers a way to avoid an outbreak of violence between Romans and Israelites, between Jews and other Jews. Jesus' death is intended to reconcile the warring parties. In this rationale, Jesus functions as the lightning rod. Girard emphasizes that Jesus put an end to the scapegoat mechanism by dying. In his view Jesus' death puts an end to sacrifice, for the crucifixion revealed the nature of sacrifice. According to Girard the gospel, then, is not ultimately about the exchange of victims, but about ending the bloodshed.

### 3. Scapegoat and substitution

Girard's interpretation is one that concerns society. A more individualistic interpretation is that of substitution. The sacrifice can be seen as vicarious suffering, where Jesus takes the place of sinful humans. Substitution is the central theme in the philosophy of Jewish philosopher Emmanuel Levinas. To Levinas, vicarious substitution and responsibility for the other are equal terms. In encountering the other I am, as it were, captured by his gaze. There is no escape. You cannot ignore the gaze of the other and neither can you transfer the responsibility to a third party. The impossibility to refuse responsibility renders substitution to a sphere beyond ethics, into religion. Dorothee Sölle emphasizes that it is about *substitution*, not replacement. Unlike replacement, substitution does not decrease one's own responsibility. Her vision meets the objection (see below) that the person whose place is taken has no personal involvement.

The role of people is here: to open up to the gaze of that one fellow person who appeals to you. Note that no one can decide this for you. Responsibility is thus, contrary to what one would suspect from a first reading of Levinas, linked to freedom. If there is a lack of freedom then the sacrifice becomes a dogma.

### Objections

This brings us to the objections to Christian sacrificial theology. Even with a more individual approach to the cross as substitution, there are objections from both the feminist and the liberal side.

## 1. Feminist criticism regarding sacrifice

From a feminist angle criticism came regarding the sacrifice of Jesus as a model for women. The self-sacrificial death of Jesus has been criticized as 'cosmic child abuse' by feminist theologians (for example, Rita Brock) or, in comparison to the sacrifice of shedding Jesus' blood, as 'birth done better'. In this criticism, God the father seems to be the agent who sacrifices his beloved son, instead of Jesus as the agent who gives his life for his pupils. Some feminist theologians avoid the subject, preferring to focus on God as mother (for example, the Goddess Movement).

Feminist criticism also refers to suffering especially. The sacrifice can be seen as vicarious suffering. The problem is that it is only a small step to glorification of suffering. Obedience and suffering are propagated in reference to Jesus' sacrifice. Combined with the order to follow, this could have a disastrous effect on women. However, sharing the suffering with Jesus can also have a meaningful positive impact, for women too. One example is the legend of the Lamed-waf, the 36 righteous ones. According to this ancient Jewish legend the world falls on 36 righteous ones, who carry the suffering of the world, in order to keep the misery from the people within bounds. They are indistinguishable from ordinary mortals, and often they don't know themselves they are a righteous one. But if there would only be one of the Lamed-waf missing, then 'the suffering might even poison the heart of the smallest children, and humanity would die out crying'. The fate of the 36 righteous is therefore: to suffer vicariously for the people. In the opera by Poulenc, based on Bernanos' *Dialogues des Carmelites*, the protagonist is a vicarious, suffering woman. Throughout the story, the young nun, Sister Blanche, is afraid to die and actually also afraid to live. She leaves the convent out of fear. At the close of the story, however, she freely joins her fellow sisters, who are beheaded at the guillotine. Voluntariness is essential here.

On the other hand the suffering of Jesus may also be experienced as support. In *My Bright Abyss: Meditation of a Modern Believer* the American poet Christian Wiman writes:

I don't know what it means to say that Christ 'died for my sins' (who wants that? who invented that perverse calculus?), but I do understand – or intuit, rather – the notion of God not above or beyond or immune to human suffering, but in the very midst of it, intimately with us in our sorrow, our sense of abandonment, our hellish astonishment at finding ourselves utterly alone, utterly helpless. (2013, p. 134)

What people need most in a hopeless situation is someone who is there for them, listens to them and sits beside them.

## 2. Liberal theologians

For many liberals atonement is an indigestible theological construction. It may have worked for many centuries, but nowadays it is more obstructive than helpful. The central point of the criticism is the lack of a person's individual contribution.

A liberal objection is the lack of input from people regarding the sacrifice of Jesus. A poem by the Dutch poet J. B. Charles (1987, p. 200) is, precisely at this point, pretty cynical about the sacrifice of Jesus:

Oh God, what are we rascals,
oh Jesus, see us weep together
and be ashamed.
Just keep hanging there. Amen.

Another, related point is the uniqueness of Jesus' sacrifice. This is aptly reflected in the poetry of the Dutch poet Tjitske Jansen (2007, p. 29):

There was the teacher who asked which of us would have agreed to die in Jesus' place. I put up my hand. I could see myself. On the grassy slope beside the Barnevelds stream. On a big wooden cross. I did not think about the pain. I did think about the fact that after three days I would rise up from the dead and that I would be a hero then. Raising my hand was not the right answer. The right answer was that Jesus was the only one who would want that, who would be able to do that, who would do such a thing for mankind.

Jansen's poem raises a number of questions: how can the sacrifice of one person, Jesus, save the rest of humanity? And is Jesus' sacrifice unique? Is Jesus the only one in the world, in history, who can be a substitute for another? What about the Polish priest Maximilian Kolbe? From May 1941 Kolbe was in the Nazi concentration camp in Auschwitz. After an alleged escape attempt by a prisoner in Kolbe's barrack, ten men were sentenced to death by starvation in a bunker. Kolbe offered himself as a substitute for a father of two children. 'Take me,' Kolbe said, 'I'm single.' And what about the American teacher Victoria Soto who hid her children in an abandoned room during an attack in 2011 and told the shooter that they were on the other side of the school, and was shot instead?[3] And the countless nameless heroes who sacrifice part of their lives to care for someone else? Does that not count, because the only sacrifice is the self-sacrifice of Jesus? Where are the people, where are we in the story? And do we really need Jesus' sacrifice on our behalf? Where is our own responsibility?

## The sacrifice of Jesus in the Gospels

What image do the stories in the New Testament reflect regarding Jesus' sacrifice? Let's take a look at how the Gospels end. Right away we have a problem, as all four end differently. In Mark's Gospel, the oldest story, a mysterious man awaits the women at the empty tomb. He tells them Jesus can be found in Galilee. Horrified, the women run away from the empty tomb. No triumphant resurrection from the dead here. With Matthew's Gospel, this is actually more the case. In his Gospel, the earth trembles when an angel from heaven comes down to roll away the stone from the tomb. He tells the women that the crucified Jesus is no longer there. He is now the risen Jesus. Matthew concludes his Gospel with such glossy theological language that it seems too good to be original. Luke's Gospel talks about two angels and also the story of the friends on the road to Emmaus. The image of the person walking next to you when you are struggling, comes into view the most in this Gospel. John gives the most mundane image of Jesus after his death. His story finishes the same way it began: Jesus meets the disciples fishing at the lake shore, and eats some fish. Most Bible scholars are of the opinion that John 21 is not part of the original text. Was it added later? And who added it: the author himself or a third person? If the latter is the case, what else has been changed?

When you start comparing and trying to analyse the stories of the resurrection, the text falls apart right before your eyes. You can't make head or tail of it. The stories are not consistent with each other; moreover they are chronologically inconsistent, the number of key players varies and events where no one was present are reported. Why aren't the evangelists more clear? After all, this is the core of the Christian faith. Perhaps this is exactly why it is not intended to give a clear eyewitness account. Perhaps the form is consistent with the content. Perhaps the content is so complex, ambiguous and mysterious that it can only be talked about in veiled and confusing terms.

One thing is certain: nowhere in the Gospels do we get the idea that Jesus is a victim or that he did not know what the risks were, or that he had no other choice. Jesus gives himself to death. His death was not the result of an avenging God who sacrifices him, but a well-chosen self-sacrifice. Unlike the films about Jesus of our time,[4] Jesus' death in the Bible is not dramatized with much violence and blood. The evangelists' accounts are sober and restrained. In all cases the story ends with the disciples' reaction to his death. Only after his death do they understand for the first time the meaning of his life. For the four Gospel writers it is probably not so much about a detailed description of the drama, but about the disciples' reaction, our reaction. After his death, the disciples realize that Jesus was special. Only then do they understand that he didn't want to liberate Israel by force, or to heal all vulnerable people like a magician, but that he wanted to be close to people and to rid them of their fear and loneliness. In his footsteps, they get up and try in their turn to form a community and help people in need. From that point of view, Easter can perhaps be seen as the resurrection of the disciples, following in Jesus' footsteps.

In the context of a compassionate Jesus, it might be better to speak of a substituting *gift* rather than a sacrifice. In this context, the French philosopher Jean-Luc Marion talks about givenness. Jesus was not sacrificed in the sense Caiaphas the high priest put it, 'It is good that one man dies for the people' (John 18.14). He gives himself away. The idea of a sacrifice as a self-giving compassionate love provides a new perspective. Marion says this love can be recognized in a glance, a glimpse, a trace, but you cannot have it or hold it. Givenness differs from a gift. When people give each other a gift, a relationship is expressed: you are worth so much to me. An extreme example is the envelope containing £20, which goes around the family at every birthday. That envelope doesn't even need to be opened any more. The envelope is just being sent back and forth and has lost its function as a gift. In contrast, a sacrifice is tantamount to unconditional love.

Did Jesus' sacrifice out of love make sense? In her study on self-sacrifice and care ethics, Inge van Nistelrooij addresses the meaning of Maximilian Kolbe's sacrifice, mentioned earlier. She states that Kolbe did not give his life in vain, although his self-sacrifice was not likely to save the life of the father. At the most his life may have been prolonged. Although there was no receiving of his life, Kolbe thought his action of value. The value might be the inspiration it arouses among everyone who hears his story. Likewise, Jesus' self-sacrifice might inspire us to give of ourselves.

## Cinematic and literary approaches to the sacrifice of Jesus

In this book we like to turn to art, film and literature to exemplify theological thoughts. It strikes me that so many modern films have this personal substitution as a central theme. They are, as it were, anonymous Jesus films. Examples include *Babette's Feast, Breaking the Waves, The Lord of the Rings* and *As It Is in Heaven*. The Chronicles of Narnia and Harry Potter series can also be seen in this light. I will discuss these last two examples.

C. S. Lewis wrote The Chronicles of Narnia as a Christian allegory. The main character, the lion Aslan, is the Christ figure. He allows himself to be killed so that the evil powers will release those they hold hostage. The idea of this exchange is proposed by the evil powers. The sacrificial process is known to all from the earliest times; it is the law that an innocent one may die on behalf of others and so free them. It is called 'deep magic from the dawn of time'. Although the evil powers approve of this arrangement they unfortunately have no intention of keeping their side of the bargain after Aslan is dead. The resurrection comes into this story as an unexpected development, from what Aslan calls 'deeper magic from before the dawn of time', something about which the evil powers knew nothing. Very symbolic, and in line with Girard's thought about Jesus' sacrifice that ends the idea of sacrifice once and for all: when Aslan rises, the ancient stone altar on which the sacrifice was offered cracks and crumbles in pieces, never to be used again.

J. K. Rowling has Harry Potter act as a Christ figure too, especially during the finale of the series. He is known as 'The Chosen One', who is destined to fight evil and save the Hogwarts community. Despite the expectations of, for example, his mentor Professor Dumbledore, Harry undertakes his sacrifice as a willed and intentional act. His devotion to Lord Voldemort is done for the sake of a higher goal. Then how is his self-sacrifice different from the one of a suicide bomber? Isn't he doing it for a higher purpose too? The love of a self-sacrificing terrorist is limited to a certain group and damaging another group. In contrast, Harry's love is extended to all others, even to Voldemort. Besides, his surrender is not a death wish. His intention is to carry out a life-bringing mission. What is sacrificial about Harry's death is not his willingness to die, but his determined commitment to let others live. That J. K. Rowling modelled Harry Potter after the example of Jesus might be part of the series' success (compare, Coenradie, 2016b).

## Conclusion

The figure of Jesus is associated with images of victims, scapegoats and self-sacrifice. The sacrificial metaphor gives a lingering unsatisfying feeling if there is not a form of participation accompanied by it. This can be found in the experience of compassion. That is, the compassion of Jesus with those who suffer, and not vice versa. The emphasis can also be on the living Christ, and as such his sacrifice may inspire us to be there for others in immediate care, which requires sacrifices. Not because it requires sacrifices, but because they are unavoidable. In addition you may experience that even the sacrifices you undergo, can give you satisfaction. There can be receiving in care, as the fictional Marion experiences at the beginning of this chapter.

---

### Questions for Reflection

What meaning do you find in Jesus' death?

How do you respond to the feminist and liberal critiques?

How do you view sacrifice in the light of Jesus' self-giving?

---

## Notes

1 Cf. Coenradie (2016a), p. 290.

2 To allow Peter anonymity names have been changed and the situation he talks about has been simplified.

3 http://vickisotomemorial.com/, accessed 21 November 2016.

4 Mel Gibson's film *The Passion of the Christ* (2004) comes out on top when it comes to violence.

# 3

# Vulnerability

SIGRID COENRADIE

## Stories about Vulnerability in the Bible

According to the Oxford Dictionary 'vulnerable' means: 1. exposed to the possibility of being attacked or harmed, either physically or emotionally; 2. in need of special care, support, or protection because of age, disability, or risk of abuse or neglect. The Bible covers both meanings. The first meaning stands out the most. People exposed to disaster is not an uncommon appearance in the Bible. Vulnerability is already present in Genesis 2. Eve picks an apple from the paradisiacal tree of knowledge of good and evil, and lets Adam have a bite too. Then they discover they are naked, they feel ashamed and hide. The vulnerability is felt. Shortly thereafter, they must exchange this paradisiacal life for a life with the pain of childbirth, the sweat of labour, and there is always the threat of death. Where does this come from? The story is explained as a matter of overconfidence: humans wanted to be like God, and they are not entitled to that. But let's admit it: an appealing tree of knowledge of good and evil in the middle of the garden, that you should not eat from, screams as it were: 'Eat my fruits!' A human's curiosity can't but take the bait and set off into the wide world. The challenge is to make the earth into a habitable garden. In liberal tradition, one therefore says that life's suffering is no one's fault. It is associated with the *condition humaine*, with our being human, which happens to be vulnerable.

This *does not* apply to the suffering we inflict on each other – directly by wars, attacks, domestic violence, and indirectly by overfishing, deforestation, trade agreements that exclude poor countries. What distinguishes us from the rest of creation? We know things: we have eaten from the tree of knowledge. And we can judge: it is the knowledge of good and evil. Therefore, we are higher than the animals, because they do not know the difference. But the risk of that knowledge is that we are also able to not use it properly. We can hurt someone physically, but we can also hurt with words. Even silence can lead to a frosty atmosphere in families. Therefore, our profit, our understanding of good and evil, is at the same time our loss.

In the New Testament vulnerable people are the central theme. Jesus connects with vulnerable people 'in need of special care': the blind, the lame, people with leprosy. He does not feel superior. He enters Jerusalem on a donkey, not astride a horse. He says of himself that he has no stone to lay his head on (Matt. 8.20). In his home town of Nazareth, people wonder how a carpenter's son could make it so far, and Jesus is not welcome there (Matt. 13.54–58). In short, Jesus himself is a vulnerable outsider. So, what about the miracle stories? The writers of the Bible want to demonstrate that Jesus is the Son of God. Jesus healing the blind, the lame, people with leprosy and other people with physical or mental disabilities, puts him on a par with God himself. The story of the resurrection of Jesus from the dead has that same function: vulnerability, death, is overcome. Is vulnerability dealt with here? It is probably more complicated. Strikingly, in the description of the miracle stories in Mark's Gospel, the miracles are painstakingly kept secret. Jesus implores those he healed not to disclose it (Mark 1.44, 5.43, 7.36, 8.26). One might think that is the best way of spreading the stories. Nonetheless, Jesus' disciples do not understand the miracles. Jesus is even asked to leave the area immediately after curing the possessed. He is as it were, bullied.

## From an almighty God to a vulnerable Jesus

This Jesus is vulnerable himself. He is mocked, ridiculed, humiliated and laughed at. This is clearly not the Jesus that is depicted in medieval paintings with a crown and a sceptre. It is not Jesus the king on the throne next to God, but the suffering Jesus. Personally, I think 'Christ on the cold stone' is a moving image to illustrate the suffering Jesus. It is an image or picture of a nearly naked man sitting on a platform, a rock or a wall, hands and feet tied, with a crown of thorns on his head. It represents the figure of Christ just before his crucifixion. This moment, which might very well be taken from the life of Jesus, is not described in the Bible. It goes back to a translation of the book *Vita Christi* by Ludolf of Saxony, a fourteenth-century author: 'Oh dear lord, how sad you are, sitting on this cold stone, shivering with cold and pain.'[1] This image moves us because of the extreme vulnerability it exudes. From this vulnerability, Jesus suffers with the people who were and are being excluded by others. According to Luke, he prays on the cross: 'Father, forgive them, for they know not what they do' (Luke 23.34). On seeing *The Passion* on Dutch TV, the event in which the Passion is depicted with modern music and well-known singers and actors each year in a different Dutch city, a refugee said: 'Look, there's one of us, he understands what it is like to have to flee.' And so even today this image provides comfort. In the compassion of Jesus or one of his disciples, it is about something that goes beyond a shared emotion. The point is that the person commiserating with the suffering person, in this case the refugee, shows that he matters. Fleeing threatens your identity. If it lasts a long time, you can internalize the disclaimers and stress and moreover become a victim of guilt and self-loathing because of it. The compassionate person breaks the dehumanization associated with the suffering: the shame, humiliation, loneliness (see also Sarot, 1995, pp. 155–68). This is where the second meaning of the word 'vulnerable' comes into play: sensitive. Jesus is especially sensitive to the needs of vulnerable people.

## A Japanese Jesus

A compassionate, sensitive Jesus is also outlined in the literary work of Shūsaku Endō (1923–96), a Japanese author. The main character in *Silence* (1980), the priest Rodrigues, experienced a complete turnaround in experiencing Jesus. At the beginning of the book he imagines the face of Jesus. It is the face that he is in love with since childhood. It radiates glory, courage and bravery.

Rodrigues fosters this image and he wants to be a martyr in the footsteps of this victorious Jesus. Martyrdom is certainly not imaginary, because we find ourselves in seventeenth-century Japan. During that century, the country was on 'lock-down': foreigners, and certainly missionaries, were not welcome. The Japanese Christians are ruthlessly persecuted, and forced to go into hiding. During these unwelcoming times, Rodrigues goes undercover and sets foot on Japanese soil. Initially he feels useful and meaningful. He secretly baptizes the hidden Japanese Christians and hears confessions. But just as Jesus in the Gospels, Rodrigues is betrayed for money by Kichijirō, a Judas figure. In prison, where the inquisitor interrogates him, Rodrigues is given a choice. If he openly renounces his faith, his fellow prisoners – a few Japanese Christians – will live. If he refuses, they will be killed. The way to show you turned away from your church and faith was by stepping on a picture of Jesus. In seventeenth-century Japan, authorities forced people to step on a *fumie* (literally *fumi-e* means 'stepping on' and 'picture'). Thus, they proved not to be a Christian.

At the end of the book Rodrigues is led outside and placed in front of a *fumie*. He is determined not to give in. But then the face of Jesus on the *fumie* is looking at him. There is nothing triumphant about it. It does not emit courage, but rather fatigue, exhaustion and suffering: 'It was not a face of Christ filled with dignity and pride. Neither was it a face that magnificently endured suffering. Neither was it a face that could resist temptation, nor a face overflowing with strong willpower. The face staring back at him was thin and exhausted.' Then something extraordinary happens. The face on the *fumie* speaks to him: 'You may trample. You may trample. It was to be trampled on by men that I was born into this world. It was to share men's pain that I carried my cross.' Rodrigues tramples the *fumie*. The inquisition lets him live and gives him a new Japanese name and a Japanese wife. He spends the last 30 years of his life in this forced identity, helping Japanese authorities in their hunt for Christians. Nonetheless his fascination with Jesus remains. 'He loved Him [Jesus] very differently now than before' (1980, p. 226). Rodrigues suffered under God's silence in all the suffering of persecution, hence the title of the novel. But perhaps the silence was broken by his denial in front of the *fumie*. Just as in the Bible stories, Jesus is introduced through a quote. But Endō also expresses scepticism. According to Inou, the inquisitor, it is self-deception. According to him, Rodrigues heard the voice in his head he wanted to hear most. In Endō's stories, contact with the sacred remains ambivalent, just as in Bible stories where God is only encountered indirectly – and often in contact with an other.

Endō's stories offer a different perspective on the substitution function of Jesus.[2] Instead of the idea of Jesus being sacrificed to compensate for the sins of the people, we see a Jesus who wants to be so close to vulnerable people that he also takes on the consequences of such sustained love. The liberal reading of the story of the (almost) sacrifice of Isaac[3] emphasizes a God who refuses the sacrifice of a child. Why should it be different in the story of Jesus' sacrifice? Endō's literary work resounds a perspective that deviates from the Christian dogma that 'Christ died for our sins'. Here there is no sacrifice in the sense of Jesus as a lamb being led (passive) to slaughter, but in Endō's eyes, as a faithful dog that goes through thick and thin for his master and who sacrifices (active) himself as a substitute to take the blows. The Jesus on the *fumie* does not take away Rodrigues' pain, but the fear and loneliness that comes with it. Rodrigues is not alone in this.

Shūsaku Endō also wrote a biography of Jesus (1973). This biography does not focus on the miracle stories, but on the compassion of Jesus. Endō describes Jesus as the substitute for the person who suffers. And in *Deep River* (1996), the last novel he wrote, he compares the figure of Christ with the suffering servant in Isaiah 53. In the novel, one of the main characters, Mitsuko, reads a Bible passage about this servant:

he had no form or majesty that we should look at him,
nothing in his appearance that we should desire him.
He was despised and rejected by others;
a man of suffering and acquainted with infirmity;
and as one from whom others hide their faces
he was despised, and we held him of no account.
(Isa. 53.2–3)

This description is perfectly applicable to the other main character in *Deep River*, namely Ōtsu. Mitsuko and Ōtsu met at university, where she studied French and he studied theology. As a student, Mitsuko made fun of the lanky Ōtsu; she thinks his study and faith are reprehensible and bets her friends to seduce him and thus prove that he is a wimp, and his God too. Ōtsu indeed falls for her, but that did not stop him continuing his studies. After they sleep together, she drops him like a hot potato, but despite herself she is still touched by his honesty and steadfastness. In later life, they keep in touch. Ōtsu is expelled from the seminary because he believes that Christianity is not exclusive. Truth can be found in all religions. He leaves for India, where Hindus have him join an ashram. His task is to take the sick and dying along the Ganges River to their final resting place. When Mitsuko is on vacation in India, the two meet each other. Ōtsu indicates that he is perfectly happy with his current life. A few days later, the group of travellers, including Mitsuko, make a trip to the Ganges. In the group, there is also an arrogant, ambitious photographer who wants to shoot a prize-winning photograph of the corpses burning along the river. However, it is strictly prohibited to take such pictures, as it shows little respect for the dead. When the photographer sets up his camera at an unfortunate moment anyway, he is nearly lynched by the crowd; because of the recent assassination of Indira Gandhi, tempers are overheated. Ōtsu, who saw the event unfold, sees what is about to happen and throws himself between the angry mob and the photographer. As a substitute, he suffers the blows and breaks his neck in all the violence. It is far from certain at the end of the book whether he survives it.

Shūsaku Endō portrays the Jesus figures in his literary work as anti-heroes. They are awkward, they are bullied and are being used by nefarious individuals for their own purposes. And yet they remain faithful like dogs. Faithful, in the sense of 'not letting down', being there for the other person, is one of the characteristics of Jesus, as Endō describes him. In his autobiographically tinted stories the Jesus figure is no more than a loyal, mangy, miserable mutt.

## The compassionate Jesus

How can Bible stories offer hope when Jesus is portrayed as a compassionate, vulnerable figure? In his last album *You want it darker*, Leonard Cohen sings, referring to the Bible: 'there is a lover in the story, but the story is just the same'. What difference did Jesus' death – and his life – make? What do we do with a Jesus who cannot do anything? Or should we indeed refer to the healing stories? After all, without exception these stories are about liberation from vulnerable situations. The stories of Jesus healing people are rarely just about overcoming injuries, but rather about rejoining the community. We can find an illustration of this in John 5, the story about a lame man, who has been lying beside a pool for 38 years. When the water in the pool starts bubbling, it has healing powers. The first person to reach the water is healed. The main character in the story, unfortunately, is always too late, partly because, apparently, he has no one to throw him into the water fast enough. Perhaps his lust for life is gone and he is lying there hopelessly waiting for a better life. Why did he not ask anyone to lay him near the edge? Does he push everyone away, because others cannot empathize with what it must be like to lie there day in and day out? Or does this man's fate lie in the hands of some magic the Bible doesn't care about? Who knows? In any case, the text doesn't mention that. But do you notice: here we go again. It is our apparent uncontrollable tendency to find a cause for this man's suffering, and to put the responsibility for his suffering on him. His own fault. Seen as such, when linked to sin, punishment or a test, healing stories are not exactly an example. Such an interpretation of biblical healing stories can promote feelings of guilt and a sense of inadequacy. So, it is for these debts that Jesus died on the cross. The idea that Jesus died for our sins is related to the sins of the people. Adam and Eve ate the apple. We would have done that too, because we are vulnerable as well, and thus came about the idea of original sin. Jesus, also called the second Adam for this very reason, assumes the sins of humankind and dies on the cross as a substitute. This is a theological structure that liberal Protestantism cannot do much with. Then how is the man cured in the end? Jesus asks the man if he wants to be healthy, and then orders him to take up his bed and walk. The man's initiative is explicitly required. Note that Jesus leaves the water out, emphasizing that magic is not involved.

## Strength in weakness

In his 1973 biography of Jesus, Shūsaku Endō emphasizes the re-action of Jesus' sustained vulnerability on his disciples. He argues that the disciples understood only in hindsight what Jesus meant to vulnerable people. In their turn, they wanted to move on in his footsteps. They met secretly to keep the stories of and about Jesus alive, far into the surrounding area.

Paul is the disciple who made Christianity known in the entire Mediterranean region. He went from being one of the persecutors of the Jesus movement, to being the leader. Tirelessly he travels around to spread the faith. Not everyone welcomes him with open arms. It is no accident that he writes about vulnerability. His letter to the Corinthians says:

> He [the Lord] said to me, 'My grace is sufficient for you, for power is made perfect in weakness.' So, I will boast all the more gladly of my weaknesses, so that the power of Christ may dwell in me. Therefore, I am content with weaknesses, insults, hard-ships, persecutions, and calamities for the sake of Christ; for whenever I am weak, then I am strong. (2 Cor. 12.9–10)

And a little later:

> I will not be lenient – since you desire proof that Christ is speak-ing in me. He is not weak in dealing with you, but is powerful in you. For he was crucified in weakness, but lives by the power of God. For we are weak in him, but in dealing with you we will live with him by the power of God. (2 Cor. 13.2b–4)

The image Paul gives is that the weakness of the prophets, Jesus and the disciples, including himself, is forged into strength by God. Paul states that Jesus' vulnerability resembled the vulnerability of the people he met, so after his death, Jesus became an inspiring example for those who suffer. In his letter to the Hebrews 5.2 he writes: 'He [Jesus] is able to deal gently with the ignorant and wayward, since he himself is subject to weakness.'

Following the example of Jesus, Paul tirelessly travels to found communities. And when he moves on, he tries to keep in touch with them as much as possible by writing letters. The nice thing about Paul is that he is realistic in his letters about his own failures and therefore it makes him so recognizable. He writes in a letter to the Romans: 'What I do, I do not see through, because I do not do what I want, I do exactly what I hate.' He lives with the communities, he is involved and therefore often disappointed and angry. Karen Armstrong, who devoted a study to Paul, says in an interview with the Dutch newspaper *Trouw*:

> I learned to identify with him: just like him, I was extremely vulnerable. I was ill for years, and then went through a long, deep depression after leaving the convent ... First I wanted to project my problems onto Paul, but I began to realize that he himself was a wounded and sick man. And lonely ... But he did say: 'do not let yourself be crushed by injustice. You are free! Do not let anyone enforce a yoke on you.' He did what Martin Luther King did later, who gave African-Americans back their 'sense of somebodiness'. You are somebody. You matter.

Is vulnerability also a characteristic of God? Yes, if God is seen as being incarnated in a child, born in a manger and nailed to the cross. On 16 July 1944 Dietrich Bonhoeffer wrote a letter from prison to his friend: 'God lets himself be pushed out of the world on to the cross. He is weak and powerless in the world, and that is precisely the way, the only way, in which he is with us and helps us. Matt. 8.17 makes it quite clear that Christ helps us, not by virtue of his omnipotence, but by virtue of his weakness and suffering.' This, and other letters, was published in 2010. Etty Hillesum also speaks to a helpless compassionate God in her diary (published in 1986). On 12 July 1942, she writes:

> I shall try to help You, God, to stop my strength ebbing away, though I cannot vouch for it in advance. But one thing is

becoming increasingly clear to me: that You cannot help us, that we must help You to help ourselves. And that is all we can manage these days and also all that really matters: that we safeguard that little piece of You, God, in ourselves. And perhaps in others as well. Alas, there doesn't seem to be much You Yourself can do about our circumstances, about our lives. Neither do I hold You responsible. You cannot help us, but we must help You and defend Your dwelling place inside us to the last.

Remarkably, Bonhoeffer equates God to Jesus. Not only do many Christians believe that Jesus shows us who God is throughout his life, but that Jesus *is* God. Many liberals do not go that far. For them, Jesus is an example and a source of inspiration. Remarkably, Hillesum sees people as teammates of God, as commiserating servants. Both break with the idea of an omnipotent God who must guard humankind from vulnerability. Both write during times of war, when life is anything but obvious. Right at the edge, at the breaking points of life, God is meaningful to them as a compassionate, vulnerable companion. By fully living life, with all the ups and downs that go with it, we are indeed vulnerable, but we are also intimately connected with others and with God.

## Paradox

So, that's it then? Should we simply open up, and risk being hurt? What does the Bible say about this?

In the Bible stories, there is something paradoxical about showing vulnerability: it seems a sign of weakness, but it is a sign of courage. We recognize and appreciate this courage. 'I do not believe in God,' I recently heard someone say in a museum of religious art, 'but Jesus was a cool guy.'

Jesus was courageous and vulnerable. He was not ashamed to get involved with people on the edge of society or to stand up for them. That was not only true for vulnerable people, the sick, widows and children, but also for tax officials working for the occupying forces. He did not hesitate to cast out the money-changers from the Temple. Not to cleanse the Temple, but because the prices went through the roof. His sustained vulnerability led to his death, but that was not where his love ended. Precisely because of his ultimate vulnerability Jesus is still an example for us today. Sometimes he withdraws and chooses to be alone for a while. He shows that there is always a choice: Do I put myself in a vulnerable position? With whom can I be vulnerable? Are there limits to my showing this vulnerability?

Living vulnerably, a theology of vulnerability, as the Dutch theologian Christa Anbeek addresses in *Delivered to the Heathens* (2013), is that at all possible? Religion can also be a strategy to avoid vulnerability, in order to cling to certain thoughts and ideas and to exclude other truths. But we can also use it in a positive way. By listening to each other and by not immediately coming up with a solution or a platitude like, 'It could be much worse', 'But at least you still have your kids', or 'God probably has a hidden intention, perhaps you were spared from something much worse.' Sometimes this comes to mind when, during a home visit, or in a group meeting or a celebration, a special atmosphere develops. When someone shows vulnerability in faith discussions, it can be contagious. There is an openness to explore together what you do and don't believe, in relation to your own life, in order to grow together. Because if you share this with one another, you are going to help each other naturally, provide each other with stories that have helped you. Often people will recall the well-known poem about someone walking on the beach and who sees four footprints: God walks with her. But when the going gets tough in that person's life, and she has to drag herself through the sand, there is only one set of footprints to be seen. 'Why now, God, did you leave me just when I was having such a hard time?' she asks. To which God replied: 'You were not alone. When you needed me most, I carried you.'

## Questions for Reflection

How do you react to the idea of a vulnerable God?

What do you think of Endō's interpretation of Jesus' vulnerability?

What positive ways do you see for vulnerability and religion?

# Nobody wants to be vulnerable

When I taught at a secondary school, one of my pupils (Yvonne, 16) came to my desk. The lesson was about key moments in life: having a child, getting married or entering into a partnership, achieving something in a job, emigrating, becoming ill, becoming physically disabled, the death of a loved one; in short, the vulnerable moments in life. 'I think I'll just stay single and childless,' the pupil said, 'I don't want to get attached to someone, because in the end it makes you dependent.'

Vulnerability is not a popular theme. At a time when we greatly praise autonomy, independence and self-reliance, vulnerability is seen as something negative. People who become ill or get confused or become so old that they are no longer able to take care of themselves, are sometimes afraid to burden family and society. The ideal is an autonomous, powerful citizen, who is in charge and who can live at home as long as possible. Self-management and self-reliance are paramount and form the central thread in developments such as closure of nursing homes, shorter hospital stays and reducing the number of admissions in psychiatric wards.

While sooner or later everyone will be exposed to injuries of a psychological, social, economic or physical nature, we relate vulnerability to groups: vulnerable elderly, vulnerable young people, and even vulnerable neighbourhoods. Policies are being developed for these vulnerable categories. These groups then get professional help to fight their vulnerability. And woe betide if that approach fails. There is a threatening climate in which vulnerable people are almost being blamed for needing care. The implicit message is: you have created your own vulnerability. Our society is almost obsessively concerned with happiness, health, beauty and success. And if you are ill or you age and are able to do increasingly less, then you are deviating from that standard, you are hindering progress. That is why it is not easy to be ill or old or disabled. You may feel a failure and unappreciated. And that makes it even more difficult. And if we are not ill ourselves, but are faced with illness in our environment, we tend to run away or stay away. We find that annoying, and we feel powerless too. But perhaps deep down, something else is going on: could it be related to our inability to face our own vulnerability and mortality?

Henri Nouwen is someone who kept on going until he became overworked. In the framework of the ministry of compassion, he writes:

> Let us not underestimate how hard it is to be compassionate. Compassion is hard because it requires the inner disposition to go with others to place where they are weak, vulnerable, lonely, and broken. But this is not our spontaneous response to suffering. What we desire most is to do away with suffering by fleeing from it or finding a quick cure for it.[4]

When Nouwen became stuck and was lost in the academic world he was a part of, a friend invited him to come and live with people with intellectual disabilities. In 1985 Nouwen moved to the L'Arche movement. At first, he was inconvenienced, but he soon discovered that disabled and non-disabled people can be valuable to each other. He became friends with Adam, a man who was not able to talk and suffered epileptic seizures. *Adam* (1997) tells the story of this friendship. In this book he describes the role of the 'wounded healer'. The 'wounded healer' is one of Carl Jung's archetypes. Nouwen gave it a spiritual twist: only he who is aware of his own injuries and continues to connect to his wounds, figuratively speaking, is able to commiserate with the other wounded. So it becomes a mutual encounter. Nouwen discovered that Adam was not only 'wounded' but he was also a 'healer'. In his view, Jesus is the 'wounded healer' par excellence.

Vulnerability is about daring to lose control. It can create uncertainty: having a child, entering into a relationship, doing something where you are not sure it will succeed, becoming ill and/or growing old, dying. You do not have it under control. As such it resembles shame. If everyone sees that you peed your pants, you do not know where to look. You blush and cringe with shame. Your body lets you know how vulnerable you are at such a moment. A very uncomfortable feeling. 'Nobody wants to be vulnerable,' I told my student, 'however life is just full of risks. But you know, those vulnerable moments really matter, because the relationship with a child, a partner, or a person who wants to take care of you, creates opportunities to feel deeply connected with the other person. Just when you are at your most vulnerable, you can appreciate life.' In the words of Henri Nouwen:

> Every time we make the decision to love someone, we open ourselves to great suffering, because those we most love cause us not only great joy but also great pain. The greatest pain comes from leaving. When the child leaves home, when the husband or wife leaves for a long period of time or for good, when the beloved friend departs to another country or dies ... the pain of the leaving can tear us apart.
>
> Still, if we want to avoid the suffering of leaving, we will never experience the joy of loving. And love is stronger than fear, life stronger than death, hope stronger than despair. We have to trust that the risk of loving is always worth taking.[5]

Student Yvonne shares such insight when she tells me about her old, frail grandmother, who lives in a nursing home. In the beginning she thought visiting her grandmother was embarrassing, but nowadays her family is more light-hearted about it. 'She likes it when we visit. And when my grandmother wets her pants, my father makes a joke about it, so she doesn't feel so bad,' Yvonne says, 'but then we call the nurses to change her, because that is not something my father or we could do. He would be so embarrassed.' Maybe, I think, dependency is not the end of the world when there is attention and good care.

## Care

So, what is good care? André Mulder and Ruth Hessel, both employed at Windesheim University College, did research on the care of people with physical disabilities. They wrote a guide to inform health-care providers about the religious background of people with disabilities (Hessel and Mulder, 2014). In Judaism, Christianity and Islam, people with disabilities are seen as full members of the community. Whether they experience this as such, depends on how caring for each other takes shape. Charity can be experienced as humiliating. Mulder and Hessel give the example of a young guy in a wheelchair getting a care package for Christmas every year. The fact is that it is customary for the elderly and people who are ill to receive such a gift. But people in wheelchairs are not necessarily ill, and do not necessarily want to be seen as helpless.

Many people have indicated they find it difficult to be seen as vulnerable, as long as 'vulnerable' is defined as 'pathetic, dependent and needy' (2014, p. 65). In their follow-up research Mulder and Hessel focus on the life story of the elderly, with a view to caregiving. Part of their research is conversations among professional caregivers about their own vulnerability. The idea behind it is that anyone who recognizes his or her own vulnerability, becomes more aware of the vulnerability and needs of others. After all, no one is free from suffering, sorrow, deterioration with age, illness and death. Facing one's own vulnerability is a suitable base to be open to others and their vulnerability. In addition, the authors make a plea for being able to receive comfort and help. In our society, however, the emphasis is on independence and self-reliance. The biblical statement that it is more blessed to give than to receive resembles a widely held belief in our time. You are considered a hero if you give help rather than receive it. You are considered weak if you need help. We forget that sooner or later everyone will become vulnerable. Therefore, Mulder and Hessel, against the *zeitgeist*, plead for recognition of interdependence. People with and without disabilities need each other, as Henri Nouwen also found in the community of L'Arche.

The same reciprocity applies to ill, vulnerable people and their care-givers. As a minister, I often visit people in nursing homes. It strikes me that the tasks of the care-givers are defined. Bringing coffee, measuring heart rates, applying eye drops, giving pills, taking meal cards – it is all done by different people. Sometimes it happens that someone walks in and out three times during my visit. A resident's heart rate and blood pressure are closely monitored, but it is often not known what kind of person this resident is. What is their philosophy? What are their hobbies? What was their profession? Where did they live? Do they have family and friends? Do they enjoy Bach or The Beatles? In short, what are the meaningful facts? And how do they play a role in their life now? Is music (still) important or not? If more were known about the person behind the resident, could the care be more qualitative? This requires residents to be open and the care-givers to be careful with confidential information. But above all, the willingness to commiserate. Henri Nouwen writes: 'What really matters is that in moments of pain and suffering someone be close to us. More important than any help or any advice is the simple presence of someone who is emotionally involved.'[6]

Andries Baart describes in a critical essay how health care lacks in this regard and thereby completely misses its objective. The health-care sector is characterized by an aversion to vulnerability and by working unrelationally or 'doing your own thing'. Doctors and other care-givers rarely align with what is going on in the person needing care. They easily hide behind techniques, perform (often unnecessary) scans, and prescribe expensive drugs and treatments out of powerlessness. In *De zorgval* (2013) Baart outlines how people inadvertently go from bad to worse in today's care. He lashes out against the Social Support Act regulations, that encourage self-reliance and own strength, but in the meantime have no regard for the vulnerability of school dropouts and asylum seekers. Baart calls to revalue vulnerability and have it as the basis of any health and welfare policy. He advocates a 'presence-approach' to protect care of its own downfall. A downfall that probably takes down with it and short-changes those in need of care: the trap of the care sector. According to Baart the care sector too easily perpetuates the problems instead of helping. Prescribed protocols and methodologies sow the seed, the system logic and perverse incentives of the care sector feed this mechanism. However, Baart also outlines examples of care that works. Not because of its advanced technology, but by interested attention, through involvement with the other. *De zorgval* is a double-sided 'turn-around book' in which criticism of the care sector has two faces. Baart's essay is on one side of the book. When turning the book around, the other side offers engaging and intimate practice portraits of care recipients who fell in the trap – or didn't. Journalist Christa Carbo states in this part that humanitarianism and personal contact are under pressure because they cannot be tallied and there is no business model for it. A friendly conversation or an arm around your shoulder can't be checked off a list.

However, she also describes examples of considerate care. Mulder and Hessel also note a change in health care. Gradually, more attention is being put on the quality of life in nursing homes.

## Wit

All this is aptly portrayed in the film *Wit* (Mike Nichols, 2010). The main character, Vivian Bearing, is a successful scientist, an authority in the field of seventeenth-century English poetry. Vivian is 48 years old, single, childless and has stage 4 ovarian cancer. The film starts when her doctor informs her of her diagnosis and at the same time proposes to participate in an eight-month long experimental chemotherapy. He does so in a clinical, detached way, without a trace of sympathy. He smartly appeals to her scientific interests and challenges her to be 'very brave' because there are 'some side effects'. And so Vivian, always proud of her strong-willed and independent spirit, begins an agonizing journey. She does not want to lose face and undergoes the complete therapy. Science must be helped forward. The loneliness of her total isolation in a bare hospital room is harrowing. 'Should we inform someone, family or friends?' the nurses ask. No, this won't be necessary; no one will visit. As Vivian's disease progresses, her attitude changes somewhat. To her own surprise, she eats an ice cream with the nurse, whom she tells about a bunny from her youth. In flashbacks we get a picture of her life. We see her as an enthusiastic teacher, but when a student comes to her desk, she says: 'You probably want to retake your exam because your grandmother passed away, don't you?' 'How did you know that?' the student asks, stunned. 'Because I've heard that excuse so many times,' says Vivian. 'You'll just have to wait till next semester.' And her memories go back even further, to the time when she was still a student. The time when she had a conversation with her teacher, E. M. Ashford, about a poem by John Donne, number ten in his 'holy sonnets' series, 'Death Be Not Proud'. Bearing, an analytically strong student, decomposed the poem very well technically, but her teacher is far from satisfied. The essence of the poem has been totally ignored by Vivian. Apparently, it is all in one detail: the punctuation in the final lines. Where are the commas? Some versions read:

Death, thou shall be no more;
Death, thou shalt die!

Death with a capital letter, is too great an honour according to Ashford. Death does not deserve a big stage. The poem does not want to deal with death, as if it were the greatest enemy. The poem gives death a modest place, and avoids all the strict boundaries between life, death and the afterlife:

And death shall be no more,
death thou shalt die.

A single comma marks the borders as a sigh. We can learn something from this interpretation of the poem, notes Ashford in the film.

What is it then? At the end of the film Ashford visits Vivian on her deathbed. She is in town to visit her great-grandson who is celebrating his fifth birthday. The university referred her to the hospital. The ill Vivian is barely able to recognize her teacher, who puts an arm around her. Ashford asks whether she wants to hear a poem by Donne. 'Oh no,' Vivian groans. And so her teacher reads from the book she bought as a gift for her great-grandchild: *The Runaway Rabbit*. It's about a bunny who wants to run away. He tells his mother that he wants to run away. 'Then I'll follow you,' says the mother. 'Then I'll turn into a fish that can swim,' said the rabbit. 'And I'll be a fisherman who'll catch you,' replied the mother. 'And I'll be a bird that can fly,' said the rabbit. 'Then I'll be a tree that you can hide in.' 'You see, Vivian,' explains the teacher, 'wherever we go, God goes with us.' But by then Vivian has passed, unnoticed, leaning against her shoulder.

The film ends with the ambitious young doctor. However, he is totally focused on the experimental treatment she is getting. 'How are we today?' is the only thing he asks every day in the same merry tone. He does not wait for an answer. To him, she does not exist; she has been reduced to her body. He tries to resuscitate her, although he knows that she signed a non-resuscitation statement. The nurse has the greatest difficulty to stop him. Now that she is dead, finally there is no more tinkering with her body.

The film begins with the position of the student Yvonne mentioned earlier: the protagonist tries to deny her vulnerability, to overcome it by a brave no-nonsense approach. The student prefers not to begin a life in which she will love, and therefore be vulnerable towards others, a partner and children. In the film *Wit* we see how her desire for stability and independence tears up the protagonist. The pivotal point in the film is, as it were, repeated in the weight 'death' gets in the final lines of John Donne's poem. Do we write the word with or without a capital?

Another film that is of interest in this context is *Arrival* (Denis Villeneuve, 2016), in which the protagonist, Louise Banks, is able to see into the future thanks to her contact with aliens. She sees that she gets married and has a daughter. But she also sees that she will lose this daughter to cancer and that her husband is not able to handle that loss, resulting in divorce. This does not stop her from marrying this man and longing for this child. Because she has also seen the beautiful, loving moments that these relationships provide her in the future.

## Allowing to suffer and to be vulnerable

In a critical article in *Speling* (December 2016) Peter Nissen, professor in spiritual studies, points at the tendency to overcome vulnerability through the use of spirituality. Spirituality is then a way to optimize your happiness. In many popular self-help books, such as *The Secret* by Rhonda Byrne, it is about positive thinking. If you ban all negative thoughts, for example of suffering and vulnerability, you can take on the entire world. The wellness gurus claim that perfection is within everyone's reach. That is a totally different approach than Brené Brown's. She actually warns us that we do not need to want to be perfect. The title of her book *Daring*

*Greatly* (2012) leaves little room for guessing in this regard. Christa Anbeek, professor with the Remonstrants and lecturer at the University of Humanistic Studies, also pleads to allow suffering and vulnerability. She has suffered many personal losses in her life. The losses prompted a quest for stories and ideas that supported her. Together with Ada de Jong she published *De berg van de ziel* (2013). This book contains lots of comforting ideas and stories. However, the authors also received well-intended, but inappropriate advice on how to overcome mourning. Anbeek advocates a 'theology of vulnerability' in which people come together in small groups to talk about sensitive key moments in life. What went wrong in your life and what helped you to get back on track? Where did you lose something, or where were you given something special? The latter is also part of it. Happiness, beauty and wonder cannot be made; they are afforded us. Anbeek sees talking about it in small groups in a broad perspective. Not everything can be explained in words; other forms of expression are appropriate such as art, music, rituals, silence. Anbeek does not see spirituality as a way to feel less vulnerable, it is the other way around: the stories of vulnerability constitute a starting point to share with others, and from there to experience grace and spirituality.

In her ecumenical lecture of 2016, Anbeek quotes the philosopher Judith Butler, who points to the fundamental uncertainty of existence, which is felt in experiences of grief and violence. We are exposed to others. The grief at the loss of a loved one is felt first hand. The other is not only next to us, but also within us. By entering into intimate relationships, we are more connected than we take for granted and much more vulnerable than we like to pretend in our imagined autonomy. Experiences of violence make it painfully obvious how vulnerable our body is. Our body can be hurt and violated, and even killed. Now that we live longer, we are also dependent for longer. In our culture that is a terrifying spectre. We want to be independent for as long as possible. Dependence is experienced as humiliating, a lack of freedom, shameful. The more dependent we become, the harder it is to keep our self-respect. We experience it as undermining our sense of self.

At the same time, vulnerability offers a precious ability to get in contact with others, but it seems we forget this as we get older or that we are so afraid of being hurt that it is our ideal to become invulnerable. While physical dependency is something we share with others.

Once I was with a secular girlfriend on holiday in France. Because of the heat, we went into a church. The church had a Pietà, a statue of the dead Jesus on his mother's lap. The mother, Mary, looked at her son, but her gaze was also directed at the audience, as if she asked for protest; at the same time her gaze was also introspective. Her gaze depended on the position of the viewer. As I walked in admiration around the image, my girlfriend had tears running down her cheeks. The relationship with her husband was on the rocks, and in the sight of this Mary she recognized her grief. A few weeks later I was also touched by a Pietà by the Dutch artist Rini Hurkmans, in the form of a video-installation titled 'Dear Son' (2005). The six-minute video installation in the Catharijne convent showed a seated female figure who is continuously folding a white shirt on her lap. While the surrounding space in which this endlessly repeated action takes place, and the position of the woman doesn't change, the colours in the interior and the clothes of the woman are constantly changing. The patterned pieces of textile date from different periods of history and are from all over the world. One sees the colours going from light, springlike colours to nuances of greys and blacks.

During the film there is an 'interior monologue' in which the voice of a woman reads a letter to her dead son, which I associate with the Mothers of the Plaza de Mayo in Buenos Aires. Every Thursday at 15.30 these mothers walk to the Plaza to bring attention to their lost children, grandchildren or their siblings.

Showing your vulnerability is therefore by no means an easy task. American researcher Brené Brown analysed many life stories of vulnerable people. She discovered that sincere people are able to be vulnerable. However, most people do not want to deal with it. Indeed vulnerability involves an emotional risk and a life full of uncertainty. Vulnerability may feel like loss of control, like a free fall. We would give an arm and a leg not to be vulnerable. There are basically three strategies: the first is to try to maintain control through perfectionism. Not delegating because you do not want to risk the other making mistakes. Or, the other way around, instead of doing everything alone you lapse into inertia. Then we are just like the person from the parable in Matthew 25.14–30 who buried his talent for fear of making mistakes, because he was afraid he would lose it. And the hard lesson is that that is exactly what happens: the man had his one talent taken away, a talent he had done nothing with.

The second way is that we try to keep up a shield of invulnerability. We act as if nothing can touch us. Feigning invulnerability is a shield, however it is anything but an effective shield. By pretending to be bigger and stronger and keeping going while you are actually lonely and tired, and never ask for help, you exhaust yourself. The third way to keep vulnerability at bay, is perhaps the most damaging: we numb our fear of being vulnerable. We surrender to binge eating, taking too many sleeping pills, we lose ourselves in shopping, alcohol or other addictions. So we are wasting a lot of energy in our lives by avoiding vulnerability. However, says Brown, emotions do not allow themselves to be selectively suppressed. If you do not want to feel vulnerable and you do not want to be ashamed, then you also deprive yourself the opportunity to feel positive feelings, such as happiness, joy and satisfaction. Avoiding vulnerability means avoiding life. Fear and faith come from the same source. As Leonard Cohen sings in 'Anthem': 'There's a crack, a crack in everything, that's where the light comes in.' But there is more. According to Brown vulnerability provides opportunities. Vulnerability is the source of innovation, creativity and change. Therefore, it takes courage to dare to be vulnerable, Brown concludes. She showed that courage by openly talking about the impact of her research on her personal life. In a TED talk[7] she tells how she became depressed by the results of her own investigation. In fact, she had a nervous breakdown when she discovered that in her own life she had the greatest difficulty to show vulnerability. She is a perfectionist and hails from a Texan family whose motto was 'Lock and Load', in other words suppress your feelings and be ready to shoot to defend yourself. In this way, aggressiveness can be understood as fear. At the first appointment with her therapist Brown said: 'Look, no family stuff and no childhood traumas please, I just need some strategies.' It kept her out of the running for a year. Striking detail: her therapist said what happened to her was not a 'nervous breakdown' but a 'spiritual awakening'. And that was exactly the other side of vulnerability that Brown now discovered through her own experience: vulnerability can also be the source of creativity, innovation and 'belonging'.

In the film *Still Alice* (2014) a young scientist, Alice Howland, ends up in an extremely vulnerable position. She is married and has three adult children. Because Alice can't help but giving well-meant but unwanted advice, she often clashes with her youngest daughter, but they keep in touch. Alice is a professor of linguistics. Let's just say language is her thing. Suddenly one day she is not able to utter a word in front of a packed lecture hall. It turns out this is the beginning of more amnesia. The diagnosis is devastating: Alice appears to be suffering from Alzheimer's disease at a young age. We see her struggle, her family's and her social environment's struggle with the disease. At the end of the film her husband can no longer handle the situation. Remarkably, it is her youngest daughter who takes her into her home. Alice entrusts herself to the child of whom she had been so critical. They understand each other without speaking a word.

Vulnerability is not something you can learn from a book. It does not feel comfortable, because whether it is related to work, relationships or parenting, it is not easy to take risks without the guarantee of success. But it is worth it, because it connects you with others. Love involves a willingness to take risks. The ability to risk vulnerability is rather, therefore, a sign of strength than of weakness.

## Conclusion

Vulnerability is necessary to act in connection with others. That is scary, because you may be rejected or receive a reaction along the lines of: 'Fortunately, you still have so and so', or 'So and so has that too and much worse.' You do not feel that your vulnerability is recognized, let alone that the other person commiserates. However, if that person sits down next to you and puts an arm around you, and says, 'Me too, you are not alone', it helps more than well-meant advice, statements, accusations or any rational response whatsoever. In *De berg van de ziel* however, the authors say:

> Pastors said it is important to be able to tell how bad the situation is you are going through and that there is someone there who listens. It is not necessary to change things, just being there and looking into the abyss with the other person. ... Personally, I do not settle for people who look and listen with me. I want something to be whispered, a breath, a light breeze, so I get distracted and look up. ... The whispering does not have to come from people, perhaps preferably not. (2013, p. 170)

There is no recipe for dealing with vulnerability, whether it is your own vulnerability, or the vulnerability of others. The writer talks about an 'undertone of sadness' ever present in the background, and sometimes in the foreground. But occasionally, the undertone goes away. She notes that it is important to share, that there is someone who knows what you are going through when you have been through major losses (p. 171). But *the* perfect reaction does not exist. Perhaps ultimately the reaction is less important than the presence. The knowledge that no matter how vulnerable we are, we have a loyal companion.

Jesus' reactions to the suffering of others stands out. He only visits his dying friend Lazarus after he has already died. Why? Because he does not want to favour his loved ones before others? Or because he does not want to assign great importance to death? We can only guess. He lets Jairus, the father of the little girl, wait because he first wants to address the bleeding woman. Remarkably, Jesus asks the man who has been lame for 38 years: 'Do you want to be healed?' Do you want to commit, despite your possible disappointment in people? It is not a rational question – because that would make it incomprehensible: of course the man wants to be healed, that is what he has been waiting 38 years for – but rather a relational question. Jesus' response to the Emmaus pilgrims is similar. He does not say: 'You fools, it's me. Don't you see it, where is your faith?' But he walks beside them, listens patiently, empathizes with their situation and from that point of view gives an explanation regarding the Scriptures. In other words, Bible texts are contextual. In a different time and for a different audience they can mean different things, and that is precisely their strength. The relationship between the stories and the readers is thus also relational. A connection between the stories and the readers is only possible if a reader can identify with the text and is willing to share in the vulnerability.

---

### Questions for Reflection

How is vulnerability visible in your context?

What is the gift of vulnerability?

What is the role of presence in responding to vulnerability?

---

## Notes

1 www.christusopdekoudesteen.com/index.php?option=com_content&view=article&id=1&Itemid=2, accessed 21 November 2016.

2 See 'He died for our sins', p. 50.

3 Ibid.

4 www.goodreads.com/quotes/179950-let-us-not-underestimate-how-hard-it-is-to-be, accessed 18 March 2017.

5 www.goodreads.com/quotes/492915-every-time-we-make-the-decision-to-love-someone-we, accessed 18 March 2017.

6 Ibid.

7 www.ted.com/talks/brene_brown_on_vulnerability?language=nl, accessed 21 November 2016.

# Interlude: Bible, Literature and Film

## SIGRID COENRADIE

In the previous chapters many books, films and songs have been discussed in relation to the Bible. The following chapters include some more. Time for an interlude where we pause and reflect on their use. Why do we use so many examples of literature and film in this book when referring to Bible stories? And do we actually use them as *examples*? Or do we use them to convey something else? In this interlude we provide detailed answers to these questions. The fact that we include them underlines their importance.

Until the Reformation and the invention of the printing press, paintings and sculptures in churches were an important means to 'tell' Bible stories to believers. And sometimes this is still the case. Recently I was talking with someone who was looking for the story of Jesus who descended into the underworld between crucifixion and resurrection in order to retrieve the dead from their graves, starting with Adam and Eve. He was shocked to hear that the story is a legend, and does not appear in the Bible. He asked if I had a different Bible. He was convinced this story was in the Bible, he remembers it from his youth. He explained that he had often seen this image while on holidays abroad and that he was disappointed that such a biblical story was not in the Bible. Pictures often say more than words. In church history, pictures were always more welcomed than words. Sober pictures were allowed, but the use of novels in relation to the Bible was not obvious. In the sixteenth century, the Roman Catholic Church drew up a list of banned books. We have come a long way since then. Since the 1960s it is generally recognized that art and literature offer clarification to human existence in their own way. To connect to the world, the Bible needs art. Art reflects what is going on in culture. Looking at art does not leave one unstirred; a sculpture or painting or photograph can change the viewer. Art is more than an illustration with the story. Art shows something new, gives a voice to experiences that are not obtainable through theological concepts.

What is the spiritual function of a literary text? Walter Jens (1991) outlines three aspects of literature's significance:

## 1. Mythical figures as role models

According to Jens, we posit ourselves using a reordered set of mythical figures. We establish that order ourselves. He writes: 'We interpret our beliefs about ourselves and our world indirectly, by subjecting Job and Antigone, Abraham and Don Juan, Hamlet and Faust to a metamorphosis' (p. 7).

## 2. Open fictional characters

In his hermeneutics Ricœur (1984, pp. 52–87) distinguishes pre-figuration, configuration and refiguration. Prefiguration relates to the author of the text. It is the world in which he lives and from which he draws his story. Configuration is the world within the text or the story, with its own laws. Refiguration is the world evoked by the story, the image created in the mind of the reader. The reader empathizes, the reader can identify with different per-spectives in the story and, as it were, try what it is like to live like that. The more perspectives available in a story, the more identi-fication possibilities for the reader. Thus a world of possibilities opens up to the reader.

## 3. The intertwining of form and content

Because both content and form of a literary work go hand in hand, abstracting and paraphrasing the meaning without some loss of meaning is impossible. This also applies to the Bible. After all, the literary form is the only form in which the Bible is accessible. Even in Jesus' time this was difficult. Mark often writes about Jesus' disappointment with the limited ability of his disciples to appreciate his metaphoric style as such (for example, Mark 8.19–21). More than 2,000 years later, reading metaphors in the Bible is still difficult. According to Wright for example, there are determined attempts 'to read Ezekiel's chariot of fire in terms of spaceships' (1988, p. 14). In my opinion, the metaphor of sacrifice in John's Gospel about the death of Jesus, has become a rigid doctrine instead of being a tool. Taking the text and ideology too literally hinders the function of literature in theology. In fact, biblical literature lives exactly because of metaphors, symbols and paradoxes that require the reader's imagination. The ambiguity of the language used makes literature what it is. That is precisely what provides enjoyment and opens up new perspectives.

The stories did not only have a meaning within the Gospels for the people in Jesus' audience; they also have a meaning for today's reader. They provide a framework for reflection on the individual's experiences. Because good literary works are characterized by openness, they allow for different interpretations in different times and circumstances. That is why Shūsaku Endō's historical novels *Silence* and *The Samurai*, both situated in seventeenth-century Japan, still move us. Because the faith of the protagonists themselves is evolving and because their views change in the course of the story, readers are invited to mix the given environment with their own memories and imagination. What applies to Endō's novels, also applies to the Gospel stories. Precisely because the world of these novels differs from the contemporary Western reader's world, they evoke emotions that call for interpretation.

As such, art and literature provide a contemporary expression of, or comment on, Christian-inspired ideas. At the end of the twentieth century and partly due to the decrease of the obviousness of Christianity in the Western world, literature and film received a prominent place. Most modern theologians are inclined to embrace all religiously inspired cultural expressions: from Dostoyevsky's *The Brothers Karamazov* to the musical *Joseph and the Amazing Technicolor Dreamcoat*.

Theologians have included an increasing amount of modern literature and film in their discourse. Conversely, writers have incorporated biblical stories in their literary work, or rewritten Bible stories, for example Thomas Mann's *Joseph and his brothers*. However theologians, writers and film-makers all approach it differently. Below we look at five different ways in which the relationship between literary texts and biblical texts takes shape. A complicating factor with this is that the Bible itself largely consists of literary texts; or, the Bible is considered among the most high-quality pieces of literature. This immediately marks the first way of reading the Bible: as a literary text.

## 1. The Bible as a literary text

The Bible is full of stories. Yet only in the twentieth century, in response to the historical method of reading the Bible, was explicit attention given to the Bible's literary aspects. This has many benefits. If we consider the Bible as literature, we have an eye for the game played by the writer. For example, that the writer says one thing but means something else, or exaggerates or downplays something (understatement). The fact that the reader is sensitive to the literary forms used by the writer increases the possibilities of interpretation. The person who is speaking is important here. By this I do not mean the author of the story and their context, because in the case of the Bible these are usually impossible to identify. I am talking about the narrator. The writer can for example provide a multitude of characters and change the point of view from which the story is being told. The story gets an additional meaning when you discover that the story of Jairus' 12-year-old daughter is interrupted by the story of a bleeding woman, who has been suffering from her illness for the past 12 years. The difference in knowledge between the characters, the narrator and the reader is a common narrative technique as well, which allows for different depths. A good example is the familiar story of David and Bathsheba in 2 Samuel 11. David is in love with Bathsheba, Uriah's wife. David wants to get rid of Uriah, but he does not succeed right away. Then he sends Uriah to the army with a letter for Joab, the army chief. In this letter, David requests Joab to send Uriah to the front lines, so that he will most probably die. Uriah does not know he is carrying his own death sentence, but the reader does. The reader thinks: 'Oh dear, this is not going to end well.' The reader's knowledge increases the dramatic effect and consequently also the reader's involvement. And ultimately, that is what it's all about. Robert Alter provides a few fine examples of this in his book *The Art of Biblical Narrative* (1981).

## 2. Literature and films as illustrations to or actualization of the Bible

The second, and most obvious way to connect the Bible with literature and film is that literature and film are used as an illustration to or actualization of the Bible. The relationship between literature and religion is thus that life confirms the doctrine. Ministers include quotations or excerpts from books and films in their sermons. It often involves a few lines of poetry, or a scene from a film.

## 3. Literature and film as a commentary on the Bible

The film *Son of Man* (2006) is a good example of the actualization of the well-known story of the resurrection. The film is a powerful retelling of the life of Christ set in a contemporary country, possibly South Africa. In terms of story, there are no elements of surprise in the film. As an adult, Jesus travels to the capital, gathering followers along the way from the armed factions of rebels across the land. He demands that his followers give up their arms and confront their corrupt rulers with a vision of non-violent protest and solidarity. In terms of representation of the well-known story, all you will see are surprises. It is amazing how director Dornford-May is able to provide every known element of the story with a refreshing new interpretation. As a result, those well-known stories sound more powerful than ever. He has managed to make tangible the essence of the gospel, much more so than Gibson did in his film *The Passion of Christ* (2004). Jesus and his disciples travelling in the back of an open truck, or the adulterous woman being doused with gasoline and threatened with being set on fire instead of being stoned are not alienating elements, but rather bring things right up close. One of the very beautiful scenes shows a paper bag on a table where everyone can deposit their guns or other weapons. We watch through the eyes of the disciples and see what violence they have been subjected to since childhood. The call to renounce hatred and to try doing things without the use of violence confuses them, but is liberating. Jesus does not hesitate to seek confrontation in public. He calls on people to stop allowing themselves to be lied to. Judas records everything with his camcorder. Inevitably, Jesus attracts the attention of the Judean tribal leaders who have struck a power-sharing deal with the aloof Governor Pilate. The Son of Man is tortured and killed in a back room. Remarkably, the cross only appears after Jesus has died. Analogous to the Bible, a resurrection scene is not pictured. However, after Jesus' death his mother Mary gets his body out of the grave and puts it on a cross on a hill, for everyone to see. The cross is both a place of deep mourning and the place where people decide not to be terrorized any longer. The resurrection is also their own uprising. When the gathered military threatens the crowd, they start to dance. They are standing up. On the one hand, the film is a retelling of the story of the resurrection, but on the other it does more: it delivers very hard criticism – and a clarification – of twenty-first century oppression and power politics in a country in Southern Africa ravaged by civil war.

Such comments can be of a social nature, as in *Son of Man*, but can also be very personal. A playful, free association with Genesis 22 characterizes 'You want it darker', a song with lyrics by Leonard Cohen featured on his latest CD bearing the same title. Cohen's handling of the text not only offers an actualization, but also a personal contextualization. The recurring refrain in the song: 'Hineni (I'm ready my Lord)' appears in three key moments in the story of sacrifice: when God tells Abraham to sacrifice Isaac, when Isaac asks where the sacrificial animal is, and when the angel puts a stop to the sacrifice. In one of his last interviews, Cohen states that 'Hineni' is

> a declaration of readiness no matter what the outcome. That is a part of everyone's soul. We all are motivated by deep impulses and appetites to serve, even though we may not be able to locate that which we are willing to serve. It is just a part of everybody's nature to offer oneself at the critical moment.

At the same time Leonard Cohen surrenders under protest. In an earlier song, 'The Story of Isaac' on the CD titled *Songs from a room* the willingness of Isaac, son of Abraham, to be sacrificed turns into protest against the violence in the world, against the fathers who are prepared to sacrifice their children without a higher power requesting this from them: 'You who build these altars now / To sacrifice these children / You must not do it anymore / A scheme is not a vision.' Cohen's protest not only applies to violent states of war. In an interview (1988), Cohen states that he

> ... was careful in that song to try and put it beyond the pure, beyond the simple, anti-war protest, that it also is ... it isn't necessarily for war that we're willing to sacrifice each other. We'll get some idea – some magnificent idea – that we're willing to sacrifice each other for; it doesn't necessarily have to involve an opponent or an ideology, but human beings being what they are we're always going to set up people to die for some absurd situation that we define as important.[1]

Cohen, however, makes an exception for Abraham. Unlike the perpetrators of violence in today's world, Abraham had a vision, a dream of the future, of a nation that is larger than the universe. And, despite all proof to the contrary, father and son stubbornly hold on to it. Just as Abraham challenges God to be the God of this promise in a liberal interpretation of Genesis 22, Cohen seems to surrender under protest: 'You want it darker. We kill the flame.' Besides a sign of surrender, despite the darkness of the world in which people are killing each other and the darkness of his impending death, in his song Cohen also refers to the Kaddish, the Jewish prayer for the dead. Just as in his song, the word 'death' does not appear in the Kaddish; it is all about life and about love. In the face of death Cohen on the one hand seems to protest against the 'paradox' of people murdering in the name of God, and on the other honours God: 'magnified and sanctified be Thy Holy Name'. We also hear an echo of 'Hallelujah': 'And even though it all went wrong / I'll stand before the Lord of song / with nothing on my tongue but Hallelujah.'

## 4. *Literature as a handmaid of theology; literature and film as a substitute for biblical texts*

The use of literary texts and films can, however, be overshot, whereby the focus ends up entirely on literature/film. In this fourth way literature, art and film take the place of theology. As the powerful evocative image of Bible stories decreases in a secularized world, art increasingly replaces religion. Many people are moved and touched by the *St Matthew Passion*, by the funeral of Princess Diana, or by the opening ceremony of the Olympics. Does not a sold-out football game meet the religious needs of contemporary people more than a church with 25 per cent attendance?

For many, the replacement of Christian theology by secular mass experiences is taking it a step too far. The religious sense of belonging is fierce, but does not last long, and it lacks reflection. Novelists are then expected to answer existential questions. Dutch author Connie Palmen talks about how she received a phone call from a boy who asked her about the meaning of life. The writer was not able to give him an answer. 'And you should run very hard and very far from any writer who does try and give you an answer' (Hagdom, 1991, referred to by van Heijst, 1992, p. 64). Literature, film and art have a specific, own expressiveness. Their imaginative and literary character do not lend themselves to making them into theology or philosophy. Dutch theologian Annelies van Heijst (1992, p. 268) rightly criticizes theologians for misusing literature as a handmaid of theology. Stories are then seen as simple raw material for theology, or they take theology's place. Van Heijst provides the example of a study by Jonneke Bekkenkamp, a feminist theologian. To offer opportunities of recognition and identification for women, Bekkenkamp (1993) reads *Twenty-One Love Poems* by Adrienne Rich, alongside the biblical Song of Songs as a theological text. Van Heijst's objection to this is that women can't but confirm the stories, and that in this way Bekkenkamp only presents a continuous reading, and omits discontinuous reading. In this way, the irritant, contrarian and 'difficult' texts remain untouched. While literary texts and art and film are ambiguous and open and ambivalent, and bring about

individual experiences, theological stances are a totally different ballgame. If the difference between the two linguistic playing
fields is not recognized, the theologian is likely to take literary
texts or cinematic scenes out of their context, thus compromising
their identity. In my opinion, the biggest disadvantage of this way
of doing things is that when the distinction between literature
and theology is lost, the excitement disappears as well, making
literature a substitute for theology. Literature would no longer
have anything to contribute. When you subject a literary text, for
example Nietzsche's famous text about 'God is dead', to general-
ized philosophical speaking, then the text only confirms what you
already knew. A discussion occurs when questions arise along
the lines of how does literature/film question the Bible passage?
What other views on reality does the story provide? Which view
is relevant to the reader? Those questions are disregarded when a
theologian merely looks for an illustration in art with an opinion
they already had.

## 5. The interaction between literature and theology: a meeting point

And finally, my preference, the fifth way, which begins by taking
the ability of writers and film-makers to create new meanings 100
per cent seriously. Wright (1988, p. 4) writes that there is a creative tension between the two, which makes literature work in a
spiritual way. 'The whole point of reading literature, its importance as a humane discipline, beyond that of giving pleasure
(which is by no means unimportant), is that it says something
about life which cannot be said in any other way.' So literature is
not an illustration or ornament to the statements of theology and
philosophy, but it is valuable because it can create new meanings.

Exactly at the point where literature/film and the Bible meet,
something new can develop. An example is the resurrection of
Harry Potter in the last film of the series, *Harry Potter and the
Deathly Hallows*. Analogous to Jesus, Harry undertakes his
sacrifice as a willed and intentional act, delivering himself to
Voldemort. Undefending, he exposes himself to the evil wizard,
and Voldemort does not hesitate to cast the Death Curse. Fortu-

nately, the Death Curse does not work properly, since Voldemort unknowingly carries a part of Harry's soul within him. Then a very interesting scene follows. Harry finds himself in a kind of afterlife on an all white (heavenly?) railway station: King's Cross. Here Harry meets the school's headmaster Dumbledore, who died and now repents that he has been using Harry to fight evil and save the Hogwarts community. Then Harry wonders whether he still has a choice, which Dumbledore confirms. Harry can either take a train, or return to finish the job of battling Voldemort. However, it is the school population who make the final decision. Voldemort is trying to demoralize them: 'Harry is dead! Do you understand now, deluded ones? He was nothing, ever, but a boy who relied on others to sacrifice themselves for him!' (It is of note that Voldemort accuses Harry of what he himself has done all his life.) However, the community reacts furiously. In contrast to the book, the film shows us a very biblical reaction at this point. Neville Longbottom steps forward to oppose Voldemort. 'Harry is dead', he shouts for everyone to hear, 'so many have died in this battle, but they now live in here [points], in our hearts. We will go on.' This inspires Harry to engage in the final battle of Hogwarts, which of course they win. The point is that Harry's sacrifice arouses the anger of his friends and inspires them to fight, which relativizes the resurrection altogether.

## Openness of literature and reader

Unlike arguments and pamphlets, novels have an open character. The involvement of the reader is typical for literature. The reader becomes a participant in the story. We do not observe literary characters from the outside, but we live with them, share their worries and fears, joys and sorrows. That explains the fascination we feel for fictional characters like Anna Karenina and Emma Bovary, and perhaps Jesus. The ability to touch the reader, to evoke emotions, is an essential characteristic of literature. The question is whether participating in the literary game of make-believe goes beyond the transformation of emotions, and that it also means it can change our faith and our way of life. Can literary imagination create the possibility that something in our ideas and beliefs changes when we 'participate' in a literary story? According to philosopher Martha Nussbaum (1986) it can. She claims that literature can serve as an illustration to ideas, or as an analytical tool, for example a narrative structure of reality, a 'laboratory of the experience'. In the encounter with fictional characters in novels, we move from an objective perspective to a subjective one. The encounter makes the reader take on the perspective of the fictional character. The encounter itself is and will remain fictional, so that the 'knowledge' we gain with this encounter is not a first-hand 'experiential' one. The process of reading literature brings about knowledge that cannot be falsified or authorized by objective means. The solidified experiences of others will have to do for us, readers.

According to N. Verbin (2006) it is exactly this dual perspective, typical for narrative stories and not for historical and scientific arguments, that gives the reader the opportunity to make a choice: external or internal perspective. When a fictional work requires us to take a moral position that contrasts with ours – for example, if it promotes racism and slavery – we go into 'imaginary resistance' and look at things from the perspective of the outsider. But the opposite can happen as well. Some subversive literary works may have such an imagination that they have an impact on the reader's views. For example, think of *Max Havelaar* by Multatuli (1987, 1860). Verbin writes:

> In such cases, we are dealing with subversive works of fiction, which engage the imagination in such a manner that the fictional game-world completely reorients the participant's life. Instead of leading its participant to place the fictional narrative within the framework of her ordinary life and conception of reality, a subversive narrative leads her to place her life within the framework of the narrative. (p. 191)

In this way, according to Verbin, Bible stories operate as subversive stories. The fate of Jesus as described in the Gospel stories, can touch the reader in such a way that they get involved and thereby arrive at a different interpretation of the term 'salvation', for example, from glorious victory to desperate humiliation.

In line with the transformation undergone by Shūsaku Endō's fictional characters at this point, the perspective of his readers can also drastically change.

Whether that happens depends on two factors: the ability of the text to touch the reader, that is to captivate the reader in such a way that they are drawn into the story, and the willingness of the reader to participate in the fictional world of make-believe in the specific language game offered by the text. This requires the text to be open. Texts that are opening themselves up to the reader are classic novels such as Dostoyevsky's *The Brothers Karamazov* and Graham Greene's *The Power and the Glory*. If you identify with their main characters while reading, your view of reality will change. Not the pope at the altar, but the whisky priest, the drunk in the pub, gives an insight into the judging and giving Jesus. Likewise, Dostoyevsky depicts a Christ figure who is neither a representative of power nor a saint, but someone who is dealing with epilepsy, impotence and eventually even with madness. The openness of the text also means that you do not have to go along with the imagination of the author. As D. H. Lawrence exclaimed circa 1910: 'But Dostoyevsky, mixing God and sadism, he is a foul.' But in the meantime it gives you food for thought. This openness is true for the Bible stories in two ways: the stories can be read in different times and cultures, without sacrificing any impact. And they are open because they provide the readers with room for interpretation and invite them to accept a role in the story. One example can be found in the Chapter 6 of this book, in a playful adaptation of the book of Ruth.

## Reading the Bible as literature

Lastly, we discuss more extensively the way of reading the Bible itself as literature. The Bible stories themselves being literary texts provide opportunities to play with the text and to recognize yourself in the text or, conversely, to make the text work in your own life. Roland Barthes emphasizes that it is not about the author, but rather about the text. This is certainly true in the case of the Bible. Because of the centuries that passed between writing and reading, it is impossible to determine the intentions of the authors of the Scriptures. And even their context is subject to a guessing game. Barthes points out that the author not so much writes about something, but rather writes *something*. The author does not give the text an unambiguous meaning, which the reader would have to pick out; the writer merely gives his or her text. Readers then derive multiple meanings from the text. The sheer difference in culture and time make the written texts in the Bible very different from the texts that are read. If it is high-quality literature, and in the case of the Bible it certainly is, the author *cannot* possibly write a text that seamlessly reflects his opinion. Good literature is characterized precisely by a certain openness. The story is open when it leaves room for ambiguous interpretations. In addition, the literary inspiration also transports the author into the story. David Jasper writes about this:

> Certain kinds of religious experience and the experience of the creative writer have this in common – that the subject or artist becomes a vehicle more inspired than controlling. A writer in this case is not to be judged by his intentions, moral or religious, but only by the fruit of his creation. (1992, pp. 46–7)

Bible stories contain no truths which are to be distilled out of the stories, and transformed into doctrines by the reader; rather, they are contagious. It is up to the reader whether or not to give meaning to the text. With a good story and a reader who is touched and involved, two worlds confront each other: the text's figurative world and the reader's real world. Ricœur (1991) points out that understanding aligns with the reader projecting himself in the text, but the reader receives a wider self from the world of the text.

Dutch theologian Ria van den Brandt (1999) also argues for openness; openness of the different disciplines. When theologians work together in an interdisciplinary way and theological, philosophical and literary discourses intermingle, other texts and other perspectives will come into view. She distinguishes three functions of the literary text. Literature can illustrate and complement a theological discourse, and (ideally) form a new source for theological discourse. With the first two functions the goal is not another theological content, but a more contemporary discussion about God. In the latter option things become exciting. This is where the theological language game puts itself at risk. Literary texts then have their own powerful meaning. They do not only present a new language, but also a different meaning. They form a new source.

In this book we use the stories in novels, films and lyrics as such a new language. Not only to illustrate the theological notions of forgiveness and reconciliation, or as a more modern way to demonstrate these topics, but rather the other way around: to reinterpret the Bible stories with what we find in cultural expressions. It is therefore not our intention to stretch the definition of 'theology' to a 'hermeneutics of existence', in order to make literature and film fall under theology (Bekkenkamp). Nor do we see art, poetry and literature as a replacement for theology. I see the relationship between literature and religion in the same line as David Jasper, who emphasizes the creative dialectic between literature and religion. Bible and literature cast a mutually different light on each other. Literature can save religion from the dangers of dogmatism and apologetic; trivial direct evangelization, he says. While religion provides the necessary ethical and theological standards to remind literature of the dangers of beauty in the service of evil, literature can provide critical commentary to the Bible or be a source of reinterpretation of the Bible.

According to Jasper, it is a far from harmonious relationship. The great merit of literary imagination is that it can be a powerful instrument in the 'remaking of theology' (p. ix). Good literature 'rubs', puts question marks behind theological concepts. Jasper explains:

> The text itself remains as a complex structure with a particular relationship to creator, reader and critic. In the end we trust the tale and not the teller, and it is the tale which professes an enduring and profound moral significance, perhaps, as in the case of the Pensées (Pascal), of such significance as will need to be described in religious terms, and which has the capacity to rediscover and enliven truths of theology and doctrine – the mysteries of grace and salvation. (1992, p. 54)

## Reading the Bible: a delightful pilgrimage

Finally, two comments when reading the Bible: it is fun and it takes you on a spiritual journey, a pilgrimage. Bible stories are not usually seen primarily as a source of entertainment. They often have a comforting, encouraging, exemplary or socio-critical function. Literature and film can also be helpful here, by breaking up theological formulations of metaphysical notions with the play of words. Furthermore, the capacity to read requires the capacity of humanity to listen and to get involved in the story, to become an insider, as in the process of faith. In this form of spiritual reading the reader does not control the pages; he moves in its interior, reading himself into them. He sees and feels with the author, and 'behind' the author, for especially in the case of biblical narratives, the story says more than the author intended to write. Spiritual reading is active: it questions mind and heart. The text might become a mirror for the reader, inviting him to reflect on his own story. Therefore, to understand a book is to understand a part of oneself and one's presence in the world. Reading the Bible is like a journey, a pilgrimage. It is a commitment and a challenge.

---

### Questions for Reflection

Which of the five types of relationship between Bible and literature, film, plays do you prefer, and why?

To which of the five types of relationship between Bible and literature, film, plays do the examples given in the previous chapters belong?

What is your favourite novel, film, song or play that reflects or comments on a biblical story? Why?

---

## Note

1 www.leonardcohenfiles.com/rte.html, accessed 1 January 2017.

# 4

# The Planet

## BERT DICOU

### To be a human on earth: Bible and ecology

To be a human on earth
in these times
means to come out of the water
and stand in the desert
not a god among the gods
no angel and no animal

(Willem Barnard, excerpt from the song, 'To be a human on earth',
a popular Dutch hymn – Liedboek 2013, no. 538)

Ever since humankind has been able to think reflectively, myths
have been told and poems and songs have been written. Images
have been drawn about the place of humans in nature, their relationship to the animal world, their relationship to the forces that
are greater than themselves – the gods. All cultures have developed philosophies about the place of humans in the totality of
everything that exists, and what the special task of humans in
that totality could be. The Bible is similar. The above fragment
may refer to how the author saw the original state, when there
was nothing. Waters covered the earth. There was no light. Then
creation began. 'Let there be light' was the first creation task. In
seven days, everything was created. Rather, in six days, at the end
of the sixth day God had finished. On the seventh day he rested
and enjoyed his work. The intention of this story is undoubtedly
that people should also rest on the seventh day and enjoy creation
and let their thoughts go to the Creator. That is also how it is
expressed in the fourth of the ten commandments:

'Remember the sabbath day, and keep it holy. For six days you shall labour and do all your work. But the seventh day is a sabbath to the Lord your God; you shall not do any work – you, your son or your daughter, your male or female slave, your livestock, or the alien resident in your towns. For in six days the Lord made heaven and earth, the sea, and all that is in them, but rested the seventh day; therefore the Lord blessed the sabbath day and consecrated it' (Ex. 20.8–11)

People and animals were created on the sixth and last day. People were created after the animals and differed from the animals. God had something special in mind for them.

And God said, 'Let the earth bring forth living creatures of every kind: cattle and creeping things and wild animals of the earth of every kind.' And it was so. God made the wild animals of the earth of every kind, and the cattle of every kind, and everything that creeps upon the ground of every kind. And God saw that it was good. Then God said, 'Let us make humankind in our image, according to our likeness; and let them have dominion over the fish of the sea, and over the birds of the air, and over the cattle, and over all the wild animals of the earth, and over every creeping thing that creeps upon the earth.'

So God created humankind in his image, in the image of God he created them; male and female he created them. God blessed them, and God said to them, 'Be fruitful and multiply, and fill the earth and subdue it; and have dominion over the fish of the sea and over the birds of the air and over every living thing that moves upon the earth.' (Gen. 1.24–28)

Humans are beings who, on the one hand, are a normal part of the created reality, conjured up on the same day as the animals, but on the other are close to God and are God's image and likeness. Accordingly, the custody of the animals was entrusted to humankind.

The desert in Barnard's song can refer to the desert where the first phase of the history of the people of Israel took place. After God had freed them from slavery in Egypt, they headed to the land that would become theirs. But first they spent 40 years in the desert. Incidentally, they also 'came out of the water' – the exodus from Egypt began with the crossing of the Red Sea, which turned dry just as they had to cross it.

In biblical poetics this water and this desert reoccur in the story of Jesus. After he was baptized in the River Jordan, he spent (not coincidentally) 40 days in the desert. Jesus was 'no god among gods', neither 'an angel nor an animal', but fully human, with a mission on this earth.

The creation story in Genesis 1 is written as a song, with repetitions and choruses. A recurring chorus is: 'And God saw that it was good.' At the end of the sixth day, after the creation of humans, God oversaw the whole and even concluded 'that it was very good'.

## Psalm 8

This beautiful situation, the balance of all that is, everything in the right place, is short-lived. He who introduces himself to the Bible and starts reading on page 1 and then continues, will soon discover that. Although first, there is a second creation story with an equally happy starting point. Humans get a 'paradise' to reside in, a perfect garden. All they need to do to receive food is just reach to the trees with all sorts of fruits. But not even one chapter further, the humans have been kicked out of this 'Garden of Eden'. After which the real history begins. In this real history, nature is often unreliable, life is short and not always pleasant, and moreover people seem to be weak, unjust, violent and cruel. Nevertheless, fortunately there is still a lot which in the eyes of God (or the people themselves) could be called 'good' or 'very good'.

Throughout the Bible some things can be found that relate to the primordial experience that Genesis 1 talks about; we are actually living in a fantastically beautiful world. Psalm 8 is a good example which will be discussed next. The book of Psalms is a very rich collection of poetry. It consists of 150 poems that at some point must have functioned as songs. All aspects of existence are covered. Psalm 8 is one of the poems that reflect on the fact that God created everything that exists. The tone of Psalm 8 is one of joy and wonder.

> O Lord, our Sovereign,
>    how majestic is your name in all the earth!
>
> You have set your glory above the heavens.
>    Out of the mouths of babes and infants
> you have founded a bulwark because of your foes,
>    to silence the enemy and the avenger.
>
> When I look at your heavens, the work of your fingers,
>    the moon and the stars that you have established;
> what are human beings that you are mindful of them,
>    mortals that you care for them?
>
> Yet you have made them a little lower than God,
>    and crowned them with glory and honour.
> You have given them dominion over the works of your hands;
>    you have put all things under their feet,
> all sheep and oxen,
>    and also the beasts of the field,
> the birds of the air, and the fish of the sea,
>    whatever passes along the paths of the seas.
>
> O Lord, our Sovereign,
>    how majestic is your name in all the earth!

The psalm begins and ends with God's majesty. His 'name' is the most impressive 'in all the earth'. The end of the first verse talks about God's 'glory' in the 'heavens' above. God's power has no limits, both omnipresent in heaven and on earth. Moreover, God reaches his target without an impressive display of power: even with the modest means of 'the mouths of babes and infants' he is able to defeat his enemies.

The rest of the song is about the place of humans in the universe and in nature. The key words 'heaven' and 'earth' from the sections about God also prove significant as sections about humans. First the position of humankind is considered from the perspective of 'heaven'. At night, the poet looks up to the sky, 'the work of your fingers'. The celestial area with the moon and the stars clearly is God's most impressive piece of work. Humans seem so small in comparison. How is it possible that God still has an interest in such an insignificant creature?

Then the poet, on behalf of us all, continues with our position on earth. Still under the impression of God's majesty, and still deeply aware of our smallness in the context of the world above, we are confronted with a new wonderful thing. Apparently we have been entrusted with ruling over the other creatures on earth, which are also 'the work of your hands'. Not only do people receive God's relatively undeserved attention, care and love, a matter of deep wonder and gratitude, they receive even more. Their exalted position among the other earthly creatures is more reason to be surprised and delighted. God lets them rule over the other creatures, which position 'crowns' humans 'with glory and honour'. All that is more reason to praise God's majesty, which the psalmist does in the last verse of the song.

As often noted, Psalm 8 seems to be a reflection on or a poetic variant of the story of creation as told in Genesis 1 and what was said about the relationship between God, humans and animals. Both texts are, correctly so, highlights of biblical literature. But they also raise questions concerning their views on the place of humans in all that surrounds them. Isn't this vision very outdated? In this chapter, I listen to philosophers and writers from the world of theology and the church, as well as from scientific and literary environments. I start with the world of science.

## A physicist's view on creation

For a while, faith and science had a difficult relationship where the story of creation was concerned. Believers thought the theory of evolution an attack on how one ought to think about the origin of living things. In particular, the relationship between humans and ('the other') animals was a stumbling block: the theory of evolution saw only a gradual difference between highly evolved apes and the first stages of Homo sapiens. Physics brought insights into the origin of the universe that gave the impression that one rationally knows how, from a primordial time when there was nothing, everything was created as it is now – a very large infinite universe.

Now, the struggle between believers and scientists seems to be over. Only the rearguard of the church's so-called 'creationists' or their contemporary variants, still fight against a scientific view that does not seem to necessarily need God as originator or director. This, however, raises the question whether it is still possible and useful in our scientific time to continue to speak about 'creation', a word from religious language, or whether this has become passé. I spoke about this with physicist Peter Kluit, a believer and scientist. Peter specializes in elementary particles and works for Nikhef, the National Institute for Subatomic Physics in the Netherlands. He is, among others, involved in the ATLAS experiment at CERN in Geneva. Using an impressive particle accelerator, research is done into the subatomic base of our existence. He is an active member of the Remonstrant community of Haarlem.

*Peter, you said you find it interesting to think about the role of nature in faith. As a natural scientist and a believer you enjoy the thoughts about the relationship between these two worlds.*

Yes, I've long been interested in the relationship between science and faith: knowledge and what exceeds it. Not only did I study physics, I also studied philosophy. In the Middle Ages a lot of thought was given to science and faith. At that time they were faced with the task to unite the ancient thought of Plato and Aristotle with the biblical texts. This led, among other things, to the fact that they started to think critically about how to deal with the Bible and how literally one should take the texts. Thinkers like Thomas Aquinas, in the footsteps of early theologians like Augustine, succeeded nicely in reconciling the ancient way of thinking with the biblical one.

But since the Enlightenment (and the scientific revolution of the seventeenth century), everything has changed. Since then, faith is no longer the solid framework for interpreting reality. We have realized that the way the Bible formulates views fits the thinking of ancient Israel. That world view is completely dated. Nevertheless, the creation story in Genesis 1 appeals to me. In particular, how it sees the whole of reality in one great cohesion, the place of people between the animals and beneath the stars.

Moreover, Genesis 1, surprisingly, portrays a picture of the origin of the universe that fits how we now think about it in natural science. It starts with (almost) nothing, then you will successively see space and time develop (from a physics point of view), light, the material world, life, plants, fish, birds, other living beings, and humans. It all happens in a creative process in which new things emerge, of course, not literally in seven days, but you can distinguish stages and periods. In Genesis, God creates by speaking; speech determines what appears. In the history of the cosmos too, rational structures – the laws of nature – began to apply when for the first time there was talk about a universe, and from that time on they started to structure reality.

*Most Christians agree that the Bible is not intended as a scientific account of the natural history of the earth and the universe. It is a different kind of literature. The question however remains whether it is possible to accept all hypotheses and experimental evidence brought forward by science, but to continue to speak of God as Creator and nature as creation.*

I do not think that the scientific discoveries in the last centuries limit or contradict the scope of the religious view of life. Beyond the limit of your knowledge there is an unknown and partly unknowable reality. Physics has a lot to say about the origins and workings of the universe. Yet we have no idea of the answer to a number of major scientific questions: we do not understand why the universe consists of matter (and not anti-matter) and the source of 95 per cent of energy and matter is unknown. With our research, we are constantly trying to find and push the limits. This has been going on since ancient times and I think it will continue for a long time.

*What do texts like Genesis 1 and Psalm 8 tell you?*

Physics and cosmology have nothing to say about the most fundamental questions. *Why* is there a reality? What is the purpose of life? Science is not about that, however faith texts are. Faith is about issues which we *cannot* know for sure. As a believer, there are things you trust. If I can read a text like Genesis 1 with an open mind, I will enjoy it. Texts like Genesis 1 and Psalm 8 put you in the bigger picture, give you the consciousness of belonging to something greater than yourself, bigger than your mind. In my opinion, we should keep referring to God as 'Creator'.

*What aspect of thinking about nature do you now find especially relevant?*

In my view, a part of nature which we should pay more attention to, is the importance of cycles. Understanding cycles in ecosystems is essential to make good decisions about our future and the earth. But also in a philosophical sense: that everything would revolve around individual existence, the feeling of many that 'I' am in the centre, gives a distorted picture. I think it's good to consider that I was formed from elements that were there from the beginning of the universe. Quarks and elementary particles that are now in my body will reappear into all sorts of new forms of matter after my death.

In Genesis 1 there is a cycle of seven days, the seven days of the week. Then it begins all over again. That was reflected in agriculture: in every seventh year you let land lie fallow (Lev. 25), after which a new cycle of seven years began.

In industrial farming nature is forced and awareness of the original cycles has disappeared. I believe it is important to remember that existence works as such, and I derive inspiration from New Testament texts that describe such cycles:

> 'Listen! A sower went out to sow. And as he sowed, some seed fell on the path, and the birds came and ate it up. Other seed fell on rocky ground, where it did not have much soil, and it sprang up quickly, since it had no depth of soil. And when the

sun rose, it was scorched; and since it had no root, it withered away. Other seed fell among thorns, and the thorns grew up and choked it, and it yielded no grain. Other seed fell into good soil and brought forth grain, growing up and increasing and yielding thirty and sixty and a hundredfold'. (Mark 4.3–8)

'The kingdom of God is as if someone would scatter seed on the ground, and would sleep and rise night and day, and the seed would sprout and grow, he does not know how. The earth produces of itself, first the stalk, then the head, then the full grain in the head. But when the grain is ripe, at once he goes in with his sickle, because the harvest has come'. (Mark 4.26–29)

'Very truly, I tell you, unless a grain of wheat falls into the earth and dies, it remains just a single grain; but if it dies, it bears much fruit'. (John 12.24)

*Some biologists believe that humans sometimes pretend too much to be like the king of creation – we are not that special. In Genesis 1 and Psalm 8 too the position of humans is overstated.*

I think it is understandable that people emerge last in the process of creation and acquire a central position. This corresponds to the actual situation as known by the Israelites: they are people who grow crops, raise sheep, and let cows graze. It is also humans who name plants and animals and interpret their existence. Creation is *entrusted* to humankind.

For me entrusting nature to humans means also that we have to be wise in dealing with our environment. Technological progress has brought us both prosperity and severe environmental damage. But technology can also be a force for good. A number of new techniques to solve environmental problems have already been developed. It still lacks the political will and funding to actually deploy this technology. That really needs change. In addition, changes are needed in consumer spending, which depletes resources and is often polluting. Dutch physicists presented their own explanation for the Intergovernmental Panel on Climate Change (IPCC). We can and must take action now!

## The timeliness of Psalm 8

In one respect, the outline of the position of humans in Psalm 8, with regards to their relationship to nature, is more appropriate in our time than at the time this psalm was written. The psalm proclaims without reserve the dominance of humans over their natural environment.

Yet you have made them a little lower than God,
and crowned them with glory and honour.
You have given them dominion over the works of your hands;
you have put all things under their feet,
all sheep and oxen,
and also the beasts of the field,
the birds of the air, and the fish of the sea,
whatever passes along the paths of the seas.

In biblical times, people had not progressed nearly as far as that 'all', all living creatures, fell under their rule. Today, however, it seems that there are only a few ecosystems that have *not* dealt with the consequences of human behaviour. We even managed to change the climate, with serious consequences for animals and plants.

Because human influence has become so enormous, it has been proposed to refer to this time period as the Anthropocene period – a new geological period, after the Holocene period. The changes taking place right now and which will determine what the planet will look like in the future, are not so much the result of geological or biological processes, but of the human factor.

But few of these changes are positive, and a summary of the impacts offers a daunting list. It has been determined that in the last century, an alarming number of plant and animal species went extinct, and it is expected many more species will follow. Global warming threatens the living conditions of both humans and their natural environment. Higher average temperatures and drought have a negative impact on agricultural production, which leads to poverty, hunger and war. Rising sea levels threaten low-lying, vulnerable countries such as Bangladesh and Burma. A large part of the great tropical forests has deliberately been destroyed for profit. As a result, erosion is rapidly changing once fertile land into a barren wasteland. It is uncertain whether the battle to preserve what is left of the rainforests can still be won. Then there is the problem of environmental pollution. In many areas, hardly any attention is given to recycling waste. Untreated industrial and household waste are excessively found in natural environments. The resulting serious pollution of land, sea and air can only partly be offset.

## Pope Francis on the environment

The realization that the impact of humankind has – already – resulted in serious environmental damage, and that it only threatens to become much worse, is shared by a growing number of politicians and church leaders. Undoubtedly Pope Francis is the best known. His encyclical *Laudato Si'* (published in 2015, available online at https://laudatosi.com) deals with this issue. Meanwhile *Laudato Si'* is regarded as an extremely important contribution to the global debate on sustainability and the ecological future of the planet. In the first part Pope Francis gives an analysis of what is wrong. The entire above-mentioned list, and more, is described in detail. Then he looks at the biblical sources. He also addresses the charge that the Bible itself has given rise to such an irresponsible way of dealing with nature. He disagrees.

> We are not God. The earth was here before us and it has been given to us. This allows us to respond to the charge that Judaeo-Christian thinking, on the basis of the Genesis account which grants humanity 'dominion' over the earth (cf. Gen. 1.28), has encouraged the unbridled exploitation of nature by painting him as domineering and destructive by nature. This is not a correct interpretation of the Bible as understood by the Church. Although it is true that we Christians have at times incorrectly interpreted the Scriptures, nowadays we must forcefully reject the notion that our being created in God's image and given dominion over the earth justifies absolute domination

over other creatures ... This responsibility for God's earth means that human beings, endowed with intelligence, must respect the laws of nature and the delicate equilibria existing between the creatures of this world, for 'he commanded and they were created; and he established them for ever and ever; he fixed their bounds and he set a law which cannot pass away' (Ps. 148.5b–6) ... In our time, the Church does not simply state that other creatures are completely subordinated to the good of human beings, as if they have no worth in themselves and can be treated as we wish ... Catechism clearly and forcefully criticizes a distorted anthropocentrism: 'Each creature possesses its own particular goodness and perfection'.

(Pope Francis 2015: sections 67–9; cf. section 220)

For Pope Francis, the Bible actually offers the base for the opposite of brutal domination over nature. His next theme is therefore that people should take responsibility on a personal and political level. His encyclical is in essence an urgent call for change. He calls on his readers to start an 'ecological conversion', 'a new lifestyle' and calls for 'a covenant between humanity and the environment'. He writes that education should play a central role in bringing about this change. A turnaround which, on the one hand should take shape in private and which, on the other, requires radical political decisions. The planet's future is at stake. In the interests of both nature and humankind the current anthropocentric culture and economic philosophy should be replaced by a culture and a philosophy that are ecologically founded. Pope Francis speaks of environmental ecology, economic, social and cultural ecology, and ecology of everyday life.

The pope sends a pretty radical message to the world. Perhaps too radical to be implemented as he advocates. But, given his position and his popularity, he may be the most fit to preach such a message. Moreover, the message is consistent with a wider and broader awareness that the ecological state of the earth is in danger. It is good that he is able to make the connection in such an outspoken way between the urgency of the ecological question and the inspiration from biblical sources on the role of humans on our planet.

## An anti-Psalm 8 and a papal prayer

The eco-theologians of the *Earth Bible Project*, which I wrote about above regarding several new ways of reading, are a lot less positive about the biblical view of nature in texts such as Genesis 1 and Psalm 8. They are critical of a philosophy of nature that is so clearly hierarchically laid out, with humans being automatically placed higher than animals, and even given control over the animal kingdom. According to them, this is the recipe for ecological disaster. Domination can move easily into exploitation. The danger of such hierarchical thinking is that the higher-placed human will automatically feel more relevant than the lower-ranking animals; his interests should therefore prevail.[1] Instead of responsibility based on stewardship or a different hierarchical concept, they would like to develop values that connect responsibility with kinship and interdependence of humans and nature.[2] The role of people should thus be defined differently.

In part 1 of the *Earth Bible* series, *Readings from the perspective of Earth*, Keith Carley writes about Psalm 8. The title of his article is 'Psalm 8: An Apology for Domination' (Carley, 2000). From the beginning, it is clear that Carley rejects the vision of the psalmist regarding the place of humans. He argues that the psalm is both theocentric and anthropocentric, with the approach 'leave no room for the voices of either the Earth or its non-human creatures' (p. 115). 'The Earth's interests are certainly not central in Psalm 8' (p. 121). Carley's suspicious conclusion is that the psalm 'may in reality not even be so much about the glory of God as about the glory of male worshippers of YHWH and their control over all creation' (ibid.).

Carley closes his article with a version of the psalm in which he lets earth speak. Unsurprisingly, it became mainly an anti-Psalm 8.

> When I look at the sky, how wonderful the whole creation is!
> You care for sparrows, feed the lions,
> and still find time to care for human beings!
> ...

What arrogance: they think you have put them in charge!
Yet they depend on their fellow creatures
for clothing, labour, food, for air and water –
which they pollute in ways they now perceive only dimly.

You never willed them to be conquerors,
rather partners in the unfolding of your bounty.
(pp. 123–4)

It is interesting that Pope Francis also concludes his paper with a
poetic part that redefines the relationship between God, humans
and nature (section 246). It consists of two prayers. The following passages from the second prayer, 'a Christian prayer in union
with creation', could simply be considered a variation on Psalm 8:

Triune Lord, wondrous community of infinite love,
teach us to contemplate you
in the beauty of the universe,
for all things speak of you.
Awaken our praise and thankfulness
for every being that you have made.
Give us the grace to feel profoundly joined
to everything that is.

God of love, show us our place in this world
as channels of your love
for all the creatures of this earth,
for not one of them is forgotten in your sight.
Enlighten those who possess power and money
that they may avoid the sin of indifference,
that they may love the common good, advance the weak,
and care for this world in which we live.
The poor and the earth are crying out.
O Lord, seize us with your power and light,
help us to protect all life,
to prepare for a better future,
for the coming of your Kingdom
of justice, peace, love and beauty.
Praise be to you!
Amen

Remarkably, and indicative of *Laudato Si'* is that the pope does not limit himself to nature in trouble. He also explicitly mentions the poor – there are *people* who suffer heavily because of the way in which the world is organized. In the encyclical, the pope often makes the connection between environmental and poverty issues, both the result of unilateral economic choices.

Though its tone is different, content-wise there does not seem to be a big difference with Keith Carley's anti-psalm. Pope Francis is equally critical. He warns against the sin of indifference from those who have power and are rich. 'Being one with' creation is also his starting point, rather than 'ruling over'. Both authors demonstrate a sense of reverence for creation and wonder at the beauty of it; both texts are actually a hymn. The fact that we are permitted to live on this beautiful earth automatically brings about an obligation to care for it as best as we can.

## Hymns and compassion

The combination of wonder, praise and responsibility is perhaps the most essential contribution of biblical thought to the eco-logical debate.

The Israelites were unfamiliar with the major issues that we face today. So there are very few biblical passages that reflect on nature conservation or ecological risks.[3] The responsibility of people for the natural environment is not a prominent theme.[4] But what Peter Kluit proposes at the end of the interview and what Pope Francis argues at length in his encyclical, taking on that exact responsi-bility, ties in with the philosophical and moral implications of the biblical texts about nature. The world of nature is good in itself, as explicitly stated in Genesis 1. Plants, animals, mountains, lakes, seas, are valuable for no other reason than that God created them. God appreciates their existence and their beauty. Therefore they cannot simply be reduced to objects that we can take advantage of. It is the task of humanity to take good care of it.

Translated into our time, this means: responsibility for the state of the planet and every possible effort to resolve the problems that we have caused.

It could very well be that the biblical approach contributes that little 'extra' to achieving such a change of consciousness. After all, however convincing the list of rational arguments to take action in the short term, there is need for more. An increased awareness of necessity, urgency, duty and responsibility, on the basis of reasonable arguments, will definitely help. Equally, positive stimulation of a kind that is not purely cognitive, could be what we need for the decisive step forward.

This at least is the opinion of Sallie McFague, a fervent advocate of a new 'planetary theology' on an ecological basis (see for example her book *Life Abundant. Rethinking Theology and Economy for a Planet in Peril*, 2001). In her book *A New Climate for Theology. God, the World and Global Warming* (2008) she discusses her view on the core values of biblical religion – and indeed of many other religions – 'praise' and 'compassion'.

In Chapter 6 of her book, she analyses the biblical 'discourse of praise' (2008, pp. 103ff). 'Praise' is the expression of the experience of gratitude and amazement about existence. A gratitude which will also be recognized by many non-believers (p. 113). Compassion is about involvement in the other person or the other. These two are interconnected. When someone opens their eyes to the beauty of the world, they naturally get involved. He who really takes in the beauty and complexity of nature, and also sees its vulnerability, will not hesitate to stand up for her. 'One takes care of what one loves' (p. 119). Admiration, gratitude and compassion because of her vulnerability and the damage caused to her are powerful incentives to take action.

Pope Francis thinks along the same lines, as evidenced by the title of his encyclical: *Laudato Si'*. These are the first two words of the great hymn to creation by his namesake from the twelfth century, Francis of Assisi: the 'Canticle of the Sun'. In the first paragraph of his book, the pope quotes this line: 'Praised be You my Lord through our Sister, Mother Earth who sustains and governs us.' And, as mentioned, the pope adds his own praises at the end of his encyclical.

McFague likes to use the metaphor of the earth as 'God's body'. Pope Francis will not be quick to use this metaphor, but for him too, nature is a place in which God can be found (paras 84–8).

## God's Gardeners and their nature psalms

Now on to literature. Margaret Atwood's book *The Year of the Flood* (2009) takes place in a later time. By now, the ecological destruction of the planet has assumed alarming forms. Central to the book is the eco-spiritual resistance group 'God's Gardeners'. It is unacceptable to them that in their society animals and plants are footing the bill. They are vegetarians, although they have the provision that in cases of emergency meat can be consumed. They eat the products of their own secret 'garden', a rooftop garden hidden in the middle of the filthy, violent city where they live. Through their alternative way of life, the Gardeners hope to bring a better future closer by.

The group, which shows strong signs of a religious sect, is led by a charismatic leader, Adam One. The book is built around his speeches: each larger chapter begins with one of his inspiring sermons, always fitting the theme of the day (each day of their calendar is marked by a green role model or an ecological theme). After the sermon they sing a song from *The God's Gardeners Oral Hymnbook*. In total the book contains fifteen sermons and fifteen hymns. Like Psalm 8, the hymns are short, poetic reflections on the relationship between God, humans and nature.

As a reader, you get somewhat mixed feelings about those Gardeners. On one hand they make a rather esoteric and naive impression and their warm feelings are hardly taken seriously by even the most unsightly of their fellow creatures, but on the other, you'll be quick to admire their radical green lifestyle and their per-severance. They belong to a small minority who do not go along with the rampant cynicism and actually resist. The destructive social order that has become commonplace in global society, is not very exciting.

The nature hymns of the Gardeners offer the same duality. These endearing little songs are funny in their adorable naivety, but they do testify to the dedication of this group. The Gardeners do their best to keep believing in goodness and in a future where people and nature live in harmony, while everything in their world is moving in exactly the opposite direction.

The Earth forgives the Miner's blast
That rends her crust and burns her skin
The centuries bring Trees again,
and water, and the Fish therein.

The Deer at length forgives the Wolf
That tears his throat and drinks his blood;
His bones return to soil, and feed
The trees that flower and fruit and seed.
...

But Man alone seeks Vengefulness,
And writes his abstract Laws on stone;
for this false Justice he has made,
He tortures limb and crushes bone.
...

Give up your anger and your spite,
And imitate the Deer, the Tree;
In sweet Forgiveness find your joy,
For it alone can set you free.

(Atwood 2009, pp. 426–7)

Their longing for the original paradisiacal state of humankind –
the name of God's Gardeners, of course, refers to the Garden of
Eden, even their rooftop garden is named after it, the 'Edencliff
Rooftop Garden' – does not mean that they live in a bygone era.
Creationists they are not. Their eco-spirituality is clearly post-
Darwin. The evolution and the modest place of humans within it
gives them an added sense of humility. For the same reason their
relationship with animals is different from that in Psalm 8. This
is evident in the hymns they sing at the festival, 'Of Adam and all
Primates' (p. 54).

Oh let me not be proud, dear Lord,
Nor rank myself above
The other Primates, through whose genes
We grew into your Love.

A million million years, Your Days,
Your methods past discerning,
Yet through Your blends of DNAs
Came passion, mind and learning.

We cannot always trace Your path
Through Monkey and Gorilla,
Yet all are sheltered underneath
Your Heavenly Umbrella.

And if we vaunt and puff ourselves
With vanity and pride,
Recall Australopithecus,
Our Animal inside.

This is a redefinition of the relationship between God, humans and animals in light of the theory of evolution, while maintaining the idea that God gave us particularly a few special talents in his creation.

Margaret Atwood did not provide a score, but Orville Stoeber put the songs from *The God's Gardeners Oral Hymnbook* to music. They are in the style of folk songs and are available on CD (*Hymns of the God's Gardeners*). You can also listen to them on YouTube, with accompanying video.

On the website associated with the book, yearoftheflood.com, Orville Stoeber explains: 'I wrote these songs for the reasons the Gardeners themselves would have written them: for the purpose of praise, adoration, and prayer to our planet, in thanks for its animals and plants and the "primate seeds" that led to our human experience.'[5]

That Atwood is very much concerned with the ecological problem can also be seen in a different part of the website. Environmental issues are provided with non-futuristic information. For example, there is a page about 'bird friendly coffee'.[6] In different places in the novel the writer refers to the ecological damage caused by non-bird-friendly production of coffee. Not only does Margaret Atwood entertain us with an exciting book, she also wants to get through to us that we are not taking very good care of our planet.

## The blessing of a piece of land or a garden

Finally, a non-fiction example of a green religious text. It is a 'blessing of a piece of land or a garden' that I found in an alternative liturgy book: *Common Prayer. A Liturgy for Ordinary Radicals*.[7] The term 'ordinary radicals' refers to Shane Claiborne's book *The Irresistible Revolution: Living as an Ordinary Radical* (2006). This book is about the neighbourhood community called 'The Simple Way' founded by him and other 'ordinary radicals' in Kensington, Philadelphia. They call themselves 'new monastics' (new-style monks) and have deliberately settled in this disadvantaged neighbourhood in Philadelphia. It is an area with high unemployment, high crime rates and high house vacancy rates. The principles of The Simple Way are: simple life, serve the neighbourhood, daily prayer and the creation of urban gardens.

From their website:

> We have a dream of a village in the middle of the urban desert – with a little cluster of row homes sprinkled about and a neighborhood where folks are committed to God and to each other. Some are indigenous to the neighborhood. Some are missional relocators. Some have gone off to school, trained as doctors, lawyers, social workers, business folks ... and they have returned to the neighborhood to offer their gifts to the work of restoration. The houses are small, and that is all we need – a place to lay our heads ... because most of our life is lived on the streets, on the stoop, sweating in the practice of resurrection, planting gardens on abandoned lots, rehabbing vacant houses, and making ugly things beautiful again. Every morning we greet the day with prayer, and in the evenings we share a meal or grill out on the street.[8]

These 'ordinary radicals' do not form a sect, as did the Gardeners of Margaret Atwood, but they do bless gardens. In the blessing that

I found, God is praised for the 'centipedes, ants, and worms, mice, marmots, and bats'. A light and playful thanksgiving for creation, which also contains a section about creation, and which brings us back to Sallie McFague's couple, 'praise' and 'compassion'.

> God of the Universe,
> You made the heavens and the earth,
> So we do not call our home merely 'planet earth'.
> We call it your Creation, a Divine Mystery,
> a Gift from Your Most Blessed Hand.
> The world itself is your miracle.
> Bread and vegetables from earth are thus also from heaven.
> Help us to see in our daily bread your presence.
>
> Upon this garden
> May your stars rain down their blessed dust.
> May you send rain and sunshine upon our garden and us.
> Grant us the humility to touch the humus,
> That we might become more human.
> That we might mend our rift from your Creation,
> That we might then know the sacredness of the gift of life –
> That we might truly experience life from the hand of God.
> For you planted humanity in a garden,
> and began our resurrection in a garden.
> Our blessed memory and hope lie in a garden.
>
> Thanks be to God,
> Who made the world teeming with variety,
> Of things on the earth, above, the earth, and under the earth.
> Thanks be to God,
> For the many kinds of plants, trees, and fruits,
> We celebrate.
> For the centipedes, ants, and worms,
> For the mice, marmots, and bats,
> For the cucumbers, tomatoes, and peppers
> We rejoice,
> That we find ourselves eclipsed by the magnitude
> Of generosity and mystery.
> Thanks be to God.[9]

And again Psalm 8 is closer than you think: just like the psalm, the blessing refers to the faith that God made 'heaven and earth', and just like the psalm it conveys that our earthly existence must primarily be seen from that point of view. It's a nice modern version of the data so strongly expressed in Psalm 8 that the created world is the work of God's hands, with a reflection on the special responsibility that is entrusted upon humankind. Even the stars from Psalm 8 are represented. Psalm 104 is another psalm that comes to mind, which also names all sorts of animals.

---

**Questions for Reflection**

What is the difference between humankind and the rest of the animal world?

How 'green' do you think the Bible is?

How does the Bible speak into the environmental crisis?

---

## Apocalypse! Fear of what lies ahead: catastrophe and new beginnings

Perhaps humanity has always been concerned about the future, but in our time, we are inundated with dire warnings and sometimes outright disaster scenarios from both the perspective of science as well as the perspective of popular fiction. Raw materials are being depleted, the number of people on the globe is growing too large, water and food are becoming scarce. In one region, global warming will cause droughts and people will be unable to live there. In another region densely populated areas will be inundated. Moreover, technological changes are happening so fast that we can barely keep up with them. Not all of it will have a positive outcome. The fear is that artificial intelligence could very well take over human initiative. No one even dares to predict where genetic manipulation of plants, animals, and possibly in the future even people, will lead to.

The biblical authors obviously had no idea of the technological or environmental issues in the current era. The world looks completely different now from how it did to them. But even they were aware that the future would not be a natural continuation of the present. They knew that a period of calm assurance could be followed by a time of conflict, violence, insecurity, poverty. They knew what people can do to each other – many wars are described in the Bible; and they also knew that nature is a lot less reliable than it sometimes seems. They certainly would not have been surprised at the contemporary fears of either the consequences of extreme drought or rising sea levels and how these threaten civilization.

The people in the Bible not only knew all the uncertainty about what might happen, they also deliberately used it: the prophetic literature used all of these subjects that people feared in order to warn its audience. The prophetic books of Isaiah, Jeremiah, Ezekiel and a collection of smaller books (the 'Book of the Twelve Prophets') describe in vivid images the terrible consequences for the people and their leaders who persisted in their reprehensible behaviour. Nature would turn against them, their cities would be destroyed, their society would collapse.

Futuristic books and films of our time often have the same prophetic warning as an undertone. And remarkably enough, here and there, we find notable parallels with biblical literature. This chapter will focus on a few of them. To begin, I return to *The Year of the Flood* by Margaret Atwood previously discussed.

## The Flood, according to Margaret Atwood

*The Year of the Flood* is part of a trilogy: *Oryx and Crake*, 2003; *The Year of the Flood*, 2009 and *Maddaddam*, 2013. Margaret Atwood wrote a fascinating reflection on the end of the world as we know it. In the near future, greed and profit will push aside all other values, which will lead to the collapse of all political systems, both nationally and globally. Large companies take over. The elite is doing well for itself, the rest of the population is left to fend for themselves and falls into anarchy and crime. Ecology is at the bottom of the list, with all the associated consequences.

But the grim world which came to be is awaiting a much bigger catastrophe: the almost complete eradication of the human race. This is put into action by a bio-terrorist genius who has come to the conclusion that the planet will be much better off if this barely functioning human race would stop eradicating species and, instead, die themselves. The bio-terrorist is able to develop an extremely lethal and highly contagious genetically engineered virus. The virus spreads quickly to the ends of the earth; anyone who comes into contact with it dies.

As the title indicates, *The Year of the Flood* deploys a biblical image for the extermination of the human race, namely the flood. In Genesis 6–9 God destroys humanity which has become totally corrupted in a short time. He does this by opening the floodgates of the heavens and all the springs of the great deep, after which the earth is flooded up to its highest peaks. Only an ark full of animals, and one chosen family, Noah's, is allowed to survive the flood.

The radical action of God in Genesis 6–9 is the Bible's most comprehensive and notorious 'natural disaster'. It is in fact, an almost complete reversal of creation. After all, in Genesis 1 creation emerged *from* the endless waters. That desolate state is now re-established, quite a few generations after Adam and Eve. In a short time the violence and wickedness of people has become so great that God gave up all hope of improvement. He found that he could only cleanse the earth by drowning the entire human race and almost all animals. Fortunately, Noah and his family had received the message that they had to build an enormous boat for themselves, and for the animals. In any case, they had to save all animal *species*. Their task, after leaving the ark, was to start the world all over again. And thus the plan is worked out. Afterwards, God promises that he will never again strike the earth with an all-covering flood.

In Atwood's book, God's Gardeners recognize themselves in these biblical images. Apart from writing eco-friendly psalms and maintaining an illegal rooftop garden in the urban jungle to provide for their own subsistence, they prepare for the catastrophe that visionary Adam One sees coming. They do this by building arks here and there – places for survival once it starts happening.

They hope they will survive, not only because they really want to, but because they feel they will hold a special role in the period after the flood. They will be the ones that will restore the lost connection between humanity and nature. They believe that their participation in the 'new creation' will contribute to making the earth whole again. They call themselves 'Adams' and 'Eves' and, in anticipation of the Year of the Flood, they had already started their own calendar with a new 'Day of creation'. On the first lustrum of that day Adam One spoke the following words:

> Dear Friends, dear Fellow Creatures, dear Fellow Mammals:
>
> On Creation Day five years ago, this Edencliff Rooftop Garden of ours was a sizzling wasteland, hemmed in by festering city slums and dens of wickedness, but now it has blossomed as the rose.
>
> By covering such barren rooftops with greenery we are doing our small part in the redemption of God's Creation from the decay and sterility that lies all around us, and feeding ourselves with unpolluted food into the bargain. (2009, p. 11)

They know of God's promise in the Bible, never to flood the earth again, but that of course does not exclude the coming of a 'Waterless Flood'. Indeed, it proves to be such a flood when in their 25th calendar year 'The Year of the Flood' begins.

Although the story of the flood in the Bible does not refer to the future, but to a terrible past long ago, in the era of Adam and Eve, it still sets the tone for what may lie ahead. If people are making too big of a mess of it, God will not hesitate to intervene with firm actions and destroy everything.

According to the apocalyptic current in biblical literature, it is inevitable that the history of humankind will expire this way.

> Just as it was in the days of Noah, so too it will be in the days of the Son of Man. They were eating and drinking, and marrying and being given in marriage, until the day Noah entered the ark, and the flood came and destroyed all of them. Likewise, just as it was in the days of Lot: they were eating and drinking, buying and selling, planting and building, but on the day that Lot left

Sodom, it rained fire and sulphur from heaven and destroyed all of them – it will be like that on the day that the Son of Man is revealed. (Luke 17.26–30)

This passage establishes a link between the future moment when God decides 'enough is enough' and the Son of Man will return to earth to set things right, and two 'moments' in the past, when God also acted in a similar way. The flood on the day of Noah, and the day of the destruction of the city of Sodom. Sodom disappeared through God's intervention under a volcanic rain of fire and brimstone. That was God's judgement on the city. Lot escaped, but his wife looked back for one moment and changed into a pillar of salt.

At an unpredictable point in the future, history will come to an end in a catastrophe of cosmic dimensions. A minority of elected people will be saved. The others will be lost, just as with Noah and Lot. That sounds serious, but such texts are not only meant as a warning but also as an encouragement: despite the enormous danger, those who persevere for the good turn out to be among those for whom a bright new future is set aside.

The apocalyptic book of Revelation in the New Testament follows that same pattern. Although it announces a terrible final confrontation between God and the forces of evil, in which everything that exists will be given up to destruction, in the end the message is largely optimistic. The universal destruction is not the end, because a renewal of creation follows. The final chapters of Revelation describe 'a new heaven and a new earth' (Rev. 21.1) in words and images that refer directly to the Garden of Eden and the creation stories in general. On that new earth, the relationship with nature is totally fine once again.

Then the angel showed me the river of the water of life, bright as crystal, flowing from the throne of God and of the Lamb through the middle of the street of the city. On either side of the river is the tree of life with its twelve kinds of fruit, producing its fruit each month; and the leaves of the tree are for the healing of the nations. (Rev. 22.1–2)

In his book on ecology and the Bible, Richard Bauckham calls this beautiful new world biblical 'Ecotopia' (2010, pp. 175–8).

Returning to the trilogy by Margaret Atwood: there is little hope for the vast majority, but a renewal of creation seems to present itself. (This is not a spoiler, because Atwood starts her novels with an episode from the end of the story.) In the opening scene of the first book, *Oryx and Crake* a new kind of human seems to have been created, a genetically adjusted type. Genetic engineers have managed to remove the most problematic of the moral weaknesses of humans. I will not say what role God's Gardeners play in this new future (which is really the subject of the third part of the trilogy). It is true, however, that they have fully and correctly assessed that the stories from Genesis about Adam, Eve and Noah might very well provide the model for the future that would come soon.

## Flood stories in movies

Noah's flood was the subject of Darren Aronofsky's *Noah* (2014). In his version the story turns into a mythical, eco-apocalyptic fable. Not everyone recognizes the biblical Noah in the film's Noah. Brian Godawa for example thought he was more of a modern day environmental fanatic gone crazy, someone 'who concludes that people do not deserve to survive because of what they've done to the environment and to animals'.[10] In a strange coincidence, the same Aronofsky has been named as the one who is going to turn Margaret Atwood's trilogy into a TV series for HBO.

Although according to the Bible there would not be another global flood, this did not stop Kevin Reynolds using the idea in a science fiction film. His film *Waterworld* (1995) describes a world where one is forced to adapt to a life without solid land underfoot. Humankind has not succeeded in halting global warming and the resulting consequences show it. The polar ice caps have melted. The whole planet is flooded. Civilization is gone. Those who are still there, lead a primitive life on boats or artificial floating islands. A new genetic variation develops: people with webbed toes and gills behind their ears.

A rather reluctant hero is the protagonist of this film, a so-called 'drifter' who is joined, against his will, by a woman and an orphan. The girl is being sought for a map tattooed on her back, the map of a mythical country, 'Dryland'. Although all memory of the former civilization is gone, there are still stories about a country that is different from their 'Waterworld'. Dryland lies somewhere beyond the horizon.

A number of ocean dwellers who find out about the map see an opportunity here. Fertile soil is only available in the form of laboriously extracted sediment from the seabed. He who finds the way to a piece of 'dry land' would be a rich man in no time. But there are also people who would like to find Dryland for other reasons. They yearn for a world that is less hard and unjust. Life on the ocean is not only difficult because of the harsh conditions, it is also hard because those who are the strongest and most violent call the shots, at the expense of those who lose out. For the latter, it would be a paradisiacal situation to just live their daily lives in peace and quiet. So there are two groups that are very keen to gain access to the map on the girl's back. A confrontation is inevitable.

The final scene of the film shows the glorious moment when dry land is reached and the story comes to rest. A beautiful beach, green nature: the viewer knows that all is not lost and the 'exiles' are permitted a new start.

In Genesis too there is much attention on the moment when they can disembark the boat. Noah and his family set foot on solid ground after impatiently waiting. When everything and everyone has left the ark and history can resume, God makes his great covenant with humankind. This covenant should avoid it all getting out of control again as before the flood: an important provision is that people should not shed each other's blood. The sign of the covenant is the rainbow. God tells Noah and his family:

'When I bring clouds over the earth and the bow is seen in the clouds, I will remember my covenant that is between me and you and every living creature of all flesh; and the waters shall never again become a flood to destroy all flesh. When the bow is in the clouds, I will see it and remember the everlasting covenant between God and every living creature of all flesh that is on the earth.' (Gen. 9.14–16)

## Future doom – the prophet Isaiah

Although the biblical authors did not have to worry about future floods of global proportions, plenty of other catastrophes could emerge. For the biblical authors there was a clear link between disasters and human behaviour. They saw catastrophes as a result of religious, ethical or political failure.

Ecological and other catastrophes were God's instrument to punish Israel or any of the other nations. For example, a severe drought would be interpreted by the prophets as God's way of sending a message. Similarly, they could predict such disaster in the future. They would also interpret or predict military defeats and horrors of war as a signal from God, instead of as simply the result of international political developments.

Isaiah 19 contains an oracle of doom against Egypt, a major player in international politics in Isaiah's time. The prophet predicts that fertile Egypt, rich in food, a thriving economy, abundantly nourished by the waters of the Nile will turn into a wasteland, an ecological disaster area.

The waters of the Nile will be dried up,
   and the river will be parched and dry;
its canals will become foul,
   and the branches of Egypt's Nile will diminish and dry up;
   reeds and rushes will rot away.
There will be bare places by the Nile,
   on the brink of the Nile;
and all that is sown by the Nile will dry up,
   be driven away, and be no more.
Those who fish will mourn;
   all who cast hooks in the Nile will lament,
   and those who spread nets on the water will languish.
The workers in flax will be in despair,
   and the carders and those at the loom will grow pale.

Its weavers will be dismayed,
and all who work for wages will be grieved.
(Isa. 19.5–10)

Isaiah is without doubt the biblical author who makes the most of this type of imagery. Chapter 34 is another ecological oracle of doom from his book:

And the streams of Edom shall be turned into pitch,
and her soil into sulphur;
her land shall become burning pitch.
Night and day it shall not be quenched;
its smoke shall go up for ever.
From generation to generation it shall lie waste;
no one shall pass through it for ever and ever.
(Isa. 34.9–10)

In this chapter it is not only the land of Edom that turns into an active volcano, the whole world will turn into a doomsday landscape. People will no longer inhabit it, only creepy animals and demons (exhaustively listed in this chapter) will populate the wasteland. Nevertheless, Isaiah is not primarily a prophet who provides us with doomsday scenarios. The book of Isaiah also contains some of the most exuberant visions of hope. Remarkably, these visions also make extensive use of ecological imagery. Isaiah 34 is in the first part of the book. The second part, Isaiah 35, continues as follows:

The wilderness and the dry land shall be glad,
the desert shall rejoice and blossom;
like the crocus it shall blossom abundantly,
and rejoice with joy and singing.
The glory of Lebanon shall be given to it,
the majesty of Carmel and Sharon.
(Isa. 35.1–2)

## Isaiah 32: from catastrophe to bright future

An apocalyptic final battle seems to be fought in Isaiah 34–35, in which the destruction is set aside for the enemies who threaten the people. The people will experience just the opposite. But in the vast majority of cases, the people of Israel itself are the object of prophetic tirades. In the case of Israel, it is consistently the case that the current or future calamity is caused by ignoring Israel's covenant with God. This is not the covenant God made with Noah, which concerned *all nations*. God made this new covenant with the people of Israel, after he delivered them from slavery in Egypt. On the way to the promised land, in the desert, Moses received the provisions of the covenant on Mount Sinai. The contents of the covenant can now be found in the Torah (in the books of Exodus to Deuteronomy). It contains detailed rules not only on religious matters but also on issues concerning social justice. When the leaders of the people did not follow those rules, which happened often, they could count on prophetic criticism.

No matter how intense this criticism, and no matter how complete the self-inflicted devastation, the harsh language is always interrupted by or interspersed with words of hope. Isaiah 32 is an interesting example. The chapter begins with a look to a bright future.

> See, a king will reign in righteousness,
>   and princes will rule with justice.
> Each will be like a hiding-place from the wind,
>   a covert from the tempest,
> like streams of water in a dry place,
>   like the shade of a great rock in a weary land.
> (Isa. 32.1)

But in the meantime, the people are facing a catastrophe. From verse 9 the prophet addresses the women, and tells them: 'In a little over a year you will tremble, you who still feel secure. The grape harvest will fail, and the harvest of fruit will not come ... Upon the land of my people shall come up thorns and briers; yea, upon all the houses of joy in the joyous city.'

For the palace will be forsaken,
  the populous city deserted;
the hill and the watch-tower
  will become dens for ever,
the joy of wild asses,
  a pasture for flocks.
(Isa. 32.14)

But then the prophecy surprisingly continues with a turn for the better:

until a spirit from on high is poured out on us,
and the wilderness becomes a fruitful field,
and the fruitful field is deemed a forest.

Then justice will dwell in the wilderness,
  and righteousness abide in the fruitful field.
The effect of righteousness will be peace,
  and the result of righteousness, quietness and trust for ever.
(Isa. 32.15–17)

God's 'Spirit' will come down and change everything. The recovery is painted in ecological terms, fitting the foregoing oracle of doom; however it is striking that the trees not only produce tasty fruit but also valuable fruits such as justice, peace, tranquillity and confidence. 'My people will abide in a peaceful habitation, in secure dwellings, and in quiet resting-places' (v. 18). After the inevitable horrific devastation, God holds a future that is better than they had imagined. As mentioned, the tone for this had already been set in the first verses of this chapter.

Those first verses – on the king and the leaders – immediately answer the question of how this future of peace and justice should take shape. As in many other places in the books of prophets, it is because the national or local leaders protect the weak and will not partake in corruption. These are prerequisites for the future that God has in mind for his people.

It is worth underlining again that what is discussed in prophetic literature is certainly not all fiction. Even if it was future doom, the people knew the calamities of which the prophets spoke from personal experience. Their country was on the edge of the influential sphere of the various powers of Mesopotamia and was often violently brought under control (again). Moreover, there were regular conflicts between the smaller rival nations in the region. It was certainly not exceptional that cities and agricultural lands were destroyed in a war. Populated areas would be hit so badly that any surviving residents had to start all over again and had to seek refuge elsewhere. In addition, a common tactic was to exile part of the original population.

While the prophets painted a detailed picture of the disastrous effects of Israel's bad choices and the reprehensible behaviour of their leaders, they did not pay less attention to the positive future that awaited Israel after undergoing judgement. Cities may be destroyed, an exile may have disrupted society, but in the end God will not abandon his people. Thus, the main motive of Isaiah 35 as cited above is the return of the exiles to the country through a desert that is now thriving. That same motif is elaborated on in all ways in Isaiah 40—55, which is almost a separate book in the book of Isaiah, and talks about the end of the Babylonian exile.

## Catastrophes in (post-)apocalyptic films

Fans of films that predict a fearful future, know that few films dare not tell their story without at least a glimmer of hope at the end. Some even take it a step further and show a total deliverance from evil. This pattern is very similar to what the biblical prophets give their readers. Here are two examples. In terms of environmental factors we are making the transition from floods in the films I discussed earlier to a dry wasteland. The latter variant is also the most common in the Bible. As can be seen in the above excerpts from Isaiah, the prophets saw that, with the judgement of God, especially populous and fertile regions turn into empty and barren wastelands, where only wild animals live. These are changes that people experienced for themselves.

## Interstellar (Charles Nolan, 2014)

The subject of Charles Nolan's film *Interstellar* is the desertification of once fertile lands and the fact that people can no longer survive in the country where they traditionally lived and worked, but then on a global scale. The seriousness of the situation does not immediately get through to the viewer at the beginning of the film. The world does not look any different from ours. We see a bunch of farmers who are struggling, their harvest is threatened by a plague and drought. Occasionally a sandstorm passes through which covers houses and cars. But then it turns out that this has been going on for some years, and on a global scale. Society has changed very radically: raw materials are depleted; international trade has been discontinued; the entire *high-tech* civilization to which we are so accustomed has disappeared; there are no more armies; climate change has had an enormous impact. In the worst affected areas, hunger struck so hard that there are no people left, but even in less affected areas it is increasingly difficult to produce enough food. It is impossible to cultivate a growing number of crops due to incurable plant diseases. Only a bit of corn grows, but even the corn production is likely to fall due to prolonged drought and sandstorms. The day approaches when agriculture no longer makes sense. People are starting to leave their dust-covered farms and cities, but no one knows where to go. Due to climate change, loss of vegetation and past pollution, an even graver danger presents itself; oxygen levels in the atmosphere drop dramatically.

Ordinary people continue to fight for survival, but scientists are convinced that one generation down the line it will be all over. Earth will no longer be able to sustain humankind. The only solution seems to be to find another planet and continue life there. Literally, under a 'new heaven', in another solar system in another galaxy, 'a new earth' will become the new home of humankind. However, the big question is whether it is technically possible to take all the people to the new planet. Therefore, scientists are working on a back-up plan: recreate humankind. Unlike the biblical creation, this new creation is done by the people themselves. The spacecraft that sets off is carrying a precious cargo of 5,000 fertilized human eggs. The central motif of the film is the suspense between the two possibilities. Would it be wise, or even necessary, to just give up on current humanity and completely start over? Or could there be another way? At the end it appears that *love* points the way to the answers of these questions. So ultimately it turns out to be more a religious than scientific film.

## *Mad Max – Fury Road* (George Miller, 2015)

This film is intended to be an up-to-date sequel to the successful series of *Mad Max* films from 1979–85, with Mel Gibson as lone wolf hero Max Rockatansky. Tom Hardy plays Max in the 2015 version. The situation remains the same. We find ourselves in a grim post-apocalyptic world. No trace of former technology, urban civilization or something resembling culture. Even nature is pretty much gone. People need to survive in what looks like an endlessly hostile desert. Some type of new society emerged, but because the most primitive and violent types come out as winners in the struggle for life, it is a society based on oppression, fear and randomness. So the setting is definitely more exotic than *Interstellar*, which remains reasonably close to our reality. But *Mad Max* gives a quite adequate visualization of the biblical prophecies of doom: a country where normal life and normal cities are gone, where no joy and pleasure are to be found, where nature has given up – a dangerous wasteland where it is preferable not to go alone.

The above elements were already present in the earlier series. In the 2015 version the image is complemented by a prehistoric-sounding religious leadership cult. For example, some women are kept in a harem to produce babies for the ruler of the Citadel (the makeshift city). A caste of war slaves ensures the maintenance of order. They are brainwashed to die for their leader; their sacrifice will lead them straight to Valhalla. The ruler calls himself 'Immortan Joe'. He demands absolute submission. He is forcing ordinary people to worship him as a god. They are indeed totally dependent on him, since he has control of the water supply. Water is extremely scarce in the hot desert. From time to time (but not very often) he opens the taps. His health is poor, but he hides behind a skull mask.

The story begins when Mad Max ends up in the Citadel. People from outside the community are captured on a regular basis to donate (all) their blood to the wounded. It seems that Max is to undergo the same fate, but he escapes. Coincidentally, Furiosa, a senior military leader of the Citadel, escapes at the same time and takes with her the young women of the breeding programme. Out of necessity, Max and Furiosa form an uneasy coalition. Furiosa plans to return to 'Green Place', the land where she was once kidnapped as a girl. After numerous confrontations (they are being chased by Immortan Joe and his army) they reach it. Unfortunately, this paradise does not exist any more. The Green Place has turned into a swampland. A small group of older women is all that is left of the original inhabitants.

Furiosa then realizes that she has no choice but to return to the city she became part of. Her future lies there. This is again a thoroughly biblical theme: the 'new kingdom' is neither found in the lost paradise, nor in a different world, it is our own place that will be changed and renewed. Max and Furiosa endure a series of new attacks, but in the end it is Immortan Joe who is slain. Furiosa is injured and barely survives, but returns to the Citadel as the new queen. A new, different era begins. This is symbolized in the final scene: the newly appointed queen lets the water flow abundantly; everyone can share in it.

Again we do not need to look far to find these elements in our much older source. The installation of a new, righteous ruler as mentioned in Isaiah 32 is present in many more places throughout Isaiah. And we can even turn to this biblical prophet for the sharing of the water. The final chapter of the subsection in Isaiah about the return from exile, through the desert (Isa. 40—55), portrays Israel's future as follows:

'Lo, everyone who thirsts,
   come to the waters;
and you that have no money,
   come, buy and eat!
Come, buy wine and milk
   without money and without price.'
(Isa. 55.1)

## Imagine the catastrophe

Based on the enormous popularity of this and similar films, people love being presented with as many variants as possible of the terrible fate that awaits our planet and 'all of us'. It is frightening but also fascinating, given that human behaviour could lead to a disaster that would herald the end of our way of life. Beside the fact that catastrophes in environmental terms may await us (see *Interstellar* and a host of other movies in this genre), wars at the borders of Europe and attacks in major European cities clearly show that even here stability is not unchallenged.

(Post-)apocalyptic books and movies often opt for a situation where everything went completely wrong, with the associated extreme images. Herein they do not differ from the biblical visions of impending doom. Maybe our imagination is most stimulated by such strong performances. Imagining the worst could be a good way for an optimally sharpened awareness of what is currently urgent.

We ascertained that reading or viewing pleasure is partly due to the standard pattern where the hero or the endangered group with whom we can identify, still finds a way out. The improbability of finding a solution only stimulates the hero or group to search for it nonetheless. The greater the pleasure then, when the hero succeeds.

For at least a few of the survivors there is a new future ahead. They will be able to continue some of the traditions of humanity, compassion and love – while the vast majority indulges in violence and barbaric behaviour. In the end, the underdogs take home the grand prize, not the powerful brutes. All things considered, it is exactly the strong implicit message of hope that makes films so appealing. An important spiritual contribution to our culture!

A notable exception is *Left Behind* (Vic Armstrong, 2014) which tries really hard to be a Christian film, but the aspect of hope is not present. It is the story about the fulfilled prophecy that at a totally unexpected moment God calls home the chosen ones and the rest of humanity is left to deal with the great tribulation.[11] The chosen ones have suddenly disappeared. There is little hope for those left behind.

Fortunately this is not the Bible's main contribution on the subject of the 'future'. Much more characteristic of the Bible is the hope that earth itself will be renewed, including the returning forests, resurrecting disaster areas and regained social cohesion and justice we saw in Isaiah. The ardent hope witnessed in prophetic literature ultimately determines more the tone than the certainty that the land of the Israelites, their peace and quiet, are not as stable as they themselves wish and hope.

The prophets pointed for their warnings certainly not only to shortcomings of a religious nature. It was their firm conviction that a society lacking in respect for the poor, where profit is the main motive and where leaders are more interested in power than in law, is leading to its own demise. Even in this respect, one does not have to look far to find parallels in our modern era. How strong is the social structure in Europe? Are the people at the bottom of society even here not being cast aside? Is the rise of populism not an omen that our part of the world does not remain the obvious stable, democratic, prosperous region that it was in the last half-century? It is not certain that our existence will remain 'peaceful and quiet' in the future.

---

## Questions for Reflection

How are you worried about the future?

How are current 'apocalyptic' films and stories prophetic?

What part does 'hope' play in your context?

---

## Notes

1 Also compare Primavesi (1991), pp. 84–110.

2 See e.g. Habel (2000), pp. 47f.

3 In the interview with Peter Kluit Leviticus 25 was mentioned, a chapter in which the land is prescribed to lay fallow for one year every seven years. 'It shall be a year of complete rest for the land' (Lev. 25.5).

4 The practice of animal sacrifice is a different story. As Anne Claar notes in her chapter on sacrifice, the distinction made here between suitable and unsuitable animals – 'clean' and 'unclean' – whereby the latter should not be eaten, has the

effect that the 'unclean' animals have significantly less to fear from man. Thus the unclean state of many species has a direct impact on animal protection. Some parts of nature can not be touched.

5 http://yearoftheflood.com/how-the-music-came-to-be/, accessed 16 July 2016.

6 http://yearoftheflood.com/the-bird-friendly-coffee-page/, accessed 16 July 2016.

7 Claiborne, Wilson-Hartgrove, Oroko (2010, pp. 561–2).

8 www.thesimpleway.org, accessed 2 August 2015.

9 Claiborne, Wilson-Hartgrove, Oroko (2010), pp. 561–2. The *Common Prayer* collection can also be viewed online: http://commonprayer.net.

10 'Darren Aronofsky's Noah: Environmentalist Wacko', http://godawa.com/movieblog/darren-aronofskys-noah-environmentalist-wacko, accessed 20 June 2016.

11 Compare the quote about the 'days of the Son of Man' in the first part of this chapter.

# 5

# Economy

## Introduction

ANNA-CLAAR THOMASSON-ROSINGH

With the fall of the Berlin wall and the bankruptcy of the Soviet planned economy there seemed to be just one option for the structuring of the global economy. The free market is taught as the model in all our universities, at every faculty of economy and business. Since the financial crisis in 2007, the ongoing conversation about the economic rules that structure our global society has erupted into a heated debate about the rights and wrongs of the market. This debate exists not only in politics and academia, it is a discussion that stretches into daily life, the arts and even religion.

In the UK we see the organization of 'transition towns', with some areas even introducing their own money for local produce (the Bristol pound).[1]

Transition Network is a charity which works to inspire, encourage, connect, support and train communities as they self-organise around the Transition model ... In our vision of the future, people work together to find ways to live with a lot less reliance on fossil fuels and on over-exploitation of other planetary resources, much reduced carbon emissions, improved wellbeing for all and stronger local economies.[2]

Films around the theme abound, from the blockbuster *Wolf of Wall Street* to the BAFTA winner *The Big Short*, not counting the many lesser-known documentaries easy to find on the internet. Even if we only look within Christianity we will find people claiming that the neo-liberal capitalist market economy is intended by God and clearly rooted in Scripture just as we will find others claiming that capitalism is a heresy that does not accord with biblical faith. The discussions go deeper than simply disagreements on the structures, to discussions on whether the underlying issue is greed or pride.

Although some will claim that 'theology has a place in the discussion of global economics' (Rieger, 2011, p. 36) that place is not undisputed. It is remarkable that many books on theology and economy or articles that combine the two do not draw on the Bible, especially not on the Hebrew Bible (Kidwell and Doherty, 2015; Williams, 2012). Equally remarkable is that in the discussions that emerge, people from very diverse points of view might be commenting in similar ways. Joris Luyendijk, who wrote *Dit kan niet waar zijn* (2015) which is translated as *Swimming with the Sharks* (2016), is a Dutch anthropologist and journalist who can, surprisingly, be compared to Rowan Williams (2012), the former Archbishop of Canterbury. Both talk about 'relationships of transparency and mutual responsibility' (Williams, p. 216). Although, for Luyendijk, it is worded as 'insufficient personal responsibility'.[3] More importantly both claim that 'the specialists' do not know more than we do. Luyendijk is clear in his image of an empty cockpit and Williams claims that these specialists are not more 'successful than others in mapping the territory' (p. 219). Everybody is reminded that the global economy is near not far.

Although books on theology and the economy hardly mention the Bible, biblical scholar Walter Brueggemann recently published *Money and Possessions* (2016). He gives six theses that provide a general frame of reference (p. 1). All six theses circle the central idea that prosperity is a gift from God that human beings hold as stewards. It is both a blessing and also dangerously seductive and a source of injustice. Brueggemann claims that the heart of biblical teaching is the idea of debt release (p. 47). The regulations around forgiveness of debt are a prime example that wealth is held provisionally. He acknowledges that these biblical claims 'amount to a deep critique of common practice' (p. 11) in our economy and in our own daily lives. Do these claims give any insight?

The large macro structures of the IMF, the World Bank, our national banks and governmental budgets and debts might feel like a world away from borrowing money to buy a house or the means to buy the next meal for your children. Even so all these things are implicated in the questions of what is wise in our economic practice. Nobody is untouched by these issues, everybody is making economic decisions on a daily basis. Do I buy fair-trade, or not? How much of the extra I pay is actually going where I would want it to go and how much is lining the pockets of big supermarket bosses, or of investment funds that might later be responsible for my pension? How fair is it anyway if one tea plantation is getting a lot more money than the next because they managed to go fair-trade? And then a similar string of questions for buying local and organic produce. Of course these questions are just for the rich. What if I cannot afford to pay the premium on 'fair' and 'high quality'? What if my next meal comes from the 'loan sharks'?

The macro structures remind us of the complexities and unintended consequences that lie around the corner of every decision. The personal economic decisions we make every day and the questions they raise remind us that this topic has many layers and sub-sections and our explorations will in a way only scratch the surface. The choices we make on the issues we do address are mainly given by our own reading of the scriptural text and what we find there. In the Old Testament, questions of slavery and how to deal with debt are to the point; in the New Testament the relationship between debt and sin, forgiveness and freedom come to the fore as well as the relationship between the rich and the poor.

At this point we need a health warning. The texts that we will read in the context of this theme are ancient and come from a social-historical background that is incomparable with the times in which we live. In some cases we know little of the original contexts of the texts that we read. (Often historians have used these texts to construct that context, but there is little information from outside the text.) In the following sections we are looking for associative inspiration and playful interpretations of biblical texts loosely connected to our theme. We would like to see if we can find wisdom that will help us to make sense of our current economic lives and help us not with specific advice, but with a bass line we can improvise our own melody on.

## Poverty, debt cancellation and forgiveness

### BERT DICOU

Western Europe belongs to the richest regions in the world. The level of prosperity in countries such as Germany, the Netherlands and England is many times higher than in most other countries outside this region. The level of prosperity per capita is also very high. This does not mean that there is no poverty in Europe. Rather, the average person should consider themselves as 'rich', which means that certain statements from Jesus may be perceived as unpleasant to the average British Christian.

> Then he looked up at his disciples and said:
> 'Blessed are you who are poor,
>     for yours is the kingdom of God.
> 'Blessed are you who are hungry now,
>     for you will be filled.
> 'Blessed are you who weep now,
>     for you will laugh ...
> 'But woe to you who are rich,
>     for you have received your consolation.
> 'Woe to you who are full now,
>     for you will be hungry.
> 'Woe to you who are laughing now,
>     for you will mourn and weep.
> (Luke 6.20–25)

Just as in the Old Testament, more than once the New Testament talks about having or not having money or other means of livelihood. Except that the poor in Jesus' vision have an obvious place in God's kingdom, while the rich still have to wait it out and he stressed more than once that the rich have a clear responsibility towards the poor. The poor should not be abandoned, but rather supported. He who can help the poor and does not do so, will be 'forever' scorned by God (the parable of the rich man and Lazarus, Luke 16.19–31; separating the sheep from the goats on the last day, Matt. 25.31–46). This is perfectly in line with the Old Testament. The disregard of the poor is one of the biggest violations of the covenant that God made with his people. Failure to comply with this obligation was the subject of many a prophetic tirade. Jesus is equally outspoken on this point.

What can be the reason that 'you who are poor' are told unequivocally, 'yours is the kingdom of God'? No reason is given, but it can be seen from the accompanying verse that God wants the last ones to be the first. The rich have already had their turn, they 'already had their share'. Now it is the turn of the poor. Such a reversal can also be seen in the canticle of Mary, at the beginning of Luke's Gospel. Mary has been told that she will be the mother of the new king of Israel, the Son of the Most High. She praises God because he has chosen her for this role despite her 'low status' and sings about other such reversals:

> He has shown strength with his arm;
>     he has scattered the proud in the thoughts of their hearts.
> He has brought down the powerful from their thrones,
>     and lifted up the lowly;
> he has filled the hungry with good things,
>     and sent the rich away empty.
> (Luke 1.51–53)

Later in the Gospel different statements and stories of Jesus talk about the trouble the rich may encounter on the path to God. It is an art to remain out of the grip of the god of money; loving God and Mammon do not go together (Luke 16.13; Matt. 6.24). Conversely, the poor have an advantage. A small gift from someone who can't afford to miss the money counts for more than a substantial gift from a rich person who doesn't even notice such an expense (Luke 21.1–4; Mark 12.41–44). All in all, it seems very likely that God has a preference for the poor.

A few years ago, a small Dutch group calling themselves 'Foundation for the Western Bible' published a satirical version of the

Bible, *The Western Bible. Cut out for the 21ˢᵗ century consumer*, with some Bible books including Matthew's Gospel. For the convenience of the modern Western reader, the editors had left out all the drivel about the negative aspects of money and God's involvement with the poor. Literally. The result is fascinating: some pages contain more blanks than text.

It is somewhat similar to the English *Poverty and Justice Bible*, an official publication of the British Bible Society, in which all the passages that deal with poverty and (in)justice are marked with a highlighter.

## Blessed are the poor

Even though we are rich in our part of the world, there is indeed poverty. Even in our part of the world there are those who are attracted to the message that the poor are blessed, because the kingdom of God is theirs.

In a fascinating book, *Blessed are the Poor? Urban poverty and the church* (2015), theologian and emeritus bishop Laurie Green searches for the possible significance of Jesus' statement in the context of the real existing poverty in the UK. This fits the 'contextual theology', a method he developed. Moreover, he writes, he personally has always had a great affinity with the work of the church at the bottom of society. He visits people in impoverished neighbourhoods in big cities, and writes down their stories about social isolation, the impossibility of finding work (or at least to find work that yields enough to live on), their anger on overdue maintenance, insecurity, loss of amenities, dilapidation, and also how they often find the courage to keep their heads above water in these harsh conditions.

With these stories in mind, what would you be able to imagine with regard to Jesus' emphatic promise? *Why* did Jesus call the poor 'blessed'? What did he *mean* by it?

Green stresses that it is not just any statement of Jesus. These are the opening words of his speech 'after he came down from the mountain'. The latter is an unmistakable reference to Moses, who received the terms of the covenant of God and his people on Mount Sinai and, after he descended, discussed them with the Israelites. 'Blessed are you who are poor' is the first provision of the 'statute' of this new commitment entered into by God, the installation of his kingdom, which after a long wait is about to start now (pp. 110–12).

A first answer is that God manifestly wants to begin his kingdom *with them*. The poor are not just the object – the religious obligation to care for the less fortunate: they are now the subject of this new reality that manifests itself and which transforms the existing order.

The lack of material wealth does not make one a better person. It is not the intention to glorify the idea of poverty as such. Green shows that whether you are rich or poor, your existence could completely revolve around money (p. 91) – much more than what's good for someone. Persistent lack of money, debts and so on determine how you relate to your environment. As such, frequent domestic violence in poor neighbourhoods often has as background a woman who is being held responsible by her husband for the inevitable gaps in the family budget. It is not a coincidence that criminality is rampant in these neighbourhoods.

Yet Green believes that 'being blessed' is indeed also real (pp. 123–32). Often, their background, their social situation and their way of life are associated with characteristics that definitely qualify to participate in God's kingdom. Green met a lot of poor people who had a simple, direct and pure form of faith. He was also impressed with their joy of life and interconnectedness – despite their poverty there was often reason for spontaneous fun. He also mentions their sense of dependence and readiness to trust, besides a keen eye for whom *not* to trust. Their confrontation with injustice and inequality gives them a well-developed sense of what is and is not fair; those who are able to word this towards council members can be easily compared with the biblical prophets who did the same. Finally, vulnerability – a situation that most poor people are familiar with, is not only a weakness but also a strength. In religious tradition as well, vulnerability is often the entrance to truth and action.[4]

## Loans and debts

Shortly after the 'beatitude' or 'blessing' of the poor, in the same chapter of Luke's Gospel, Jesus talks about a topic regarding the relationship between people without money and people with money. The first ones will often want or have to *borrow* from the latter. Which results in paying off *debts*.

> If you lend to those from whom you hope to receive, what credit is that to you? Even sinners lend to sinners, to receive as much again. But love your enemies, do good, and lend, expecting nothing in return. Your reward will be great, and you will be children of the Most High; for he is kind to the ungrateful and the wicked. (Luke 6.34–35)

Just as the blessings, this section is part of Jesus' speech to his disciples, 'after he came down from the mountain', the inaugural speech of the new kingdom (Luke 6.17–49). Together with its variant in Matthew 5—7, which is spoken just after Jesus went up the mountain (hence 'Sermon on the Mount'), this speech is considered the most fundamental explanation which Jesus gave his followers. Anyone who had something to say about the meaning of the kingdom of God in the later history of Christianity, automatically comes to these texts. As appears from the brief passage above, that kingdom provides a reordering of how people interact with each other, both on an economic level and in general ('love your enemies').

An interesting resource for the common practice around borrowing and debt is the apocryphal book The Wisdom of Sirach, from the second century BC. It outlines the reluctance that may exist among potential lenders, the fact that not everyone with a debt will be able to repay the debt, and even the explicit abuse of it. Nevertheless, he maintains the duties of charity and helping the poor:

> The merciful lend to their neighbours;
>     by holding out a helping hand they keep the commandments.
> Lend to your neighbour in his time of need;
>     repay your neighbour when a loan falls due.

Keep your promise and be honest with him,
and on every occasion you will find what you need.
Many regard a loan as a windfall,
and cause trouble to those who help them.
One kisses another's hands until he gets a loan,
and is deferential in speaking of his neighbour's money;
but at the time for repayment he delays,
and pays back with empty promises,
and finds fault with the time.
If he can pay, his creditor will hardly get back half,
and will regard that as a windfall.
If he cannot pay, the borrower has robbed the other of his
money,
and he has needlessly made him an enemy;
he will repay him with curses and reproaches,
and instead of glory will repay him with dishonour.
Many refuse to lend, not because of meanness,
but from fear of being defrauded needlessly.

Nevertheless, be patient with someone in humble
circumstances,
and do not keep him waiting for your alms.
Help the poor for the commandment's sake,
and in their need do not send them away empty-handed.
Lose your silver for the sake of a brother or a friend,
and do not let it rust under a stone and be lost.
(Sirach 29.1–10)

## From economy to spiritual ethos: cancel and forgive

The words of Jesus in Luke's Gospel about unabashedly lending
money to those who need it connects, as we saw, the economic
aspect with the broader moral. Just as we see in wisdom literature, we enter the sphere of mercy and good deeds. Reading Luke,
immediately following the cited verses, this is further completed:

Be merciful, just as your Father is merciful. Do not judge, and you will not be judged; do not condemn, and you will not be condemned. Forgive, and you will be forgiven; give, and it will be given to you. A good measure, pressed down, shaken together, running over, will be put into your lap; for the measure you give will be the measure you get back. (Luke 6.36–38)

In this passage, the transition to morality is made. It is not only due to the sequence of verses that these two are closely connected. It is not a coincidence that the word 'forgive' suddenly shows up here. Interesting in this regard is a story of Jesus that connects economic and spiritual aspects. It is a parable about remitting or pardoning (in Greek these two words have the same meaning) debts. At this point the focus is not to regulate social relations between rich and poor – potential or actual debtors and creditors – but it is about something else. There is an explanation based on an assumed, but probably very familiar image for the poorer audience. The situation where money is borrowed and cannot be paid back in due time, is timeless. The spiritual ethos associated with participating in God's kingdom has the same dynamics as in the economic ethos: becoming free of debt and in your turn freeing others as well, by forgiving them.

Then Peter came and said to him, 'Lord, if another member of the church sins against me, how often should I forgive? As many as seven times?' Jesus said to him, 'Not seven times, but, I tell you, seventy-seven times. For this reason the kingdom of heaven may be compared to a king who wished to settle accounts with his slaves. When he began the reckoning, one who owed him ten thousand talents was brought to him; and, as he could not pay, his lord ordered him to be sold, together with his wife and children and all his possessions, and payment to be made. So the slave fell on his knees before him, saying, 'Have patience with me, and I will pay you everything.' And out of pity for him, the lord of that slave released him and forgave him the debt. But that same slave, as he went out, came upon one of his fellow-slaves who owed him a hundred denarii; and seizing him by the throat, he said, 'Pay what you owe.' Then his fellow-slave fell down and pleaded with him, 'Have patience with me, and I will pay you.' But he refused; then he went and threw him into prison until he should pay the debt. When his fellow-slaves saw what had happened, they were greatly distressed, and they went and reported to their lord all that had taken place. Then his lord summoned him and said to him, 'You wicked slave! I forgave you all that debt because you pleaded with me. Should you not have had mercy on your fellow-slave, as I had mercy on you?' And in anger his lord handed him over to be tortured until he should pay his entire debt. So my heavenly Father will also do to every one of you, if you do not forgive your brother or sister from your heart.' (Matt. 18.21–35)

According to the introductory part, the call for leniency in the parable is intended as guidelines for situations in which a person is wronged and hurt by another. How often do you forgive that person before concluding that there is no point going any further? Peter thinks seven times is enough. Jesus keeps it at seventy times seven, or, keep going incessantly. He tells the parable to explain the point. In a parable, also called a 'comparison', the audience can interpret for themselves how the story 'compares' with the situation at hand, and which person in the story they want to identify with.

In this parable it is obvious that the audience (Peter in this case) identifies with the one who has to forgive another, as this was indeed the starting point. He will not identify with the king; after all in the parables about the kingdom of God it is determined who is the king: God, or his representative on earth, Christ. The audience/reader is therefore invited to identify with the creditor who is, in the first place, a debtor himself. The implication is that the person who is asked to forgive another, should also look at himself at the same time, especially as someone who is undoubtedly also indebted to others; and who is certainly failing when it comes to the completely new way of life associated with the citizenship in the kingdom of God – God's new world.

The 'ten thousand talents' is an absurdly high amount. One talent was worth 6,000 denarii (6,000 times the daily wage). In the parable it would have been completely logical if the debtor, to whom the huge debt was forgiven, would have forgiven his own debtor the much smaller amount – only 100 denarii.

But that didn't happen. In the kingdom of God someone who is accepted and forgiven by God, will make every effort to forgive others as well. Especially when they ask to be forgiven. It would be incomprehensible if this didn't happen. The new beginning a person receives after forgiveness of his debts, the clean slate with which he can continue his life, appears to yield a striking image for the new beginning someone receives when the metaphorical 'debt' is forgiven.

This fits perfectly with the dawn of the new reality – the kingdom of God – as announced by Jesus. Characteristic of this new reality is a totally new way of dealing with each other.

'Forgiving debtors' as our debts are forgiven, was such an important value to Jesus that he made it a part of the prayer he taught the disciples as the most pithy prayer, the so-called 'Our Father'.

> Our Father in heaven,
>    hallowed be your name.
>    Your kingdom come.
>    Your will be done,
>       on earth as it is in heaven.
>    Give us this day our daily bread.
>    And forgive us our debts,
>       as we also have forgiven our debtors.
>    And do not bring us to the time of trial,
>       but rescue us from the evil one.
> (Matt. 6.9–13)

Also in Luke 11.1–4, which contains a shorter version of the prayer, we see the request to be forgiven and to forgive others. Matthew even adds an explanatory statement: 'For if you forgive others their trespasses, your heavenly Father will also forgive you; but if you do not forgive others, neither will your Father forgive your trespasses' (6.14–15). Again the dawning of God's kingdom is the starting point of what Jesus says – see the first few lines of the prayer.

Throughout the later tradition of the Christian faith, the concept of forgiveness, in the sense of being able to forgive those who have wronged you, played an extremely important role. It is understood by many as the most characteristic value of Christian faith. Often it is emphasized that except for the one who is forgiven, it can also be liberating for the person who forgives.

## From spiritual ethos to social debate: the Bible and the 'Troubles' in Northern Ireland

Coming into debt or being forgiven a debt covers both the economic and the spiritual–ethical areas in the New Testament. Values from the economic environment are not regarded as totally different from values from the spiritual environment. A good example is the variant of 'blessed are the poor' (and 'woe to the rich') from Luke. Matthew's version of the beatitudes contains 'Blessed are the poor in spirit' instead of the obvious economic category. This means those who are spiritually poor, those without pretensions, without arrogance, those who are aware of their own limitations and accept them. Moreover, in Matthew's version the 'meek', the 'merciful', the 'pure in heart' and the 'peacemakers' are named.

A risk of that overlap of values which has meaning in both personal–spiritual and social dimensions, is that the somewhat more complex social aspect disappears. If in a given society the church becomes closely linked with the government or the national elite, that church may be less inclined to literally reprimand the rich and it is safer to regard poverty as a virtue. This is a situation which in history, up to now, has often occurred.

But in the pendulum movement of history there was and always will be reaction, in the belief that the key message of the gospel is much broader than just the personal salvation of the believer. Often the reverse movement takes place: from highly personally experienced values from the gospel one looks for the meaning in society – from spiritual ethos to public debate.

In 2015 the Dutch chapter of Remonstrant ministers held its biennial study retreat in Northern Ireland. The location was deliberately chosen because they wanted to study the role religion plays or can play when there are major social contrasts or even violence. The history of the 'Troubles' is still tangibly present in Belfast. This term refers to the very violent phase of conflict between (Catholic) Nationalists and (Protestant) Unionists which started in the late 1960s and did not end until 1998. The background of the conflict is ancient. The tensions come from English and Scottish (Protestant) settlements from the early seventeenth century, which sought to promote the integration of (Catholic) Ireland into the British Empire. When Ireland became independent in 1910, Ulster, where most Protestants lived, continued to belong to the United Kingdom. Even back then that led to bloody conflicts.

Religion was a complicating factor in the whole case. Because of the contrast between the Protestant and Catholic groups, Protestant and Catholic churches were often drawn into the conflict, although there were moderating voices coming from the churches as well.

David McMillan was a guest at this retreat, a theologian from the Northern Ireland Baptist Church. He told first-hand how the contrasts tore apart social life for decades. At that time, his own church was characterized by an apolitical stance. The focus was entirely on the personal–spiritual aspect in religious life. People still prayed for the victims of violence and for peace, but that was it.

In the 1980s, the decade that began with the hunger strike of IRA prisoners during which Bobby Sands passed away, and continued with several bombings and retaliatory actions, at home and abroad, a group of evangelical theologians, including David McMillan, decided that their churches had to take their responsibility as well, by letting them know that the gospel had a clear message in this context too. They founded their own organization, the Evangelical Contribution on Northern Ireland (ECONI). Their pamphlet in book form *For God and his glory alone* was published in 1988. The title in itself is controversial: *For God and Ulster* was the slogan of the hard-line Protestant unionists, the paramilitary loyalists.

The subtitle of the book, *A contribution relating some biblical principles to the situation in Northern Ireland* indicates what their programme was all about. A dozen biblical themes, each richly accompanied with references to Bible passages, are scrutinized. A discussion follows on how these insights can contribute to a solution for the irreconcilable social contrasts of the moment.

The insights are often derived from passages discussed above, from the central discourse of Jesus about the kingdom of God. This is not surprising, because the premise of the writers is how to transform the values of the kingdom in visions and actions that will further help their society. In the introduction to the book, they indicate that they hope to be 'peacemakers' (compare 'Blessed are the peacemakers' from the Sermon on the Mount). To date, they write, their religious background missed this relevance. When belonging to one particular Christian group just means that you belong to one of the two warring parties, that religious background is rather part of the problem than of the solution.

According to them there are, however, ten principles that indeed point towards a solution: Love, Forgiveness, Reconciliation, Peace, Citizenship, Truth, Servanthood, Justice and Righteousness, Hope, Repentance.

They write that the principle of 'Love' transcends the boundaries of culture, religion and background in biblical terms. And it is not in the first place 'an emotional feeling', but an institution; the 'active concern for the welfare and good of others'. 'We may find it difficult to love our enemies if they are terrorists, but we can begin by learning to love those of our neighbours who are from other traditions.'

In the principle of 'Forgiveness' the text that was chosen as a motto was taken from the Sermon on the Mount: 'For if you forgive others their trespasses, your heavenly Father will also forgive you; but if you do not forgive others, neither will your Father forgive your trespasses' (Matt. 6.14–15). They write:

There will be an expectation of pain in offering forgiveness. It is not easy to forgive, especially when there is 'justifiable anger' … Those who are offered forgiveness, including terrorists, will experience what it means to be forgiven only when they are truly sorry for what they have done and have a genuine change of heart and mind. However, whether this reaction is present or

not, we are commanded by Christ to offer forgiveness unconditionally.

In the accompanying study notes, they indicate that the Greek
word for forgiveness is associated with 'letting go of something'.
When God forgives people, 'he lets go', he no longer holds on to
what people have done in the past. They contrast this with the
Northern Irish practice, where people are accustomed to remember past injustice for a very long time.

With 'Peace' they note that they reject any form of violence,
and therefore distance themselves from 'the use or threat of violence and paramilitary force, even under the guise of self-defence'.

Under 'Truth' they write that for a Christian only Christ is
'true' in the absolute sense of the term and that all faith traditions
and formulations are only true in a relative sense of the term.
Against sectarianism, this opens the way to the recognition of the
truth and goodness in other traditions than their own.

Under 'Justice and Righteousness' they point out that many
of the problems of Northern Ireland arise from the injustice of
unequal treatment. The Bible shows God as someone who asks
justice from his people as a starting point. Discrimination based
on religious background must stop; a completely impartial justice
system should be put in place; when enforcing the law the legal
principles should continue to apply.

Under 'Repentance' we read that repentance is appropriate
when the reluctance to meet, speak with or become friends with
people from other political or religious affiliations helped maintain the dividing lines.

In 2013, 25 years after the publication of *For God and his glory
alone*, an anniversary reprint was released. At the presentation the
team from 1988 spoke about their motivations; a younger generation of involved persons indicated that in their opinion some of
the principles were still topical.[5] While the armed conflict ended
in 1998, the need to find positive links between the two parties
wasn't much less in 2013. One of the young people expressed
the hope that in another 25 years the whole debate would have
become irrelevant.

## About forgiveness: *Amish Grace*

The film *Amish Grace* (Gregg Champion, 2010) tells the story of the shooting at the Amish community school in Nickel Mines, Pennsylvania in 2006. Although the film seems to portray a rather liberal view of this event, the way the community responded was historic. The perpetrator was a troubled man (non-Amish), whom they knew well; he collected the milk on their farms. After raiding the school, he released the boys and shot the girls (five of them did not survive), then he shot himself. Even before the girls' funeral, a delegation from the community (including the father of one of the girls) visited the killer's widow. They expressed their condolences and offered her their support. But they had mostly come to let her know that they had *forgiven* him for his atrocities. The judgement of a person lies with God and not with us; forgiveness is the most visible expression of what God asks of us when we deal with people who do us harm. The widow does not understand, she is struggling to comprehend what the men are telling her. The film also tells the story of the wife of the father in question. Unlike her husband, she is absolutely not ready to forgive her daughter's killer.

The film is to a large extent an investigation into what it means to forgive. Even for those who do forgive, it is far from easy. Rather, it is a daily recurring trial instead of a one-time decision. But they are also aware that forgiving is liberating, that not only would they feel deep sorrow, they would also be consumed with anger and hatred.

The funeral of the killer is an impressive moment at the end of the film. Hardly anyone from his own social network is present. Nobody knows how to handle it. However, there are many Amish men and women, thus showing that they take their pledge to support the widow seriously.

Fortunately *Amish Grace* remains critical; the film does not avoid the less positive aspects of the Amish culture. We see a father who does not think an education for his daughter is necessary, it would only give her worldly tendencies. We hear from the sister who was excommunicated because she married 'an Englishman' and now leads a normal family life in the city. It is forbidden to keep in touch with her and even less desirable to talk about her. But that does not take away from the fact that the film compels admiration for the strength of this persistently sustained principle to forgive the other no matter what – and at the same time it shows how painful such forgiving can be.

## Forgiveness: unlimited?

In the discussion about the Christian concept of forgiveness we often talk about its limits, and we end up with extreme examples, as is also the case in this film. The best known example of a reflection on the limits of forgiveness is Simon Wiesenthal's famous book, *The Sunflower* (1969). In the book, he reflects on an experience he had in a concentration camp. A young dying SS officer confessed to him a number of heinous crimes against Jewish citizens. Now realizing he had done terrible things, he asked Wiesenthal whether he wanted to forgive him, as a representative of the Jewish people. At that time he was not able to and left the room. In the book, he asks his readers: 'What would you have done?' A dozen philosophers and spiritual leaders answered Wiesenthal's question. In a later edition of the book (1997), 43 new answers were added.

'Forgiveness' has become an important value in our culture. It is logical, therefore, to consider principles, conditions and limits. Is it mandatory, or even possible, to forgive everything? Given the answers to Wiesenthal's question there seem to be different ways to consider this.

It is important to realize that this rule – originally, in speeches and parables of Jesus – does not apply to the extremes, but rather applies to (more) ordinary situations, the numerous conflicts in our daily life, the contrasts between groups in mainstream society. In such non-extreme situations, distancing oneself, self-reflection and not reproaching the other on how they wronged you is an important factor in the recovery of disrupted relationships.[6]

## Questions for Reflection

How do you interpret: 'Blessed are the poor'?

How do forgiveness and the cancellation of debt relate?

What limits do you set to forgiveness?

# Surprised by graciousness

ANNA-CLAAR THOMASSON-ROSINGH

## Interest and usury

Traditionally Islam, Judaism and Christianity have been very cautious about interest. This caution is rooted in certain readings of biblical and Qur'anic texts. Within Judaism you can only receive interest on loans to gentiles (non-Jews), which is why Jews tended to be the bankers for Christians of the Medieval period. Islam has relatively recently created an Islamic banking system (www.islamic-banking.com) that tries to operate in today's global market with a completely different set of values and ideas to those found in most of the global economy. The fact that they manage this does raise the question of what loopholes there are in their way of operating banking without interest.

It seems that Christianity has forgotten that it too used to be suspicious about earning money with money. Calvin in the sixteenth century had the interesting and contested reputation of inventing capitalism. Although I think the picture is more nuanced, Calvin was the first Christian and European theologian to advocate lending money for interest. He saw the need for businesses needing investment and was willing to interpret certain biblical texts in that direction. Would it be possible for us to find inspiration when thinking about the economy in the age-old texts behind the prohibition on interest?

## The book of the covenant (Exodus 21—23)

The first time we find the word 'interest' (*neshek* – is literally 'something bitten off') in the Bible is in Exodus 22.25–27. In the grand narrative (the big story) of Exodus the Israelites, who were slaves to the Pharaoh in Egypt, are miraculously saved by God while they run away from their forced labour into the desert. In the desert at a mountain Moses receives the Ten Commandments (Exodus 20). Then from Exodus 21—23 there are laws; the book of the covenant. A covenant is a sacred agreement between God and people. This covenant contains the rules of the relationship with God. It is diverse in form and content. The form includes case law, short sayings (also called: apodictic declaration), divine communication and promise. The regulations order a wide range of daily life; sexual ethics; care of the disadvantaged; worship calendars; loyalty to God. Here we find basic principles for shaping the judicial task and the community's life. Among them we find:

> If you lend money to my people, to the poor among you, you shall not deal with them as a creditor; you shall not exact interest from them. If you take your neighbour's cloak in pawn, you shall restore it before the sun goes down; for it may be your neighbour's only clothing to use as cover; in what else shall that person sleep? And if your neighbour cries out to me, I will listen, for I am compassionate. (Ex. 22.25–27)

Around these verses we find laws about not oppressing and abusing the alien and the widow and the orphan; there is a verse about treating your leaders well and some about offering especially the firstborn.

What intrigues me about the text in Exodus is that the Hebrew word used for 'lend' in the first instance is really the word for borrow – 'if you cause my people to borrow'. Although I think that in Hebrew this is an innocent synonym, it does make us reflect on where the origin for the need to borrow is. It takes the responsibility of the need away from the people in need. The lenders are the reason why people would want to borrow: this is very interesting in our current 'buy now, pay later' schemes where it is indeed the lenders that push the loan onto people rather than people going out to ask for it.

Another interesting observation is that 'my people' is used as a parallel to 'the poor among you', as if the poor from our communities together form God's community. Again I do not claim that this is somehow the original or real meaning in the text, I just think reading the text afresh and anew raises this possibility and opens an opportunity to imagine our world in a different way. What if we would see those living on or under the breadline as God's people especially?

The real word for lending in this passage in Exodus comes only when it says 'do not be as a creditor'; do not be 'one who lends': how can you not be when you have lent the money? Although you are allowed to lend your money, you are not allowed to make your job out of it. Lending money is a kind of charity, it is not about 'making money'! You are not allowed to live off interest. This is of course different from never charging interest.

The real punch comes in the second part. It shows that the context of this loan is poverty rather than business. Giving your cloak in pawn must even in Iron Age Palestine be rather desperate. For Brueggemann (2016, p. 27) this text must be read in the context of the commandment, 'You shall not covet' (Ex. 20.17). When oppression of the poor (however legally) is at stake God wants to be involved. It is not only about the creditor and the debtor any more. Taking this into account it is clear that this passage is not about a loan to set up a new business but about a loan to survive. Those are very different and really incomparable situations (then as well as now!).

## Interest in Leviticus and Deuteronomy

There are two other injunctions concerning 'interest' in the law books of the Bible. One is in Leviticus 25.35–37 in the middle of a passage on the year of jubilee. This chapter is part of Leviticus 17—26, known as the 'Holiness Code', which is a block of material written by priests with a distinctive style and vocabulary. It tries to integrate ethical commandments (such as the Ten Commandments) with specific cultic and ritual law of the priestly tradition.

> If any of your kin fall into difficulty and become dependent on you, you shall support them; they shall live with you as though resident aliens. Do not take interest in advance or otherwise make a profit from them, but fear your God; let them live with you. You shall not lend them your money at interest taken in advance, or provide them food at a profit. I am the Lord your God, who brought you out of the land of Egypt, to give you the land of Canaan, to be your God. (Lev. 25.35–37)

In this text there is something strange going on with 'kin' and 'alien' or 'brother' and 'stranger'. Your brother, when fallen on hard times, becomes a 'stranger' and 'settler'. Who is my brother? Who is my neighbour? are the perennial questions when kindness and grace (and in these laws the right to ask interest on loans) are at stake. Jesus was asked this question as well: Who is my neighbour? Jesus' enigmatic answer is again a question: Who acts as a neighbour to the vulnerable? These are questions for all times. Who is my brother? Who is my sister? And this question becomes more pointed in the immigration crises we currently live through. We know, as did the writer of Leviticus, what an economic impact both the poverty of your kin and the strangers that live with you have. Clearly this text wants to maintain the prohibition against interest but it also subtly allows you to exploit your fellow Israelite as if he were a stranger. It might be that the idea is that you can use his labour force in lieu of interest.

Deuteronomy also has the prohibition against interest. Deuteronomy is written as a speech of Moses. The central rules of the treaty with God (organized in the order of the ten commandments) are in 12.1—26.19. It is a blend of ancient Israelite law and radical adaptation of Assyrian vassal treaty form. Interestingly here are covered similar topics as in the covenant code (Exodus 20—23). Within Deuteronomy 23 this prohibition on interest comes in the context of sanitary and ritual standards about going to the toilet outside the camp, about not giving runaway slaves over to their owners, and prohibitions of temple prostitution. There are also verses on fulfilling vows to God as soon as possible and regulations about eating from somebody else's vineyard or field: you may take what you can eat, and you may not bring a bag.

> You shall not charge interest on loans to another Israelite, interest on money, interest on provisions, interest on anything that is lent. On loans to a foreigner you may charge interest, but on loans to another Israelite you may not charge interest, so that the Lord your God may bless you in all your undertakings in the land that you are about to enter and possess. (Deut. 23.20–21)

> When you make your neighbour a loan of any kind, you shall not go into the house to take the pledge. You shall wait outside, while the person to whom you are making the loan brings the pledge out to you. If the person is poor, you shall not sleep in the garment given you as the pledge. You shall give the pledge back by sunset, so that your neighbour may sleep in the cloak and bless you; and it will be to your credit before the Lord your God. (Deut. 24.10–13)

In this passage in Deuteronomy we find the only two verses in which the verb 'to bite' is translated as 'to make one give interest'. This verb is mostly used of a serpent's bite. The image of interest as a deadly poison is fascinating. Although it might also just refer to different ways of taking interest. The 'bite' is a set 'fee' for the loan that is settled in advance while the 'profit' (used in Leviticus) is the way the money you owe becomes more and more over time through the interest that is accrued.

## The regulations compared

In one way Exodus, Leviticus and Deuteronomy all say the same thing; yet they are very different. The reference to the cloak in Exodus, the food in Leviticus and the garment and provisions in Deuteronomy put all the texts in the context of severe poverty. These loans are not for setting up businesses, these loans are for survival. If you have nothing else to give than a cloak as a pledge or security you are really very poor. Reading the text from Exodus for example you wonder whether the one who borrows hopes to be able to work the day and pay back before the night falls. Thinking about the very short term can be deduced; food and provisions are basics for survival. All three texts are clear, you do not 'use' the 'other's' need to earn lots of money.

This point on which the texts converge makes sense in our time and economy. We mark out luxurious goods from food for survival by, for example, higher taxes on the former. For certain commodities necessary for human survival – one of the things we would think of today is clean drinking water – we might want to lift other economic rules as well. In the free market economy we know how prices rise when the need grows bigger. This might not be ideal for drinking water and basic food. There might be another sharing principle in those cases which would be better than just the person with the most money buying what is available and selling it at inflated prices to earn lots of money from the hunger, poverty and misery of others. We might think that for basic necessities the free market is less than ideal. When the demand is huge and the supply is under pressure even then there should be no inflated prices for potatoes and rice. There should be no financial speculation with food. Could we agree internationally on such a sensible way forward?

The aspect of poverty of these texts also inspires us to think about loan sharks and pay day loans in relatively affluent Western societies. Justin Welby's challenge to Wonga,[7] some local churches efforts at debt counselling services[8] and the endeavour to make affordable credit available[9] are all examples of practical ways to work with the interest prohibition within our own culture.

At the same time the texts of Exodus, Leviticus and Deuteronomy have clearly different agendas. They speak into different situations, and maybe even into different historical contexts. The text in Deuteronomy is almost the opposite of the text in Leviticus. In Leviticus you are not allowed to take interest from your brother who has become a stranger, but in Deuteronomy you are allowed to take interest from a stranger. In our ears the difference between the Israelite and the alien might simply sound like racism. It brings to mind the double standards that operate in our current global economy, where some are allowed to protect their markets with tariffs and subsidies but other competitors on the global market are not allowed to do this. In this context it is interesting that in the current immigration debate, the UK would like to have different rules and laws for those who have just arrived as opposed to those who have lived in the UK longer.

It seems to me that the difference in attitude and concept between the foreigner and the Israelite is very unhelpful. It raises the question whether we would be more welcoming to the stranger in our midst if we were allowed to exploit them more. But does this critique of the text (making a racial difference is unhelpful) mean that these texts are somehow not valid any more or that we do not want to take them into account in any way? I think that some of the things we notice when we look at the texts closely, as we have done above, are extremely interesting – even in a completely different context like ours.


## Jubilee

The same is true for the ideas around 'Jubilee'. This is of course proven by the use of the term in an extraordinary number of different contemporary contexts which are all (however tentative or unconsciously) linked to the biblical text – film, art, academic research, and many others.[10] Another example is the Jubilee debt campaign which aimed to use the millennium year 2000 for a global release for the poorest countries.[11] There is an immediate association with debt release that has been used by charities the world over. It would be good to have a look at the idea as we find it in the text of the Bible. Have all those people who talk about the Jubilee understood Scripture?

The word 'Jubilee' in Hebrew is a word for blowing a horn. That is what the Israelites are commanded in Leviticus 25 to do when they herald the 50th year. This is all set in the context of the Sabbath. Every seventh day of the week you rest. Every seventh year you let the land lie fallow, so that it can rest. You can eat what the land yields but you do not sow or prune or gather. In Deuteronomy 15 this same seventh year is a time when you 'grant a remission of debts' (15.1) and when you set your slaves free (15.12). When you celebrate the seventh year of rest for the seventh time that is when it is a jubilee and the horn is blown.

> And you shall hallow the fiftieth year and you shall proclaim liberty throughout the land to all its inhabitants. It shall be a jubilee for you: you shall return, every one of you, to your property and every one of you to your family. (Lev. 25.10)

The institution of the year of Jubilee forbids anybody to sell land or property (or yourself in slavery) for ever. If you fall on hard times you can only 'sell' (lease really) your land and/or property until the year of jubilee, at that time all property reverts to original families. The jubilee year in the text of the Scriptures is about releasing land, just as the Sabbath year is about resting the land. Land cannot be sold in perpetuity for the land is God's and humans are but aliens and tenants. The year of Jubilee is about tribal boundaries. You can sell your land to another tribe, but after so many years it will revert back to the original tribe. The jubilee year is also about releasing slaves. When somebody falls on hard times and sells herself or her children into slavery it is only until the next year of jubilee. Children born in slavery know they are not always (not really) slaves – they are slaves only for the years until jubilee. This applies to Hebrew slaves but not to slaves that are 'from the nations around you' and 'the aliens residing with you' (Lev. 25.44–45). These you may keep; these your children can inherit. The jubilee also does not apply to houses in walled cities. If you sell one of those it 'shall pass in perpetuity to the purchaser, throughout the generations' (Lev. 25.30), but houses in villages without walls will be released in the jubilee.

The freedom of the year of Jubilee is about 'returning home'. *Amargi* is Mesopotamian for both 'freedom' and 'return to mother'. Ancient Israel was not the only one to make the connection between returning to your family and being free. Real freedom is the freedom to go home. As an immigrant I understand that not being able to go home would indeed be a deprivation of freedom in a very deep way. This is an idea that in an age of mass migrations seems at first strange and unusually topsy-turvy. Is not the freedom that is often sought, a freedom to leave home; to find safety and wealth elsewhere; to be liberated of the bondage of kith and kin. At the same time the notion is enthralling. Celebrating the jubilee is then about making it possible for people to go home. That is a very different proposal to a redistribution of wealth, even though the biblical jubilee does involve that as well. How would we go about making returning possible? What would it involve? Free movement of people is such a precious value.

It is fascinating that this biblical idea of jubilee, as we find it in Leviticus 25, has huge economic consequences. Just imagine all sources of wealth being redistributed every 50 years to a preset pattern of apportioning. This is far more radical than just the debt release which should really happen every seven, rather than every 50 years and for which the year of jubilee has become so renowned.

## Some critical comments

Of course the basic idea and its explanation in the biblical text have many critics. Here again the blatant racism of the text is repellent, more so because of its current reality. Few British or American children grow up in slavery but people in the West do benefit from slave labour overseas. This is a huge problem that the text seemingly condones. For outsiders, there are different rules than for us. This is something that has become unacceptable since the declaration of human rights. Or in a different reading of Scripture: this is something that has lost its appeal since the inclusion of the gentiles into the community of followers of Jesus.

Another valid critique is that although we have the description of the rule, nowhere in Scripture is this rule actually put into practice. We know of the observance of the Sabbath (Mark 2.23–28) and the Sabbath's year (1 Macc. 6.49, 53) but the year of jubilee is nowhere actually celebrated. Many will say this is for the obvious reason that it is an impracticable rule and that any government would struggle to implement it as law; it is unenforceable. Interestingly it was common practice for the victors of war to release slaves and cancel debts incurred under a previous regime. In the same way the economic practice at the end of World War II, although not a total redistribution, had an equalizing effect. For an established government, especially not one democratically chosen, this is not so easy. In an economy that is not tribal and less closely linked to the land, imagining the jubilee is even less feasible. To let the land lie fallow for a year as in the Sabbath year is a widespread agricultural practice (although one that intensive farming might have to relearn in the face of the ecological crises), but for land and other resources of wealth to ever only be on lease hold? Some will think this is worse than communism by a long way.

Even so there is a surprisingly compelling vision here. A vision that is rooted in graciousness (Brueggemann 2016, p. 98). The vision is so compelling that people keep referring to it. Both Isaiah and Jesus (reading Isaiah; Luke 4) proclaim the year of the Lord's favour, a direct reference to the jubilee year.

> The Spirit of the Lord is upon me,
>   because he has anointed me
>     to bring good news to the poor.
> He has sent me to proclaim release to the captives
>   and recovery of sight to the blind,
>     to let the oppressed go free,
> to proclaim the year of the Lord's favour.
> (Luke 4.18–19)

Bringing good news to the poor, setting prisoners free; the radical measure to keep inequality at bay and offer families a second chance at succeeding. The idea that access to resources and freedom are ultimately an undeniable gift of God to all – a human right – remains attractive.

## Spirituality and economy

The allure of the jubilee might lie particularly in God's involvement. Books on the jubilee are often about 'spirituality' rather than 'economy'. The recent *Theology and Economics* (Kidwell and Doherty, 2015) does not mention the Jubilee year other than in the name of the 'Jubilee 2000 Campaign'. But *Seeking a Free and Equal Society* is a question of spirituality according to Alice Pettit (2015). She invites us to let the 'concerns of jubilee shape how we live, pray and worship' (p. 3). Also for Maria Harris (1996), the proclamation of jubilee is *spirituality for the twenty-first century*. On the surface this might seem like a cop-out. The economic consequences of taking jubilee too seriously are too difficult so we make it all about prayer and forgiveness. But the spiritual sense that resources and wealth are a gift of God that people can only loosely have in leasehold is spirituality with practical consequences. In that vein Pettit's *Jubilee Spirituality* (2015, p. 22) speaks of banking and finance and Harris (1996, pp. 22–6) speaks of agricultural practice and actually freeing prisoners (pp. 68–70). The spirituality of jubilee is clearly one that needs to be lived out in the economic and political realities of this world. It is only this transcendent sense of wealth not being ultimately private that will drive any economic change. As explored in the Introduction, economy needs values. Jubilee supplies such a value: compelling and contested.

Mary Douglas (1999, 2004) reads Leviticus, and chapter 25 as part of that, in a different way altogether but comes to similar conclusions as Pettit and Harris. For her the whole of Leviticus is a literary masterpiece written by priestly writers to reconcile the clans of Judah and Ephraim and Manasseh (which become Samaria). In this reading the laws on jubilee and the ideas of freedom are a frame for the most important chapter of Leviticus, chapter 26, which is the heart of the covenant with God – the sacred treaty between God and people. Chapter 26 is the Holy of Holiest. Leviticus, for Douglas, is ultimately about God's justice and his fidelity to his relationship with Israel. She claims that Leviticus' 'insistence that the law will make them prosperous and able to resist their enemies is backed by this [jubilee] constitutional measure' (1999, p. 243). She explains that the absence of gross inequality in wealth-holding and the absence of a permanent underclass of slaves will foster solidarity. For Douglas, Leviticus is all about the relationship with God, a relationship that is kept going by economic measures that guarantee prosperity.

However one reads these texts on jubilee – even if they are not taken too literally – the tendency of the text against private wealth accumulation is undeniable. Even if read just for spirituality and metaphorically, not taking the text literally in any sense, there is still an overwhelming argument for equal distribution of wealth as a human institution. The question becomes whether we want to take the text seriously on that account. In an age where Oxfam reports that 1 per cent of the world's population owns almost 50 per cent of the world's wealth, this question is urgent. Are these texts antiquated myth that are simply nonsense in our complex modern economy? Or, do we find ancient wisdom in human systems that try to balance property, wealth and resources equally between people? Is there true freedom in the forgiveness of debts and how does that relate to current major debtors like Greece? Finally, is going home to your mother really freedom and who gets to go home?

## Freedom from slavery

One of the contexts in which these regulations of both absence of interest and jubilee play out is the context of slavery. The context is not so much the practice of slavery as the freedom from slavery; in Leviticus 25 the freedom from slavery in Egypt is mentioned several times.

Behind the economic laws is the constant presence, within this huge story, of God who leads Israel out of slavery in Egypt. This is the story of the exodus: going out. This is the story of fleeing slavery in Egypt to enter into the freedom of the promised land. This is the most important story in the Bible. It becomes the pattern for the interpretation of Jesus' death and resurrection, again a going-out in freedom, where it is release from the slavery of sin and, again, debt. The themes are so closely intertwined it is difficult to separate them.

In the text of Leviticus we find the issue of slavery immediately connected to the story of Egypt, the jubilee and the prohibition on interest:

You shall not lend them your money at interest taken in advance, or provide them food at a profit. I am the Lord your God, who brought you out of the land of Egypt, to give you the land of Canaan, to be your God. If any who are dependent on you become so impoverished that they sell themselves to you, you shall not make them serve as slaves. They shall remain with you as hired or bound labourers. They shall serve with you until the year of the jubilee. Then they and their children with them shall be free from your authority; they shall go back to their own family and return to their ancestral property. For they are my servants, whom I brought out of the land of Egypt; they shall not be sold as slaves are sold. (Lev. 25.39–42)

The big surprise is that in this context, slavery is never prohibited. Of course a similar surprise greets us when we read the New Testament. Slavery is condoned. The nationalism and racism we encountered comes in again when we read on: 'As for the male and female slaves whom you may have, it is from the nations around you that you may acquire male and female slaves' (Lev. 25.44).

I do not need to repeat the problematic racial implications of a text like this. I want to highlight that the tradition that is based on a flight from slavery reintroduces or simply continues the practice. I wonder, was it impossible to imagine an economy without slaves? Was slavery seen as an unavoidable social phenomenon? If so, how does that impact those who have the benefit of hindsight? Does the current global economy 'work' without slavery? Is that possible? If it is possible to have a viable economy without slavery, the question that these texts raise is: what other visions of equality and mutuality might be possible even if in current thinking they are deemed 'impossible'?

Harrill (2006) shows how difficult it was for abolitionists in the American slave controversy (those who wanted to abolish slavery) to argue their case from the Bible. He explains how embarrassing it is for today's readers of the Bible that the pro-slavery position is more defensible (p. 192). He lays bare a 'spacious argument' (p. 195) where interpreters change the rules of how to read the Bible to make it say what they want. I would like to propose – and hopefully have in this chapter shown – an equally 'spacious' and 'gracious' way of reading the Bible. There is much in the biblical text with which I disagree but there is little or maybe nothing that does not inspire me somehow. The Bible shows how difficult it is to change a particular economic practice, like slavery. From experience I have come to the understanding that an economy can flourish without slaves. This gives me hope for the economic practices that currently seem both not right and almost impossible to shift. It calls for patience and grace but also for perseverance. If we think something is wrong – change is possible.

---

**Questions for Reflection**

How can the biblical texts inform our thinking about the economy?

What might the prohibition for taking interest mean in your context?

What might economic justice look like?

---

## Islamic banking, an interview

### ANNA-CLAAR THOMASSON-ROSINGH

*I am talking with Stuart Hutton, whom I met at the Hilfield family camping holiday. This is a week for families at Hilfield Friary: a house of the Society of St Francis, Dorset (http://hilfieldfriary. org.uk/). Stuart is a Christian who works in Islamic banking and finance. He begins by telling us something about Islamic finance.*

One big difference between Islamic banks and conventional banks is that conventional banks make money out of spreads, the differences between the lending and saving interest rates. In Islamic finance this is forbidden as *riba*. People are not allowed to make money from money. Claiming interest is often seen as the rich making money from the poor. Those who have money use it to take money from those who haven't got money. This is not allowed. Another big difference is that conventional banks do not share risk. The risks are always left to the borrower. In Islamic banking the risk has to be shared. The person who lends the money risks that money together with the person who borrows the money. This works a bit like conventional shares, but then in lending. The importance about sharing risk is that the bank now has a stake in the business for which the money was borrowed. All parties involved will want to make it work. It is a more mutual arrangement.

For example, a mortgage with an Islamic bank may be based on a diminishing shared ownership contract. The bank and the person buying the house purchase the house on a shared ownership basis. For the share of the house that is the bank's, the house buyer pays rent, so creating profit out of an actual economic activity, not interest payments. Over time, you can pay the bank back the money for the bank's share in the house, so increasing your share and reducing the rent due. In this way the bank's share of ownership diminishes as the buyer's share rises. So instead of interest on the borrowed money you pay rent on the house. The beneficial ownership of the house is fully transferred to you the purchaser, so you would benefit from any growth on the property over time. In business, it is often a completely shared equity, so that growth or even loss may be shared.

*Stuart, does this way of doing finance and banking have an impact on the economy?*

In modern finance there is the inclination towards an opaque system. The population does not understand where the money comes from and very few people understand how it works. The banking institutions seem to like this. Islamic finance helps people to see what happens. Transparency is very important in Sharia law. This may also lead to more trusting customer relationships. Risk sharing means both parties have to work together. Also, in Islamic banking, contracts that are dependent on other contracts are not allowed. Contractual relationships need to be completely transparent. This often avoids complex dependent contractual relationships. You have to remember that Islamic finance is based on the trade system from the time of the Prophet and even before.

As all investment is screened for being Sharia compliant, the customer knows that no money is used in armaments, tobacco, alcohol or adult entertainment, for example. There is a moral basis in Islam. This kind of finance is very supportive for small businesses and entrepreneurs. It is also good for the welfare of broader society. Even giving to charity is built into the system, as one of the five pillars of Islam called *Zakat*, as in Sharia law you have to give a certain percentage to charity. Savers and investors are far more aware of where the money is going in their investments and have greater interest in what it is doing these days.

Of course this system is not infallible. Islamic banking does allow and encourage people to make a lot of money. At the same time it is about responsible finance and ensuring that those making money protect those in need.

*Do the values of Islamic banking clash with your faith and values as a Christian? What is the most important thing or value for you about being a Christian?*

Christian values are not really different from human values. The most significant value in my life is how I treat others; treating others as I would like to be treated. This is as kindness, generosity, love, sharing wealth (not just money) and knowledge. If everybody would do this the world would be a better place.

The differences between Christianity and Islam are mostly in the religious context not in values. Working with Muslim colleagues I do not have to give way to their religion, because we build our business on common values. Modesty can be a common value, even if Christianity does not have a problem with certain clothes and Islam does. My love for Jesus Christ and his words is not disallowed by my Muslim colleagues and is not compromised by this way of doing business.

I would not challenge the moral standards of a quarter of the world population. I share their ideas for the most part. For example although I drink a little wine occasionally, I would not invest in wine (because of Sharia compliance and also because of the impact alcohol has in society). I do think Islam is right in saying you should not earn money with money. Money is not a commodity and should not become a commodity. It is not a product; it is a means of transaction and moving wealth, a transfer medium.

*The Bible also prohibits taking interest. There is a lot about the 'forgiveness of debt' and we find the year of jubilee in the Bible. Are there parallels between the Bible and Sharia law?*

Maybe, but there are also differences. Modern Islamic finance is only about 40 years old. It has only been around for a relatively short time. It has developed in an economic context that is totally different from the situation in the Old Testament. The global financial world is now totally different. In the Old Testament the emphasis is on fairness and justice rather than on religious compliance, which might be a better way to come at the issue. Islamic finance is rather more top down, but does offer the opportunity to be individual too.

If we could really forgive all debt in the world as in the 'Our Father' it would damage the world economy. The liability would be lost and there is a moral obligation to repay debt. You should not take on more debt than you can pay back. The current world economy is too deep in debt to make the forgiveness of debt possible on a practical basis. In fact it could be devastating if cancelled overnight as this would destroy wealth as well as remove debt. It is how money and debt is created that needs to be considered in the future. In Islamic finance, the principle of supporting any debt with economic activity is a great start.

I am, broadly speaking, a capitalist. The year of jubilee is a non-starter in the twenty-first century. It would be fairly horrendous to agree politically as well as managing it. In its purest form with the complexity of systems that are currently in place it would simply not work. I would be concerned about wealth creation and preservation, and how this would be managed after hundreds of years in the current system, it is part of our culture.

Even so I am still interested. There might be an opportunity to take a modern interpretation of the jubilee. One potential would be to look at how derivative markets work. A derivative is a form of bet that the value of a certain investment will reach a certain point at a particular time. It is a form of legal gambling and in Islamic finance gambling is forbidden (*gharar*). Especially if there is an unknown element in a contract, it is simply not Sharia compliant. Maybe a modern jubilee would be one where some of the more complex areas of derivative markets would be cancelled out with the agreement of both parties and reduce the risk exposure across global markets. The derivatives market today is of a size several times larger than the gross domestic product of the world, so I am not comfortable with this.

## Notes

1 See http://bristolpound.org, accessed 1 August 2016.

2 http://transitionnetwork.org.dedi2835.your-server.de//wp-content/uploads/2016/10/TN-strategy-July-2014.pdf, accessed 15 May 2017.

3 www.theguardian.com/commentisfree/joris-luyendijk-banking-blog/2013/jun/19/banking-britain-beyond-control.

4 See 'Nobody wants to be vulnerable' on p. 74.

5 Short film on Contemporary Christianity's website (www.contemporarychristianity.net), which has since merged with ECONI. Accessed 16 June 2016. Also refer to Ganiel (2008) regarding ECONI.

6 For more on this topic see: Neelke Doorn, Bas van Stokkom, Paul van Tongeren, eds, *Public Forgiveness in Post-Conflict Contexts*. Series on Transitional Justice, Cambridge, Intersentia Ltd, 2012; Simon Wiesenthal, *The Sunflower: On the Possibilities and Limits of Forgiveness*, New York, 1969 and (extended) 1997; Alistair McFadyen, Marcel Sarot, eds, *Forgiveness and truth, Explorations in contemporary theology*, Edinburgh and New York, 2001.

7 www.theguardian.com/money/2013/jul/25/church-england-wonga, accessed 6 February 2017.

8 https://capuk.org/, accessed 6 February 2017.

9 http://justfinancefoundation.org.uk/, accessed 6 February 2017.

10 Some examples: film, http://jubileefilms.org/#projects; art, https://jubileeartsarchive.com/; research, www.jubileecentre.ac.uk/; the 'Jubilee Project' on YouTube, www.youtube.com/user/jubileeProject/about ('We wish to tell stories that inspire change! ... Doing Good is Contagious ...'), accessed 23 July 2016.

11 http://jubileedebt.org.uk, accessed 23 July 2016.

# 6

# Ruth

## SIGRID COENRADIE, BERT DICOU, ANNA-CLAAR THOMASSON-ROSINGH

If what we have said so far is true, that Bible stories are not about then and there, but about here and now, it should be possible to show how they affect us. Therefore, we end this book with a role play exercise: Walk in Ruth's shoes. Why Ruth? The book of Ruth is a clear four-page story about loyalty, money, family relationships, the future, faith, sacrifice, and the immigration issue. Almost all the themes discussed in *Re-imagining the Bible* are contained in this story.

The book of Ruth easily lends itself to be adapted into a play. Because the context is important for the interpretation of the story, an overarching task has been set by the director. The setting has been assimilated in voice-over narration. Next to the director and the actors, the audience is important, because ultimately it is about what the reader does with the Bible stories. Therefore, a few reactions from the audience have been added. Finally, inspired by the play, the audience play-out their own story.

It is up to the reader to add their own voice.

### Director, first meeting with the actors

Does everyone have a cup of coffee? OK, let's begin. I have already informed you about the kind of play this would be. Last week you received the script, I hope it matched with how you had more or less imagined it. I stumbled on this story at a lesbian friend's wedding celebration. The minister quoted a section from the Bible story, and the vows were a literal quote:

Where you go, I will go;
where you lodge, I will lodge;
your people shall be my people,
and your God my God.
Where you die, I will die –
there will I be buried.

In the original biblical text it turned out to be a vow of loyalty between two women, the young Ruth and the older Naomi. It is Ruth who never wants to leave Naomi. Moreover, both women are widows, and Naomi is Ruth's mother-in-law, as you already know by now.

I found it rather intriguing that a Bible quote was used in a celebration to bless the marriage of two women, while you usually hear that the Bible is against homosexuality. And most church-going people seem to heartily agree with this. Afterwards, I asked the minister what this was all about. She said that these words are very often used in marriages between two women.[1] And more-over, churches are on average fairly nuanced when it comes to relationships other than male–female, even though the opponents cry blue murder that they are an abomination to God. As if they would know that.

At home I looked up the quote and it seemed it was taken from a book in the Old Testament named after the young protagonist, Ruth. Well, 'book' is a big word, actually it's a booklet. It is four pages long, nothing more. But a lot goes on in those four pages! It is told in a concise way, and in those few pages you get a lot of information. Moreover, the author was someone with an eye for subtle detail and even had a sense of humour. I was not able to place everything right away, so I started reading around the story. And the more I read, the more interesting it became. I would not directly characterize it as a lesbian love story, halfway through the book Ruth hooks up with a man, but there is definitely something special between the two women. We will return to this at a later point. What intrigued me most – apart from the great story – was the political and economic aspect. In our society, the subject of immigration has quickly come to the top of political agendas. What do we do with refugees? Do we just want to take in war refugees or should there be room for people who want to come to our country for economic reasons? The person who cries out the loudest that we should not want that, has the political wind in their sails these days. We seem to be growing increasingly afraid of immigrants, and even seem to increasingly dislike foreigners in general.

That book of Ruth from the Bible is about a migrant family. To be exact, it is about economic refugees. A small landowner can't make ends meet on his own land any longer. Nature is not cooperating, the rain is holding off, crops fail and famine is the result. It may be OK for a while, but eventually everything is gone and there is really nothing left to eat. The farmer and his family pack their things and head to the nearest country, where nature has wreaked less havoc. In this case, 'the foreigner' is not the migrant family, it is a family from Israel.

With this story, the writer of Ruth aligns with other stories from the Old Testament. The Israelites had no qualms telling those not-so-glorious stories about themselves. At one point, their ancestors had gone to Egypt because of famine, they recounted. There they became a nation and were terribly exploited by the Egyptians. You could easily speak of forced labour and slavery. After they fled, they were a hungry nation, adrift on the way to a new country. For the next 40 years they wandered around a desert area. Migration is therefore a very logical theme for them.

In the book of Ruth, Naomi and her family are thus forced to move to a different country. But the book makes it all just a little more complicated. The sons in the family marry – women from the neighbouring country of Moab. Ten years later the situation has changed completely. Naomi's husband is dead, but the two sons have died very early on too. Who is left? Naomi and two daughters-in-law, Orpah and Ruth, both still childless. Naomi wants to return to her country. Although she implores the girls not to go with her, one of them wants to do just that. And so now Ruth is the immigrant, the one who leaves behind her family, her country, her culture, and seems to be headed to a life of absolute poverty, because make no mistake, a woman was not able to just independently build an existence in those times. And it is not very helpful when this migrant comes from Moab.

The Israelites very much disliked people from Moab. Moabites were not good enough. Every nation likes to tell a great origin story about itself. But this was how the Israelites spoke about Moab: after an adventure gone wrong, their ancestor Lot found himself in a strange, empty land. Destitute and narrowly escaping disaster, Lot and his two daughters had to build a new life. The daughters saw it coming, they concluded that for them there would not be a man, so their family would become extinct. Unless ... they got their father drunk and both, in turn, slept with him. Thus it was that two sons were born, and they became the ancestors of Moab and another nation, Ammon (Genesis 19). What a fine story to tell about your neighbouring nation!

One of the great prophetic books of the Old Testament, Isaiah, speaks of a vision of the big day that will come when God comes to save and comfort us: all evil on earth will be done with, all tyrants will be dealt with, there will be no more injustice, even death will be abolished. God organizes an immense feast for all the people, everyone is welcome. Everyone except the people of Moab, who will be trampled on this day of reckoning 'under God's feet, as straw is trampled in manure' (Isaiah 25).

An interesting detail you may wonder about is why the Moabites wanted to give Orpah and Ruth to the two sons of those paupers from Israel? Perhaps there was something wrong with both women, were they non-essential? According to one commentary, Naomi's sons did not politely ask for their hand in marriage, but they had kidnapped them somewhere.[2] But the most salient detail, the punchline of the whole story, is that at the end of the book, this same Ruth, the girl from that despicable nation, turns out to be the mother of the famous royal house of Judah in Jerusalem; her son, Obed, is King David's grandfather. The same King David, who is the example of kingship par excellence in perpetuity, and who in turn is the ancestor of the Messiah.

In that book of Ruth things are turned upside down in a revolutionary way; don't think ahead, from David to the Messiah, rather start with David and think back, go back in history and see where his ancestors came from. That whole ideal royal bloodline then seems to start with someone who did not belong, a foreigner, a childless widow, someone with no rights, no money and no prospects. The only thing that she has going for her is her exceptional loyalty to Naomi, expressed in the words I just quoted. In word and deed actually, that is what you read.

My intention with this play will become clear to you. I think this story is a great find, original and strong material, and so suitable as a mirror for present-day discussion. And you saw that I immediately thought about starting that discussion during the play. We will keep the lights in the room on and if anyone from the audience wants to add anything, they can feel free. Difficult for you, but a form which I like to experiment with occasionally. If someone from the audience reacts, just wait a moment, and then continue playing where you left off.

Enough about the background now, let's go to work! We are doing scene 1, hence: Orpah, Ruth, Naomi in action. In the book, the whole prior history is not part of the main story. So we will cover that with voiceover narration before you come on stage.

For now, this is what we have, but it needs some further work.

VOICE: Bethlehem, Judah, a Jewish peasant family. The names are promising: the man is called Elimelech, meaning 'my God is king' – things will go his way. His wife's name is Naomi, meaning 'pleasantness'. They are grain farmers and live in Bethlehem or Beth-lehem or the House of Bread. But there is a different future set aside for them. The harvest fails, there is no more bread. They have to leave. They arrive in Moab, a country where they do not really care to be. More disaster follows: the man dies. The two sons marry. Mahlon marries Ruth and Chilion marries Orpah. The sons' names are less promising in Hebrew: weak, ill, finished. And so it goes. Both men are dead in no time. Who's left: one older woman and two young women. The older woman no longer wants to stay in Moab, she wants to return to her country and her town. What is she waiting for? She has already packed her bags. The three of them lived there together, so it seemed obvious that the two younger women would go with the older one.

NAOMI: I am going. I am returning. Even though it seems the heavens are closed and my faith has left me in the lurch I am returning. Things are well in Bethlehem. Maybe for my faith and

my ideas to work I need to be back there. God seems to pay attention to Bethlehem again so I'd better go there if I want some of
that attention too. I have had rather too little of that lately.

ORPAH: Wait! We are coming. I just need to wrap up these
figurines – I want something from home to help me when I am
going to strange places. I will need something to remember how
life was. Just give me a minute. You cannot just leave us here. Not
after all we have gone through together.

RUTH: I am ready. Let's go and see about Bethlehem. It would
be good if some god would pay some attention to us: we need
livelihoods and a future.

NAOMI: But you cannot come! You cannot return. You never
came from there. You don't know what they are like. Moab is
not the right place to come from. We will go past your mother's
house and I will drop you both off there. I can't be responsible for
you any more.

ORPAH: Our mother's house? Why not to our father's house?
You think we can still seduce a man? You think our mother can
still find us somebody? I am no virgin and no mother – what
planet are you living on. That's never going to happen. I do not
even want to be with my mother – just the little models will do.

NAOMI: If only I return. God will bless again. God will bless you
here as well as me there. God will keep his promises. You have
always been true and kind: to me, to the dead. You will be paid
back for that. Happiness and kindness will follow you. You will
find a man's breast to rest your head on again. You will find a
livelihood and a future in the house of a new husband.

[Naomi tries to hug and kiss Orpah and Ruth but they go rigid
and are unresponsive]

ORPAH: Why have you gone all pious all of a sudden? You were
never like that. Trying to hide something behind God, are you?

It's about people not about God! We are coming to meet your people.

RUTH: With all due respect Naomi, that is nonsense. How can God bless us here? I do not fancy going back to where I came from. Clearly you have something to go back to: that's why you return. I do not have anything to return to. My brothers will see me coming: another useless mouth to feed; another dowry to provide – no way. I want to start afresh with your people.

NAOMI: You do not understand! Be reasonable. Moab is a dirty word where I come from. No one will touch you even if we did have a fortune to give, which we clearly have not. What you need is a livelihood and a future: children in other words. Find a man to give you some. I cannot give you a husband. Not with my body, not from my people. It is not possible. You have the wrong faith, you have the wrong father. Believe me this is a lot harder for me than it is for you! I will be an outcast the rest of my life. People might not even talk with me just because I have been to Moab (imagine what it would be like for you!). But better an outcast than a stranger. I cannot do this to you. You do not know what it is like to be an immigrant, how you are treated, how you lose everything, including any identity, any community. You can go back, be at home, find one of your own, return to your own culture, be normal.

ORPAH: Oh, Naomi, I will miss you so! I got used to everything being a bit weird you know. Nobody will quite understand where I am coming from now. But these [holding her figurines high] will go in their proper place again. Will I ever see you again? [Cries, hugs, kisses and leaves the stage with her suitcase and her figurines]

[Ruth cries, hugs, kisses – but does not let go]

NAOMI: Look at Orpah, she is sensible, go with her and you can be together. Believe me you do not wanna be a refugee.

RUTH: Stop! Naomi stop! You cannot stop me, do not try. I will follow you anyway. Where you go, I will go. Where you stay, I will stay. Your people are my people. Your God is my God. Where you die, I will die and there will be my grave. Before God and before you I promise: we will be together till death us do part.

[Naomi walks off the stage empty-handed without another word or another look at Ruth. Ruth picks up the two suitcases and leaves as well]

## Ruth – the premiere

A few months later: the director has made the latest changes and discussed them with his actors. Rehearsals are over and the play begins its theatre tour. We go and see it too! The beginning of the play took place in Moab. Meanwhile, Naomi and Ruth have travelled to Israel. They recently arrived in Bethlehem, the place where Naomi used to live, the 'House of Bread'. It still is a name with a slightly bitter aftertaste for Naomi. After all it is *still* problematic how they will get food. In a patriarchal society such as the one Naomi lives in, it is out of the question that women would earn their own money. Well, unless they sell their bodies of course. Her husband's inheritance – the piece of land he once owned – is theoretically still in her possession and that of her heirs, at least, they have the right to buy it back, but they cannot do anything with it, because they are not men. Not only was it a sad return because she had to report that her husband and sons had died, she also had to mourn the loss of economic independence and, unfortunately, she was dependent on the favour of others for her livelihood (and now also the livelihood of her daughter-in-law). Hence there is little to celebrate at Naomi's return to Bethlehem and the atmosphere is sombre. Note that Naomi means 'pleasant', Mara means 'bitter'.

> When they came to Bethlehem, the whole town was stirred because of them; and the women said, 'Is this Naomi?' She said to them, 'Call me no longer Naomi, call me Mara, for the

Almighty has dealt bitterly with me. I went away full, but the Lord has brought me back empty; why call me Naomi when the Lord has dealt harshly with me, and the Almighty has brought calamity upon me?' (Ruth 1.19–21)

When the actress who played Naomi addressed this monologue full of self-pity and reproach towards God, a first member of the audience dared to interactively participate in the performance. It was Yitzchak, an Aramaic-speaking Jew from the beginning of our era.

Yitzchak: Yes, excuse me. I'm quite sorry for you, Naomi. And for that poor Ruth you necessarily had to bring back to our country. But is it not taking it a bit far to blame God for your woes? Did not God himself say that he didn't want anything to do with the Moabites? 'No Ammonite or Moabite shall be admitted to the assembly of the Lord. Even to the tenth generation, none of their descendants shall be admitted to the assembly of the Lord.' (Deut. 23.3)

No, it is clear to me. It is better to blame yourself: you and your husband have allowed your sons to make mistakes, and the consequences showed it.

They transgressed the decree of the Memra of the Lord, and they took for themselves foreign wives from the house of Moab ... And because they had transgressed the decree of the Memra of the Lord and had married into foreign nations, their days were cut short. And both Mahlon and Chilion also died in the unclean land, and the woman was left bereft of her two sons and widowed of her husband.[3]

He finds little support from the rest of the audience. Disapproving mumbling. What ancient rules. But some people think to themselves: on the other hand it is quite a coincidence that these two young men both died suddenly ...

## Barley Harvest

In the programme booklet, the audience was able to read that Naomi and Ruth returned to Bethlehem just when the barley harvest began. Which seems to offer prospects for their chance to obtain some food. One of Israel's 'welfare' requirements was that at harvesting time leftovers should be left for the benefit of 'the poor and the alien'.

'When you reap the harvest of your land, you shall not reap to the very edges of your field, or gather the gleanings of your harvest. You shall not strip your vineyard bare, or gather the fallen grapes of your vineyard; you shall leave them for the poor and the alien: I am the Lord your God'. (Lev. 19.9–10; cf. 23.22)

In the variant of this commandment in Deuteronomy, 'widows' are also explicitly named.

When you reap your harvest in your field and forget a sheaf in the field, you shall not go back to get it; it shall be left for the alien, the orphan, and the widow, so that the Lord your God may bless you in all your undertakings. When you beat your olive trees, do not strip what is left; it shall be for the alien, the orphan, and the widow. When you gather the grapes of your vineyard, do not glean what is left; it shall be for the alien, the orphan, and the widow. Remember that you were a slave in the land of Egypt; therefore I am commanding you to do this. (Deut. 24.19–22)

When the two women talked about this with each other, it quickly became clear that the task would fall upon Ruth. Naomi did not see herself walking along the fields. But the young, energetic Ruth would be able to do that just fine. While they discussed it, the name of Boaz was mentioned briefly. He was actually one of Naomi's relatives on her husband's side (Ruth 2.1). He was certainly someone where something could be picked up, he was one of the richest farmers of Bethlehem. A prominent man in society. Besides, his name means something too. Boaz was in fact the name of one of two pillars at the entrance of the temple; the one on the right was called Jachin, the one on the left, Boaz. Could this mean that the farmer from Bethlehem was a pillar of society?

## Ruth's monologue

What do I want?
Feed myself and my mother-in-law?
Prove that she has not come home empty!
That she has me.

What do I want?
Be together with Naomi?
She has stopped speaking to me!
She couldn't care less.

What do I want?
Be the perfect daughter-in-law?
I used to love Naomi!
Bitter indeed.

What do I want?
Keep busy?
Just not think about the stupidity of coming here!
It is harvest, work enough.

What do I want?
Be noticed?
Not by the hostile stares!
I am more than just 'Moabites'.

What do I want?
Feel at home?
The field of Moab is no different to these fields!
Breaking my back for a little scrap will do the trick.

What do I want?
Get to know people?
These Ephrathites will not want to know about me!
Chatting will not keep me from work.

What do I want?
Belong?
But not belonging is also freedom!
That will never last.

What do I want?
Have a family?
Yes, keep dreaming girl!
Not in this lifetime.

What do I want?
A bit of fun on the fields?
I will probably not get pregnant anyway!
I never did with Mahlon.

What do I want?
Am I available?
And if the fun changes to violence!
I know about that.

What do I want?
Some adventure, courting danger?
Nobody knows to protect me!
That could go wrong.

What do I want?
The boys or the girls?
Probably both if I may be so bold!
I know, I may not.

What do I want?
Does it matter?
Nobody cares what I want!
The question has not entered my head.

Can I bear the shame? – now, that is the question!
Of feeding myself and my mother-in-law?
Proving that she has *not* come home empty!
That she has me.

Can I bear the shame?
Of being together with Naomi?
She has stopped speaking to me!
She couldn't care less.

Can I bear the shame?
Of staying at home?
Penniless widow, scrounging foreigner!
It cannot get worse.

Can I bear the shame?
Of working the field?
My inner strength protecting my inner dignity!
I might as well give it a go.

## Comments from the audience!

Kim (36), a fashion model, has just introduced her own fashion label on the market.
Kim: 'Can you believe this? This Ruth is a silly child. So naive! She lets herself completely be taken in by that Naomi. She just has her working hard in the fields, where she is an all too easy target for all those young men. Of course there's going to be quite a bit of messing around in all that hay. Finally a woman in the Bible who is the protagonist and it is yet another compliant twit and ideal daughter-in-law!'

## Ruth 2 – In the Field

[On stage a group of men is working on one side of a field and a group of women is working on the other side. Ruth comes up and joins the group of men. Then Boaz comes up. Boaz sees Ruth,

Ruth sees Boaz and it is clearly love at first sight. Boaz greets everybody very loudly and piously]

BOAZ: The Lord be with you.

CHOIR: The Lord bless you.

[He then calls one of the men and whispers, the only thing we hear is]
BOAZ: Whose is she?
[Further whispering the man goes back to the group of men. Boaz calls Ruth. He drops on one knee]

Now we hear the full conversations:

BOAZ: Little one, don't be afraid, stay here. My field is big enough for all you need. Do not go to other fields. Stay with my women. [He gets up and walks holding her elbow to the group of women on the other side]
Do not look at the boys. Look at the harvest! Here is food for you and your mother-in-law. If you follow these women, there will be plenty. I have told the men not to bother you. Nobody will touch you here. You are safe. Let me show you where we drink, you can join us for lunch.

[Now Ruth falls on her knees]

RUTH: Why do you look at me? What do you see? I am a refugee!

BOAZ: Gossip travels fast in Bethlehem. You have looked after Naomi after Elimelech died. I am not so sure about Elimelech taking his family to Moab, but the lovely Naomi – now that is a different matter. I trust her judgement. Also, you have chosen us as your people. You have left your home and house; your father and family to be family to Naomi. May God take you under his wing. You sought refuge with God. All the good you have done will be rewarded by Adonai the God of Israel.

(Ruth gets up and flirts)

RUTH: Please look out for me. You are my solace. You are so kind. I will serve you maybe also in other ways than your other servants?

When the public understands that the pious and wealthy Boaz is quite impressed with Ruth, someone shouts: 'And, Yitzchak, what do you think about this now? Boaz is having special feelings for a young Moabite woman.' The Aramaic-speaking Jew from the beginning of the era mumbles something about another commandment that applies here, about male family members being responsible for widows. And then he says, exasperated: 'I have absolutely nothing against Moabites in general, you know. And certainly not against Ruth. I admit, she truly is a special lady. How she helps her mother-in-law, how she is simply willing to live in a different country ... Besides, only male Moabites are not welcome at the assembly of the Lord. Boaz also explained the command as such, he says that she is welcome to take shelter under the wings of the Eternal.'[4]

It seems like he wants to rehabilitate himself for that earlier unkind remark about Naomi. But he also seems to be stirred by what Ruth said in her monologue.

Zilpah (24), a Jewish woman from 1000 BC is also sitting in the audience.
Zilpah: 'What beautiful rules our faith has! Glad to see there is always a solution at hand for widows and orphans. It is the hand of God that ensures Ruth ends up exactly on Boaz's field, a distant relative who can help out Naomi and Ruth.'

[Everybody leaves the stage, but Ruth while she keeps working says]

RUTH: What do I say to Naomi? How can I help her understand I must stay on Boaz's field? Do I want to go ahead with this? He is so old. How available is he? Can I talk with Naomi about this? Maybe just leave that till the end of the harvest. I can stay working on this field for that time. It solves the food problem for this year. I will tell her I am with the boys, see if she picks up the hint. I wonder what she can tell me about Boaz.

Sylvie (62), a lady from Amsterdam from our era, comments out loud. Max (38) is also in the audience; he recently divorced.

[Silvie (to her neighbour Els (59)] 'Oh God, look at her, what a lovely lassie. I wish I had a daughter-in-law like her. My son once had something with a Turkish girl, but do you think she ever did any grocery shopping for me? Forget it, you could not have her do the grocery shopping; she would come home with Turkish bread and olives and stuff. Great for bowel movements, but it's not your old-fashioned pot of stew. Hey, look, what is she doing now, that chick? She makes herself beautiful to go to see her lover. She'll get him, you'll see. Handsome man, you know. A bit older, but that's how it is these days huh? Either you have this young man who has nothing, no money, or a divorced guy who's already made it and feels like a second go-around. Well, I'll take the latter ... Oh look, he's a real gentleman, he sends the young guys away and gives her food. Yes, the way to the heart goes through the stomach, right?' [Sylvie is silent for a moment, then picks up her handkerchief and wipes a tear]

Max: 'I watch porn on a regular basis – yes, who doesn't? About 95 per cent of men do it, and the rest don't admit to it. That Boaz fellow is smart, surrounded by all those women who work for him. Of course as a rich, old man he had no trouble finding young leaves. And of course, those from foreign lands are simply appealing, aren't they? The grass is always greener on the other side of the fence. In Thailand, during my holidays ... all those girls are gorgeous and they all want to come to Europe. But what to do with such a girl who has so much experience? I don't like that. That Boaz immediately says that his men should stay away from Ruth. I'm curious to see how it goes.'

## Ruth 3 – At Home

[Naomi and Ruth are sitting at home]

NAOMI: Ruth, dear, it is time we start dreaming about a future again. This Boaz, he is an interesting fellow. You know the story about his mother Rahab? I think you can learn from her. There are more ways than working on the field to provide for yourself you know. Rahab was a prostitute before she settled down with Salmon. She is long gone now; I wish you could meet her. Boaz is a close relative, a redeemer even. He might want to fulfil the role of next of kin. For your future you need a son.

RUTH [whispers to the audience without her mother-in-law hearing]: Mmm, I wonder is this for *my* or for *her* future that we are talking about sons again. I wonder what she wants from me now.

NAOMI: Look Ruth, they have started winnowing. Boaz will be at the threshing-floor tonight. It is your chance. You will not be the only woman there, nobody will notice. Boaz will eat and drink and enjoy himself. He will need somebody to keep him warm. You just need to present yourself right. Wash well, use a nice smell, dress your best – you know what I mean. Let yourself not be seen. Wait till you know where Boaz sleeps. Go when he is alone. Undress and lie at his feet. Boaz will tell you what to do. He is a man with experience. Just do as he tells you. It cannot go wrong. It is the right time of the month for you, is it not?

RUTH: What a good idea mother Naomi. I will do exactly as you say.

Kim: 'Come on now. Naomi gets Ruth raped! It was not so smart of her to say that she was working with young *men*, whereas she was working with young *women*. That's how you mislead your mother-in-law. As if you feel like a good screw. Or is Ruth double-dealing: giving her mother-in-law the impression that she's doing everything to get a roof over her head? And presenting Boaz as the ideal son-in-law; allegedly he would have told her that morning "not to arrive empty-handed at your mother-in-law's". Fortunately, that night she heads to the field in a sweater and jeans and not in a little black dress, as Naomi would have it. At least she shows some sense of honour! It's too cold anyway in such a sexy dress. Maybe she wants to test Boaz? To see if it's about her or her body? She's certainly not sitting there waiting for a one night stand.'

## Threshing floor

Winnowing is the next step in the harvesting process, after cutting and drying. The action moves to the threshing floor, where the winnowing takes place. Naomi has a plan to take advantage of this special moment in the harvest season. After months of effort (ploughing, sowing, growing, and reaping) the time has now come where the cycle has been completed and crops can be collected. After threshing the time has finally come: there's the grain. Bread can be baked again. It is a festive moment. Which undoubtedly came with good food, drinks and partying. 'When Boaz had eaten and drunk, and he was in a contented mood, he went to lie down at the end of the heap of grain' (Ruth 3.7, cf. 3.4).

## Ruth 3 – At the Threshing Floor

[On stage Boaz is lying behind a heap of grain; Ruth tiptoes around the heap of grain and starts stripping at Boaz' feet]

RUTH [whispering to the audience]: I am not sure about this. Not at all, do I want Boaz? Is this a good idea? I wonder whether he will be as good as Mahlon. I do not believe in just doing as the man says though. Do you think Naomi really did that with Elimelech? Boaz needs to know what this is about otherwise it will backfire on us. I am not just seducing him.
[Ruth lies down. After a short time Boaz startled, turns around, and sees Ruth is shocked]

BOAZ: Who are you?

RUTH: I am Ruth, take me under your wing, you are close enough to be the redeemer. Give Mahlon a son.

BOAZ: What?! What do you mean? Oh, sweetheart. Really? You could get a younger man you know. The Moabite thing has worn off enough. God bless. You are amazing. First coming with Naomi and now this. You really understand what loyalty and kindness means. The kind that God shows us. Don't worry, don't be afraid. I will not turn you away. You are worth it, believe me. But we first do need to settle the business, there is land involved you know. And there is someone nearer, who could raise sons for Mahlon. He has his eye on the land. We need to talk first otherwise it might go badly wrong. I need to check with him before we proceed. Lie down till morning. But make sure you go before dawn so that nobody knows you were here. We do not want a scandal do we? Do not go back empty handed, take grain before you go.

Silvie [elbowing her neighbour]: 'Els, look, how romantic ... Girl, it's making me cry, it seems like a fairy tale. It's like farmer John, you know, the farmer in Canada, from that show *Farmer Wants a Wife*. And now I understand why they talked about Ruth and Boaz at Prince Willem-Alexander and Maxima's wedding ceremony. Alex is obviously Boaz and Ruth is Maxima, who came to him from Argentina. She couldn't go anywhere else either, with that father of hers of course. Nicely put, isn't it? Now they are together forever. That's what I want too, you know, for my son to find such a sweet lass, if necessary a foreigner, but then one like Maxima. And that she'd go grocery shopping for me. And then give me a beautiful grandchild ... Els, why don't you come up with a cool name for my grandchild?'

Zilpah: 'Wow, this is going completely wrong. That Ruth does not know what she wants. Now she's being a bit disobedient, she is not doing exactly what Naomi says. She should show herself from her best side, to help the future. Girl, be a bit more up front. Boaz is a healthy farmer, and certainly not ugly, and he has only had two glasses of wine. You must know your place as a woman, and the Lord will bless you with a rich lineage. Come on, it is not that big a sacrifice? You know you have no choice as a Moabite. Isn't it nice that she can pass on the family name of her deceased husband through a son? The Lord be praised!'

Max: 'This Boaz has quite the body for his age. Certainly done well for himself with all those pretty girls around him. Strange that he does not touch Ruth while she's lying there at his feet. Do you think he's impotent? No Viagra yet, in those days?'

Kim: 'By the way, it's cool that Boaz properly marries her. Personally, I'm going to pass on taking care of my in-laws. I don't have time for that, running my own company and all. The government wants me to do my mother-in-law's laundry after she broke her hip. But I cannot manage to drive another hour and a half to my mother-in-law's after work. And what if she starts getting dementia? Then I'll have to take her into our home, right? Or she'd have to go to one of those expensive nursing centres in our neighbourhood. We cannot handle this financially, with two kids in college.'

In ancient Israel, there were laws regarding land that was lost from family estates and caring for surviving widows. The following applies to land: 'If anyone of your kin falls into difficulty and sells a piece of property, then the next-of-kin shall come and redeem what the relative has sold' (Lev. 25.25).
The following applies to widows:

> When brothers reside together, and one of them dies and has no son, the wife of the deceased shall not be married outside the family to a stranger. Her husband's brother shall go in to her, taking her in marriage, and performing the duty of a husband's brother to her, and the firstborn whom she bears shall succeed to the name of the deceased brother, so that his name may not be blotted out of Israel. (Deut. 25.5–6)

The person who is the most entitled to Elimelech and Naomi's land and whose duty it is to marry the widow of the deceased heir – the nearest relative – is the first to choose. And that is not Boaz. However, the marriage arrangement also provides for a reserve measure in case the nearest family member wants to waive his duty, and be shamed in doing so:

> If he persists, saying, 'I have no desire to marry her', then his brother's wife shall go up to him in the presence of the elders, pull his sandal off his foot, spit in his face, and declare, 'This is what is done to the man who does not build up his brother's house.' Throughout Israel his family shall be known as 'the house of him whose sandal was pulled off.' (Deut. 25.8–10)

## Ruth 4 In the Gate

BOAZ: Mister so and so, come here, sit down. I need elders. Please can you come and sit, we need to sort out some business here. You know Naomi, who has come back from Moab? She is selling Elimelech's land. So I thought you need to know, you have the right to buy it. Redeem it for Naomi and Ruth. We can settle it now while we have the elders here. The thing is, if you don't want it, I am quite interested myself. And I have the first right after you. So you see I need to know whether you are interested.

MR SO AND SO: I am interested in buying.

BOAZ: If you buy the land you also get Ruth the Moabite. So you can maintain the name of the deceased on his inheritance.

MR SO AND SO: What marry the Moabite? But that would damage my inheritance. I cannot do that. You take the right to redeem.

[Mr So and So gives Boaz his sandal. Boaz solemnly declares]
BOAZ: Today you are witnesses that I have acquired from the hand of Naomi all that belonged to Elimelech and all that belonged to Chilion and Mahlon. I have also acquired Ruth the Moabite, the wife of Mahlon, to be my wife, to maintain the dead man's name on his inheritance, in order that the name of the dead may not be cut off from his kindred and from the gate of his native place; today you are witnesses. (Ruth 4.9–10)

CHOIR OF ELDERS: We are witnesses.

ONE OF ELDERS: You know this makes me think of the story of Judah and Tamar. That was also an unusual match – father-in-law with daughter-in-law – illegal even when I think about it, but Perez their son and his house have been such a blessing. Tamar was a foreigner and she was brave and righteous just like Ruth. Let us pray that the children from this marriage will be just such a blessing as Perez was.

## Ruth 4 Women of Bethlehem

[On one side of the stage Ruth is working alone. On the other side of the stage Naomi and the women of Bethlehem are sitting in front of a house. Naomi is breastfeeding a baby. The lighting focuses on Naomi and the women and leaves Ruth in the dark]

WOMAN 1: Congratulations Naomi! What is your little one called?

NAOMI: I am still thinking [she holds the baby up]. What do you think? What name would fit?

WOMAN 2: It is a miracle, for you to have life again; a son to care for you in your old age. God took care of you.

WOMAN 3: Well it was really Ruth: the daughter-in-law who is better than seven sons. I wish I had one of those.

WOMAN 1: Ruth has really loved you and served you Naomi. She has laboured so hard: on the land and in childbirth. This baby will be the same. A worker, a server: Obed. You should call him Obed.

WOMAN 2: Yes, Obed – because Ruth also trusted in our God, didn't she? She is in a way a true believer and serves God in a way more than any of us ever did. Obed will serve God.

NAOMI: Mm, Obed, I like that. Obed it will be.

CHOIR OF WOMEN: A son has been born to Naomi and Obed is his name. [A bit louder]: a son has been born to Naomi and Obed is his name. [Most loud]: a son has been born to Naomi and Obed is his name.

The light changes focus from the women to Ruth who is working on the land.

RUTH:
Mahlon asked: Who do you belong to?
My father, my family: I could belong to you.
Mahlon died: Who am I now?
Childless widow: poor beyond poor.

Naomi asked: Who do you belong to?
I choose Naomi's people and Naomi's God
Naomi schemed: Who am I now?
Labour and prostitution brings in food.

Boaz asked: Who do you belong to?
To Moab but also to Naomi
Boaz married: Who am I now?
Surrogate mother for a royal line.

Who am I?
Traitor of my people?
Friend and companion to Naomi?
True believer in the God of Israel?
Foreigner and refugee?
Illegal migrant worker?
Trafficked prostitute?
Slave and daughter-in-law?

Or wife and mother? Do I even want to be wife and mother?
The endless caring! And if I were:

How can my baby be Obed – surely I should call his name?
How can my baby be Naomi's – no blood runs the same?
How can my baby be a father – Jesse is the (grand)son.
How come that with my baby it has all begun...

Mother of ...
Obed, Jesse, David, Solomon (from Bathsheba of course)
A royal line indeed.
One that keeps flowering.
Even when Jesse's root seems dead.

Mother of ...
Jesus, again the bloodline is tenuous,
but all those other lines of: companionship, loyalty, friendship,
    faithfulness, kindness:
one woman better than seven men
all those lines
they come together
again and
again and
again.

The last scene has ended. The audience might not have found the ending very surprising – the hero and heroine are together. Yet, in the end they may have been confused a bit. A confusing end. Not Ruth herself, but Naomi is in the spotlight. 'Naomi took the child and laid him in her bosom, and became his nurse. The women of the neighbourhood gave him a name, saying, "A son has been born to Naomi"' (Ruth 4.17).

And an equally surprising end is that in the final seconds we hear that this boy has now become the grandfather of Israel's most famous king. 'They named him Obed; he became the father of Jesse, the father of David' (Ruth 4.17).

Initially, the audience's applause is hesitant. Somewhat confused. As in: 'Don't we get to hear more about that?' They do not really know what to make of this unexpected epilogue.

Zilpah: 'All's well that ends well. Ruth remained loyal to Naomi.

The Eternal has blessed Naomi with a new son who will continue the family name. What a beautiful piece. It shows that you must always believe in a new future. If Ruth had not been so bold, they would have still been hungry. She came a long way. As a Moabite, she is now the ancestress of Jesus nonetheless.'

Kim: 'Well, good thing it's already the end of the show, otherwise I would leave. Because now the cat's coming out of the bag. As in other Bible stories, it's all about posterity. There must and there will be a child, if necessary through a forced marriage. Naomi has concocted it all, and Ruth is such a naive, docile type, you can tell. What a disappointment. The pamphlet said: "A modern version of the biblical story". Well, if you ask me, this is another stereotyping and old-fashioned play. I do not understand why it's such a popular story among women. At the end, the protagonist, Ruth, has completely disappeared from the story and it is all about Naomi who is bragging about her child to her neighbours. As if it's her child! If I ever have a baby, I will raise it on my own. My parents can give advice, but that's where it ends. Isn't it just crazy that Ruth is not allowed to name her baby? It's Naomi's neighbours who come up with the name Obed. So you see, it's all about perception. As long as the neighbours don't gossip about you, your life as a woman is successful. It seems like the village of my childhood. God, I'm so glad I live in a different era.'

Sylvie: 'Oh, look at what a cutie Obed is! Looks just like his father, you can tell. Els, girl, I wish my son would just hurry up with a relationship, after all, I do not have everlasting life. I hope he marries a good woman who can earn a living. Just like Maxima, eh, promoting microcredit for women. An extra income would be great, because my son gets by on benefits. I can tell her, tell our own Max, come here with the kid. Don't worry, Grandma will spoil him. And then we go to the zoo every week. I think tomorrow I'll go to the market to get some wool. So I can start knitting some baby clothes.'

Max: 'So this Boaz became a father again. I wouldn't have thought. Or do you think Ruth became pregnant by God, just like Mary?

After all, she is one of the ancestresses of Jesus? I wouldn't mind either; a young girlfriend with whom to start a new family. But without such a domineering mother-in-law, thank you very much. I think the piece is a bit moralistic. Is the rest of the Bible like this as well? Reminds me of a colleague of mine, a Moroccan. I have nothing against Moroccans, don't get me wrong, but you know what this colleague said? You must gain experience with British women, and then you marry a virgin in Morocco. When I said I considered that double standards, he said: but British women don't want to marry at all. They don't care, they have sex just for fun. And they provoke it themselves, just look at how they dress. But for six months he has had a British girlfriend. And now he's singing a different tune. His family kicked him out. They are living with her parents. Poor guy.'

## Ruth – after the performance

After the applause, everyone sits down again. Before the performance started, they had announced that there would be a discussion with the director. As the director comes on stage and speaks to the audience, the first questions are about the ending. What kind of play is this? Did we end up in a fairy tale? The director tells the audience what hit him in the story.

Yes, it does seem a kind of fairy tale. But at the same time this story throws you right in the middle of the harsh reality of extreme poverty, where women become victims even more than men, and of the role of prejudice and group hate. I imagine that at the time the Israelite women came out with this book, not everyone responded enthusiastically. That there were probably many people who would have rather heard a different story about their legendary King David, first monarch of his famous dynasty and ancestor of the Messiah; a version without the Moabite woman. The hard struggle for survival, poverty, forced migration, well, that's part of the story of all the people, they could appreciate that. But a woman from that despicable neighbouring nation who gets such an important place, the great-grandmother of David, and without whom there wouldn't even have been a David? Without her, the family of Naomi and Elimelech ('my God is king!' – an explicit reference to the monarchy) would have gone extinct in this generation. That is also the essence of that last scene, which is shown with so much emphasis that *Naomi* had a son (again).

After some additional questions, the meeting seems to come to an end. But the director has another surprise in store.

We had announced this show would be an interactive play. There is still a final part. A short session, something like 20 minutes. You have already voiced comments during the show. But at that time, you had to leave the last word to the actors. Now the actors will sit in the audience and you may play. And to make it easier for you, we fast forward the time to 2017. Think about how a scene has touched you in twenty-first century conditions. You may think of anything. Economic refugees, drought and famine, nations that hate each other, poverty and dependency, man–woman relationships, love and loyalty, something from your own life ... I will give you five minutes to think about it and then we improvise a contemporary Ruth.

After five minutes, the director says: 'Okay, let's begin. We start in the first part. Ruth and Orpah have to decide whether to remain in Moab, in their own country, with their families, with their own culture, or whether they will plunge into an uncertain future in the country of their mother-in-law. She has already told them they should not go with her. Let her go. For them it is much better if they go their separate ways at this point.'

A man walks up. He introduces himself as Stef.[5] 'I'm afraid I missed the rest of the show, because I was just stuck thinking about this part the whole time. It hits close to my own life story. Because I was born in the Netherlands and I regularly visit Europe, but I live in South Africa. I fell in love and followed the woman of my life. Our children are growing up there now. But it does something to you when you leave your home country. My wife even explicitly warned me, saying, "it will not be easy for you. Are you sure this is what you want?" I knew for sure, but I have to admit that in the beginning I missed my homeland very much. The weather, the cold wind in your ears. Ordinary things, how people interact. Not hearing or speaking your own language. And that there are some things in my new country that I will never get used to. While on the other hand, I will always be the odd one out, even for the family there. I have to admit, I'm still *so very* Dutch, in thought and action. I'm a singer, I write my own songs and I just wrote a few lines that could very well turn into a song'.[6]

I am a stranger here
I left my land
I crossed your path
I followed your footsteps

You said go back
Don't put all your trust in me
But you are a part of me
What would I do without you

And I know the future is uncertain ...

But your land is my land
Your people are my people
Your language is my language
Your God is my God

The audience applauds. 'Who's next?', the director asks.

Sylvie: 'Well, my girlfriend Els here says: you've been giving commentary throughout the show, and now you can say something and then you shut up. I'm not afraid. Because I wanted to actually warn Naomi the whole time: Naomi, you can go back to your own country, but it will not be like before. Look, for more than 30 years I was together with the father of my son, he came from Suriname, he was the love of my life. But when he became ill and unable to work, he wanted nothing more than to return to Suriname, to his family and the warm climate. Are you coming, he says. No thanks, I say, I cannot stand the heat, you know, and

I like to be around when my son starts a family. I still hope my son will soon find our Maxima. But yes, there's my ex, without a penny to his name. The house he had built there was taken over by his family, who had said they'd keep an eye on it, and while he was gone, everything changed, you know. His friends went to live somewhere else; he doesn't recognize what he had left behind 30 years prior. Isn't that how it is, Mr Stef? Is that not what you encountered in South Africa too?'

Els: 'I would like to add something to that. Naomi naturally also went back to what she knew. That's what you do in times of adversity: you go back to the familiar, even though it wasn't all that wonderful either. But you know what you had back then. Even though in the meantime you may have lost your land or your home or your friends. And besides, nostalgia for the past is also often the desire for something that was never there. It was all nicer in your mind, back then. Marsman wrote: 'Never return to the place you were born, / Do not look back at your youth: / Nothing holds steady except for in your memories.'[7]

Kim: 'But the book is called "Ruth", not "Naomi"? And for Ruth it is totally different. Unlike Orpah she does not return, instead she goes on. She is the main character, but because the story is always about a child, Ruth does not clearly come into play. Therefore, I would like to redo that scene between Ruth and Naomi. Then I would have Ruth say to Naomi: "Listen, I do understand that you are obsessed with the idea of a grandchild, but I'm still here too. I can raise above the shouting matches and harassment because I'm from Moab. But there are limits. I did not come all the way from Moab with you to offer myself as a whore to a drunken farmer. What must Boaz think of me? Coincidentally I really like him. No, we are going to tackle this very differently. This is my plan. You go to the field to put in a good word for me. Tell Boaz how the inheritance of land works. And that we are very grateful to be part of it. And then you tell him that the women of Moab are beautiful and strong, and moreover 'hard to get'. If he wants me, he will have to give you enough barley for us to make it through winter so that for the time being I no longer have to perform backbreaking work in the scorching sun." There, that feels a lot better.'

God: 'Can I say something too? I am quoted in most biblical books.'

Kim: 'But not in Ruth. We are sorry.'

Then Anna-Claar Thomasson-Rosingh, one of the authors of this book, steps forward. She tells the audience about her life, which is not unlike that of Ruth at some points.

## I, like Ruth …

I, like Ruth, married someone from a different culture. I, like Ruth, moved there and had children there. I, like Ruth, am a working woman. I, like Ruth, am a foreigner even in my own country. I was born in the north of Ghana (West Africa) the very first white baby to be born in the village of Nalerigu. When I was three my parents brought me back to our (or their?) native country, the Netherlands. But my parents craved the warmth of Ghana over the cold. I went to Dutch schools but never felt quite at home. During my studies in Geneva I met the man I love. He was English. When I found a job near where he lived in the north-west I decided to emigrate. I probably thought I might go back at some point, but that has never happened. So here I am, with Ghana, the Netherlands and England all locked in my soul. With my emigrations, religious identity also changes. In the Netherlands I grew up as the daughter of the chaplain for international students. Services were multidenominational, multicultural, sometimes even multilingual. As I grew older I chose first the Dutch-Reformed and later the Remonstrant Church, as I too trained as a minister. Now I am a priest in the Church of England. The change in culture and the change in religion are bound up together, 'your people shall be my people, and your God my God' (Ruth 1.16b). It is all so recognizable. Still, reading the story, I do not want to be like Ruth. I am left with the feeling that her loyalty and friendship were misused.

I am left with a bitter taste in my mouth. A woman of such initiative and courage is left without a single line in the last chapter. It is as if she is written out of history. I am left with the question whether that is what happens with women like Ruth and like me: ultimately marginalized. But that is not the whole story. From the margins Matthew writes her back into the story. Ruth becomes one of the great-grandmothers of Jesus. Her kindness and courage validated.

I love the story of Ruth, it is so ambiguous. There are so many gaps to fill and you can fill them in very different ways. There are so many questions to ask. It could be a romantic love story. It could be a story of sexual exploitation. It could be a story about rich and poor and the market value of migration. It could be a story of cross-cultural relationships. It could be a story of interfaith dialogue. It is part of the discussion about the purity of the heritage of David and therefore of Jesus. This heritage is not pure at all from an ethnic perspective. Just like our own monarchies. The question of purity is also ambiguous because Ruth seems pure in her values and convictions. 'Who do you think you are?' Is your identity dependent on your heritage or on your choices? Maybe Ruth is a story about the boundaries of community: who belongs and who does not belong? Who is a real Israelite and who is not? Who is really British and who is not? Who is really European and who is not? A story without binding answers to the questions it raises. This ambiguity speaks to me. My life is also ambiguous.

My decisions are ambivalent and sometimes I wonder about motivation. This story is full of mixed motivations. Why did Ruth want to go with Naomi – because she loved her or because she wanted a better life? Why did Naomi want Ruth to go in the night to the threshing floor – to make sure Ruth had financial stability or because she needed that stability? Why did Boaz help – to be good to the widow and stranger or because he fell in love with Ruth? Ruth seems a story of redeemed self-interest.

Even the overarching meaning of the story is ambiguous. What does this story do in the Bible? What does it tell us about God? What does it tell us about how to live our lives? It almost feels like those real life stories that are stranger than fairy tales, and more random. There is no moralizing in this tale. That is a relief. There is no advice for us working with multicultural families. There is no advocacy for gay relationships. There is no guidance for how to deal with migration. There is no view on how to deal with grief. Within that ambiguity there are some unambiguous messages. There *is* a sense that whatever happens, there might be a possible future. There is a sense of hope and it is real. In the story the solution (the happy end – if that is what it is) is hidden within and comes out of the presenting problem. Of course Elimelech should never have gone to Moab, but out of Moab comes good. This idea reminds me of a traditional Dutch Christmas carol: 'Komt, verwondert u hier, mensen' (Come in wonder, all ye people):

> See, who is the word without speaking;
> see who is ruler without splendour;
> see who is light within the night.

In another verse:

> Give me guidance through your infancy;
> make me strong through your fragile hands;
> make me great through your smallness;
> make me free through your ties;
> make me rich through your need;
> make me happy through your suffering;
> make me alive through your death.[8]

What seems wrong, bad, dark, and even evil might still hold within itself the promise and the possibility of goodness, worth, nobility and light.

Even if life in a foreign culture seems to be difficult, even if you wish you could go home, even if the loves of the past seem more real than the loves of today, even if you long for people just like you, there is hope. Even if you think it is impossible to take in any more refugees, even if the only solution to immigration seems to be to close the borders, there is a different way to look at it. Ruth explains more strongly than any other story both how difficult and how hopeful the relationship with foreigners is. The stranger and strangeness give new opportunity and creativity. It works two ways. The foreigner enhances the host culture and the migrants lives are improved by contact with the different cultures they travel through or to. The solution both to my own homesickness and feeling of homelessness and to wider migration issues might still grow out of the difficult situation itself. A future is possible. There is a promise of flourishing for the person and the community that dares to be open.

## After we have left the theatre …

… and visit the three authors of the book *Re-imagining the Bible*, they explain that the experiment with the change of perspective, where the people in the audience become the actors, and vice versa, was not entirely a self-conceived idea of this inventive director. They brought the director to this idea in the wake of a famous metaphor from the work of Danish philosopher and theologian Søren Kierkegaard. 'The address is not given for the speaker's sake, in order that men may praise or blame him. The listener's repetition of it is what is aimed at'.[9]

It is a quote that is cited quite often, usually in reflections on church life. It is then interpreted as: it is not meant for all focus to go to the minister who is or isn't doing a good job in the pulpit. That is not the purpose of a church service. A church service should aim to ensure that the *audience*, the churchgoers, get involved in what is being said. And not to repeat, but – as the voices in our own Ruth audience showed – to give their interpretation from the connection with their own lives.

Kierkegaard writes these phrases in a discussion in which he plays with the image of theatre. A play has a prompter, actors and an audience. The prompter, the one out of the picture, guarantees the text. Right up front is the actor, who did not come up with the text, but who is handed it (as previously handed to him by the director). All the audience sees is the actor, and he seems the most important. But this is only partially true.

It works differently when repositioned to the spiritual theatre of the church. There, the speaker is not comparable with the actor, he is not an artist that needs admiration – but rather he can be compared to the prompter. And actual actors are the churchgoers. That's where it happens. They are not spectators at a show, no, they are right in the middle of that show. As Kierkegaard puts it:

> The stage is eternity, and the listener, if he is the true listener (and if he is not, he is at fault) stands before God during the talk. The prompter whispers to the actor what he is to say, but the actor's repetition of it is the main concern – is the solemn charm of the art. The speaker whispers the word to the listeners. But the main concern is earnestness: that the listeners by themselves, with themselves, and to themselves, in the silence before God, may speak with the help of this address.

If this play talks about an audience, then that audience is God. 'In the most earnest sense, God is the critical theatregoer, who looks on to see how the lines are spoken and how they are listened to'.

Now you understand how the director came up with his idea for the change in perspective! In more contemporary words: how would theatregoers, or readers of Bible stories, contextualize what they see and read? That is what it's all about.[10]

---

### Questions for Reflection

Where are you in the story of Ruth?

What would you say after the play?

How do you associate themes in Ruth with themes in your context?

---

## Notes

1 From Celena M. Duncan (2000), p. 94: 'Thousands of lesbians have repeated these words in rituals blessing their unions.'

2 Wil Gafney (2009), 'Mother Knows Best. Messianic Surrogacy and Sexploitation in Ruth', in C. A. Kirk-Duggan and T. Pippin (eds), *Mother Goose, Mother Jones, Mommie Dearest. Biblical Mothers and Their Children*, Atlanta: Society of Biblical Literature, pp. 23–36, p. 26.

3 Targum Ruth on Ruth 1.3–4, http://targuman.org/targum-ruth/targum-ruth-in-english/, accessed 8 December 2016.

4 Targum Ruth on Ruth 2.11, http://targuman.org/targum-ruth/targum-ruth-in-english/, accessed 8 December 2016.

5 Based on the Dutch singer Stef Bos. The following monologue is loosely based on what he said in a recent interview. The interview can be found at, http://zinweb. nl/nvo-video-stef-bos-lied-ruth/, also published on YouTube, www.youtube.com/ watch?v=wOd6S7v6maE, both accessed 6 December 2016.

6 English translation of the original in Afrikaans, which can be found on Stef Bos's website, www.stefbos.nl/page/Liedteksten/detail/1827/Lied_van_Ruth. There are several versions of this song available on YouTube ('Lied van Ruth'), including these: www.youtube.com/watch?v=gSpIk3cmdNA, accessed 6 December 2016.

7 H. Marsman (1940), *Tempel en Kruis*, Amsterdam: Em. Querido, p. 20.

8 The Dutch text of this hymn can be found in Liedboek (2013), no. 478.

9 From his work *Purity of Heart Is To Will One Thing*, chapter 12. The following quotes in this chapter are taken from its online version: www.religion-online. org/showchapter.asp?title = & 2523 C = 2398, accessed 15 December 2016.

10 Compare S. Wells (2004), *Improvisation: The Drama of Christian Ethics*, Grand Rapids, Michigan: Brazos Press. Samuel Wells approaches Christian ethics in his book from the model of improvisation in theatre. 'When Christians ... gather together and try to discern God's hand in events and his will for their future practice, they are improvising, whether they are aware of it or not. They – almost invariably – accord authority to Scripture, and generally to some other forms of discernment, perhaps tradition, or reason, or experience, or something similar. These provide the boundaries of their performance their stage, as it were. And on this stage they strive to enact a faithful drama ... improvisation is the only term that adequately describes the desire to cherish a tradition without being locked in the past' (2004, pp. 65–6).

# 7

# Re-imagining the Bible: Reading the Bible in the Context of Present-Day Life

## BERT DICOU

## Introduction

In the previous chapter we showed how a story from a totally different culture and from a bygone era becomes significant if we allow the story to speak to us in our own context. That context follows automatically. We can do our best to understand the original setting and to determine some of the historical background, social customs, laws and religion of that time. But we will always be reading from a certain context. We are male or female, rich or poor, native or immigrant, instinctively associated with those who are 'in' or those who are 'out'. Our appreciation of the play, the way we read and perceive it, what meaning we give to it, is undoubtedly closely related to the situation in which we find ourselves.

In the past (the nineteenth and most of the twentieth century) Bible science often sought the objective truth about the Bible. From a historical perspective: what do we know about history described in the Bible, what is there to say about the way history ended up in the Bible, and what is the literary history of the Bible books themselves? Did they originate as the books we now know, or is there evidence of gradual growth and several editions? What is there to say about the creation date and circumstances of the various Bible books? What were the author's intentions with them?[1]

Bible science also searched for an objectively ascertainable biblical message. What fundamental concept determines biblical thinking, and what does the Bible want to transfer about this theological concept?

The rise of postmodernism, however, has severely undermined the confidence in the existence of objective truths in any field. There was, and is, much focus on the subjective element. There is suspicion towards the person who claims a certain truth – do they profit from it? Do they defend certain interests?[2]

In this mindset, persons who deal with the interpretation of texts, including biblical texts, are challenged to be aware of their own prejudices and their own place in society. Conversely, readers who question their own context when reading the Bible and approach the Bible with their own, often critical questions, are defended.[3] For example, we saw this with those who warily asked questions from a 'green' point of view whether certain biblical texts about nature were actually in the interests of nature.

The theme and details regarding loss and recovery of land in Ruth, as discussed in the previous chapter, suddenly bring into view the problems of women in today's South Africa who are not allowed to own land – Mtshiselwa (2016). As a result there is relatively greater poverty among women than among men. Apparently Naomi cannot use the land that once belonged to her husband, and a male family member is needed in order to do so. Mtshiselwa argues that this patriarchal, oppressive way of doing things is not questioned in Ruth. He also finds it quite disturbing that in Ruth 4.9 and 10, Boaz 'acquires' the fertile land and Ruth (using the same verb for both), which in his opinion might as well have been translated with 'bought' or 'purchased'. Nevertheless, it is exactly this type of critical approach towards these abuses that provides an impetus for a liberative reading of Ruth.

However, a form of 'autobiographical reading of the Bible' should be part of this as well, where a scientific–analytical way of reading can be effortlessly combined with a reflection on one's own life experiences mirrored in the Bible text that is being studied.

That is how Celena M. Duncan tackles it in her contribution to the bundle *Take Back the Word*, a collection of articles with examples of 'a queer reading of the Bible'. Duncan (2000) reads Ruth as 'a bisexual midrash'. She explains that she does not interpret the concept of bisexuality relating purely to sexual attraction. For her, this also includes the intense relationship between Ruth and Naomi. Ruth's words of faith (when she insists on following Naomi to the land she originally came from) go far beyond the ordinary and are a witness of deep love. It becomes more complicated when the relationship between Ruth and Boaz is added to the picture. In between analysing the biblical story from that perspective, Duncan talks about her own long-term relationships with, first a woman and then a man, and the often unclear and ambivalent position of someone who is bisexual.

Louise J. Lawrence's *The Word in Place: Reading the New Testament in Contemporary Contexts* (2009) is a remarkable book that methodically brings together social context and Bible interpretation in an original way. For her reading projects, she uses the method of 'contextual reading of the Bible', originally developed in South America and South Africa, which we discussed briefly in the section entitled 'Ways of reading' at the beginning of this book (p. 15). The Scottish Bible Society developed a version tailored more to the situation in Europe. In 2010, they published their own methodical book: *What is Contextual Bible Study?* – Riches (2010).

Lawrence speaks of 'the folk arts of biblical interpretation'. In this method of reading and interpreting it is not the professional biblical scholar who is the main interpreter. Interpretations from groups of ordinary readers count in full, or better, this is what this method starts with. It could even lead to biblical scholars nuancing the importance of their academic insights.

> These types or contexts serve to make real and alive the links between the Bible and the world, and give the professional guild a sense of perspective on their own readings, and the modesty to acknowledge the profound insights that can come from folk voices. (2009, p. 40)

Lawrence starts with the concept of 'place'. The physical environment matters. In her fieldwork she discusses reading the Bible in a city, in a rural village and in a fishing village. Subsequently she reads the Bible with two specific groups: first with the deaf, and then with the clergy.

Co-author Sigrid Coenradie, who wrote about substitution – 'taking someone else's place' – in the chapter on Sacrifice ('He died for our sins' p. 50), adds:

> The 'place' is at the core of Western Christian theology in the sense that God's active *Stellvertreten* (vicarious substitution) in Christ was automatically understood in terms of God's stepping into my 'place' so as to save my personal place or to preserve or newly create a space where I can be. Following the example of Jesus, we can then step into someone else's place, meaning to be there for the other in a specific place and situation.[4] Reflecting together on a biblical text which is meaningful for that 'place' can be helpful in the process.

A thoroughly revised edition of the book *Let's do theology* (2009) by Laurie Green appeared in the same year as Lawrence's study. The book was originally published in 1989. Already in 1989, he advocated a context-oriented way of doing theology, even though it was quite against the academic stream, as described in his preface (2009, pp. vii–viii). Like Lawrence, he advocates theology based on reflecting on concrete experiences in specific circumstances. As he puts it, he was keen on developing a method that

> allows for the careful critical reading of each context so that our theology can derive not from abstract assumptions, but is instead substantial, pertinent theology that speaks from, and relevant to, real people in their specific culture, place and time. (2009, p. 13)

We already encountered Laurie Green in the section entitled 'Blessed are the poor' (in Chapter 5, p. 147). Green (2015) explores and describes the experiences of contemporary urban poverty in the UK and as he reflects on this he brings in the Bible texts on poverty ('blessed are the poor').[5]

His method, based on Daniel Kolb's model for 'experiential

learning', is a spiral taking in the different steps of 'experience', 'explore', 'reflecting', 'respond' and 'new situation'. The factual context comes into the picture in the 'explore' stage, the exchange with stories from the Bible and insights from Christian tradition at the 'reflect' stage. He deals with that phase of exchange in his pointedly titled chapter 'The liberation of the imagination' (2009, pp. 82–95).

I borrow a good example of how this can work from a recent 'exchange' with the story of Ruth in a Dutch context. There, the imagination is put to work in various ways.

## Example of imagination: Ruth and contemporary immigration issues

### Immigration: your land is my land?

In the autumn of 2016 the Dutch city of Amersfoort hosted a small exhibition entitled 'Ruth in een ander licht' (Ruth in a different light).[6] The exhibition showed six portraits of refugee women in the Netherlands. The portraits were made by two young photographers, the Dutchman Sander Troelstra, and the Iranian Mujtaba Jalali. The latter is a refugee himself. He lives in a refugee centre in the Netherlands. In Iran, he photographed Afghan refugees, which was not appreciated by the authorities.

At the same time and at a different location in Amersfoort, the refugee issue was approached from a different angle. A double exhibition called 'Op de vlucht' (On the run) was being held in a church on the other side of town. On the one hand, there were pictures of the 19,000 Belgian refugees who had found refuge in Amersfoort in 1916 (World War I), then a small town of 25,000 inhabitants. (This was commemorated exactly 100 years later.) Then on the other, famous and less famous recent journalistic photographs of the current refugee crisis.[7]

The site of the first of these was the connecting element between the two exhibitions: it was being held in the Tower of Our Lady.[8] The tower's bronze door, the Pilgrims' Door, shows a Madonna by Eric Claus, made in 2014. The exhibition plays with the familiar image of Mary's protective cloak, under which anyone can take shelter. At the bottom of the cloak, Eric Claus depicts the twentieth century 'pilgrims' the city of Amersfoort had to deal with, namely the large groups of refugees from Belgium.

The photo exhibition in the tower, 'Ruth in a different light', was based on a song about Ruth by Dutch singer Stef Bos (who briefly participated in the play). He recognized himself in Ruth – like him, she had exchanged her homeland for a different country to follow someone, and it must not have been an easy thing to do for her either.

The words from the story in Ruth 1 are words of devotion and loyalty, and also words that indicate quite accurately how much you leave behind: your country, your people and your familiar way of life.

'Where you go, I will go;
where you lodge, I will lodge;
your people shall be my people,
and your God my God.'
(Ruth 1.16)

Stef Bos wrote the song, which circles around his version of these words, for his South African loved one; he wrote it in Afrikaans.[9] Interestingly, he points out in this song that he takes into account that her compatriots will have trouble with him being a foreigner.

I know your people are scared
Because we are different
But I'll build bridges
Over the gap
...

And when darkness falls
And your people avoid me
I will give you love
Until the hate is gone
Because your house is my house
Your fear is my fear
You silence my silence
Your land is my land

The refugees portrayed in the Tower of Our Lady in Amersfoort, and all the others who have come to seek refuge in our part of the world, have a good chance of experiencing the 'fear of what is different' from the indigenous population and perhaps even hatred during their stay. Though they will certainly experience that others do welcome the newcomers with a high degree of openness, and look for the contact rather than the 'evasive behaviour' which Stef Bos sings about. Will bridges be built? And how does the attitude of modern immigrants contribute to it or not?

The exhibition included a subproject, set up by the organization La Scuola ('the school'), Academy of Living. They called it 'De Verplaatsing' (The Move). It consisted of a writing exercise. Participants were invited to be moved by people who had physically moved, who may or may not have been forced to leave their homeland.

Empathizing with another person is an art. Empathizing with a refugee, a Syrian man or woman, is not an easy task. And yet we challenge you to do just that. It lets you see things differently … Also empathize with Ruth, with what she experienced when she went with her mother-in-law. Experience what it's like to leave your country. Write a very short story (max. 350 words), a poem, a song about it. Or compose a piece of music or paint a picture, draw an illustration. And who knows, maybe there are other ways of expressing what moved you in this empathy. You can be inspired by Stef Bos' song 'Song of Ruth' and/or by the story in the Bible.[10]

In any case, what this project shows is that a biblical text can easily come back to life when you start asking your own questions, contextualize for yourself, and look for connections in your own environment.

Empathizing with today's immigrants is a useful undertaking in any way, and making use of the thoughts and ideas channelled through Ruth can enrich that reflection. Whether you are forced (Naomi) or you choose (Ruth) to leave for another country, where do you end up? How do you relate your culture, your faith and your values to the culture, beliefs and values of the country where you end up? How do you deal with the fact that maybe you are met with hospitality, or that you experience that not everyone is happy about your arrival? Also that people really have trouble with your 'being different'? Do you stay within your own group, or do you adapt? How important is it for you that you have your roots in another country?

To Naomi it is clear, she wants to go back to where her roots are. For the two daughters-in-law there are other considerations whether or not to migrate. What does Ruth's statement mean: 'Your land is my land, your God is my God'? Does it mean severing your own roots and completely adapt?

## Contextual Bible reading and films

As Louise J. Lawrence argues in her book *Word in Place*, 'place' should be an important factor for any form of theologizing. Any form of contextual Bible reading starts with seeing what is happening in your town, city, country, part of the world and reflecting on it.[11] In an open investigation you then look at what touches on the theme of a Bible passage that has been read in that context. Establish connections for yourself. The cultural expressions of our own era are an excellent tool for this. Not least, films, the medium par excellence are used to tell stories to a wider audience.[12] Hence, within this book you often find a short film description.

In the story of Naomi and Ruth it is not difficult to find parallels with what is happening in the world today, as can be seen from the above. This can involve a variety of ways of immigration, remaining connected to the homeland, whether to adjust to the new culture; the question whether a balance in this should or should not occur. There is a multitude of books and films dealing with this subject. Below is one example: *La petite Jérusalem* (*Little Jerusalem*).

### *La petite Jérusalem* (Karin Albou, 2005)

French director Karin Albou takes us to a neighbourhood with high-rise flats in a Parisian suburb.[13] It is a typical metropolitan suburban area of the seventies. These areas are well-known in our country too: communities on the outskirts of the city, consisting of row after row of parallel gallery-access flats. Enormous bee-hive-like complexes, large blocks often twenty or more storeys high, a rectangular 'centre' consisting of low-rise buildings of no more than five storeys, and here and there a few really high residential towers. These blocks were well suited to solve the housing shortage. The flats are relatively large, there is a lot of greenery between the buildings, and yet such neighbourhoods do not seem to make the people who live there truly happy. There is a short dialogue between the two main characters from the film, the sisters Laura (Fanny Valette) and Mathilde (Elsa Zylberstein) during a walk through the neighbourhood: 'This neighbourhood is depressing.' 'Yes ...' 'That's why I would really like to go and live somewhere else.' 'If you read the Torah, you will not see the ugliness of the city.' The two sisters are the children of a Jewish immigrant couple from Tunisia. Their father passed away. They live in a flat with their mother and Mathilde's family. Mathilde, a very pious woman, is married to Ariel and together they have four children. Laura is the sister who wants to leave. She does no longer feel comfortable in Orthodox life either. Her sister lives completely for God. Laura is a philosophy student and feels that the Torah is not the only place to find truth; her hero is Immanuel Kant. She is not so keen on the family traditions either. Much to the concern of her mother, she shows no interest in the men her mother introduces to her. Unfortunately, even the magic methods her mother brought with her from her Tunisian village, such as incensing the phone when the man in question calls, have no effect. So Laura would like to live somewhere else, but the rules of their culture are merciless: a woman only leaves home when she marries. Moreover, there is no money for her to rent her own flat.

In recent years, we mainly know the world of the French suburbs from disturbing news reports. Dissatisfaction in these neighbourhoods is high, and from time to time, things get heated and people engage in arson and clash with authority. In Laura and Mathilde's town things get rough sometimes too. There are a lot of Jews, so many that you could call it 'La petite Jérusalem' (Little Jerusalem). However, it is a 'Jerusalem' of graffiti-smeared concrete, low-flying aircraft and crammed undergrounds. But there are also many Arab immigrants, mostly from North Africa, just like Laura's family. Tensions sometimes run high. One day, Ariel gets beaten up for no reason. Later the synagogue is set on fire, after which the services are held in some type of party tent. Ariel, the man and therefore the head of the household, forbids Laura to go out on the street on her own any more. Following the example of her idol, Laura would go for a daily walk – at exactly the same time and along the same route. The regularity of the 'Kantian walk' is good for the spirit. But, not much later, her philosophical passion is all gone. She has a small job as a cleaner at a school. Every working day begins and ends with changing clothes in the locker room. There's a young Algerian boy who works there too. His locker is opposite hers. Back to back they put on and take off their daily work clothes. One day there is a spark. Then comes one of the many peculiar but beautiful dialogues of the film: 'In Algeria, a man is not allowed to get so close to a woman he doesn't know,' says Djamel and proceeds to tell something about himself. He was a journalist, he was working on a book about the first Arab woman who wrote poetry. 'Are you a mystic?' Laura asks. 'Yes. Aren't you?' 'Yes.' 'See you tomorrow.' 'See you tomorrow.'

Just like Laura, Djamel lives with his family, except in his case they are traditional Muslims. It does not take long for the two families to get wind of it. Ariel finds a note on the doormat that says 'I am your slave. Will I ever be able to taste your beauty?' The reaction on both sides is as can be predicted: this must stop immediately. Meanwhile, sister Mathilde has her own problems, despite her commitment to the world of Jewish tradition. Married (too) young, timid in front of her husband, and moreover convinced that it is not pious to enjoy sex, she does her marital duty purely as a duty and in doing so drives Ariel to despair. In a kind of belated sexual education, the woman at the bathhouse patiently explains that the Torah allows a lot more freedoms than Mathilde thinks and that it certainly does not exclude the pleasures of love.

While Mathilde finds her own way with some difficulty, Laura gets stuck. The introduction to Djamel's family ends in tragedy: they do not care for a Jewish girl. And to his own enormous frustration, Djamel is not able to break with his family, that is a too great a sacrifice.

Not long after, the family falls apart. Ariel has had it with the anti-Semitic feelings in 'little Jerusalem' and decides that he and his family should move to Israel. Their old mother goes with them. In a Ruth-like scenario, the two sisters do not opt for the same choice: despite her misfortune so far and the fact that her efforts to have her own place at the heart of this culture also failed, Laura decides to stay.

Karin Albou knows the world she depicts from personal experience. She is also Jewish–French with North African roots. *La petite Jérusalem* makes us well aware how unbridgeable the gap between different cultures can be. A protagonist who nevertheless tries to build bridges in such a situation and the difficulties experienced while doing so, reflects the story of Ruth in a context we can relate to. The rest of the family, which makes the equally understandable choice not to stay in 'foreign' France but to move to 'familiar' Israel (even though they have never lived there before!), makes it even more clear how exceptional Ruth's decision was, compared with Orpah's.

Integration of immigrants in Western Europe does not always run smoothly. Lagging employment opportunities and a sense of being discriminated against results in people feeling less at home in their new country over time. For the Netherlands this was charted by the SCP (Social and Cultural Planning Office) last year. For the population of Turkish origin we read:

43% of Turkish Dutch would want to permanently live in their country of origin ... In the past decade, in particular the number of second generation Turkish Dutch who want to permanently live in the country of origin has increased. This may have to do with the increased unease about life in the Netherlands and with the image of this group, but also the increased attractiveness of Turkey. Turkey plays an increasingly prominent role on the world stage, both politically and economically. Unlike immigrants, native Dutch believe more so now than in 2006, that the Netherlands is an open and equal country. Immigrants on the other hand, have become gloomier about it.[14]

An interesting parallel between Albou's film and the story of Ruth is how women in a culture dominated by men search for and find their own way. Despite the fact that the man in Laura and Mathilde's family is the one who determines what is and is not allowed and who decides to leave for Israel at a crucial moment, the women actually play the leading role. This is exactly how it is in Ruth. Despite the decisive role of Boaz, it is a typical woman story. There are more of those in the Bible, but the Bible is still predominantly a book focusing on the histories of men. The lineage goes from father to son. As it appears from Ruth, there is quite a difference in terms of rights and opportunities between men and women. All the more remarkable, then, that Naomi and Ruth are the actual main characters in this story. It is not surprising that in the celebration of the 100th anniversary of a North Holland Mennonite Sister Circle, the members of the circle suggested covering the book of Ruth in their festive church service. In the preliminary discussion some members indicated they were sympathizing with Naomi in particular while others identified with Ruth.

## Reversals

There are all sorts of reversals in the book of Ruth.[15] We have already mentioned the foreign woman of the despised nation, who will become the ancestress of the royal house of Israel. Then there is the reversal that is often spoken of in the Bible about the poor, the widow and the foreigner who must be taken care of – while here the poor, the widow and the foreigner are the *subject* of the story, where the woman from Israel herself becomes an immigrant. Then there is the reversal that in a history of men, women suddenly play the leading role. It is thanks to Naomi and Ruth that the royal family of Israel could come about. How Ruth decided to stay with Naomi and go with her, how Naomi put her on the trail of Boaz, and how Ruth had prepared to go along with this plan and tried her best to follow it ... these are all essential elements in achieving this result.

Gillian Feeley-Harnik (1990) highlights a number of interesting parallels with another defining moment in the history of Israel.

Just as in Ruth the birth of the monarchy is presented as a woman story, so do the stories of the liberation of Israel from slavery at the beginning of Exodus and the journey to the promised land begin with an outspoken woman story. Where the book of Ruth introduces David, the beginning of Exodus focuses on the birth of the central character in that phase of history, namely Moses. The stubborn midwives Shiphrah and Puah refused to obey the command of the Pharaoh to kill newborn Israelite boys. The mother of the newborn Moses hid him in a rush basket on the edge of the Nile, where he was found by the daughter of the Pharaoh, who took care of him. Moses' sister, who had remained in the area, successfully advised the princess to leave the small child with a 'carer' – obviously her mother (Ex. 1—2). Furthermore Feeley-Harnik (pp. 166–7) notes the role of Moab in the story of the journey to the promised land; Moab is actually the land where Moses died. She confirms her view of Ruth as an eminent women's story by pointing to the fact that in the book another heroic woman from the ancestry of David and the Messiah is mentioned by name, namely Tamar (pp. 170–1). Tamar was a widow and it looked like she would remain childless. Her in-law family ignored all the rules set in place for women in her situation. At a crucial moment, she disguised herself and seduced Judah, her father-in-law, and became pregnant (Gen. 38).[16] After he 'acquires' Ruth, the women of Bethlehem give Boaz, a descendant of the same Tamar and Judah (as evidenced by the last verses of the book) the following blessing:

> 'May you produce children in Ephrathah and bestow a name in Bethlehem; and, through the children that the Lord will give you by this young woman, may your house be like the house of Perez, whom Tamar bore to Judah.' (Ruth 4.12)

## Poland = Moab

It is not stated that the link between Karin Albou's film and the elements described in Ruth is intentional. There are interesting connections to be made between the story of the Parisian family and that of Naomi and her daughters-in-law, but the director does not necessarily need to have made that connection herself, and there are no other indications that she played with this thought. Probably this link, or rather this association, only exists in the mind of the author of this chapter.

If this were the case, then surely it would not just be a wild association that makes no further sense. After all, it is not the first time that the book of Ruth is used – reread and recontextualized – to shed light on the situation of Jews in their own, not necessarily favourable, non-Jewish environment.

In her article 'Ruth speaks in Yiddish', Kathryn Hellerstein (2006) translates and discusses two Polish Jewish poets, Rosa Yakubovitsh (1889–1944) and Itsik Manger (1901–69), who published Yiddish poems about Ruth in the period before World War II. In her poem about Ruth meeting Boaz, Yakubovitsh empathized with Ruth in particular and describes her, unlike many of her predecessors, as a confident heroine who deliberately takes the initiative. The scene is situated 'on the threshing floor of a barn that could as stand on the Polish countryside as on the outskirts of ancient Bethlehem' (p. 90).

Unlike Yakubovitsh, who was killed in Auschwitz,[17] Manger managed to escape the Nazis. He fled in 1938 from Warsaw to Paris, later to Marseilles and then to North Africa, where he wrote his poetry cycle about Ruth in 1940. Later he lived in London, and in 1958 he immigrated to Israel. In his version, the two daughters are 'blondes' and Orpah pours tea from a samovar that is simmering in the room. The Moabite village they leave bears unmistakable Polish traits. Orpah received a letter from her father. He calls her 'Orposya' in Slavic. A good man came calling for her, Antek. 'Although she has lived with a Jew,' he is prepared 'to take her as she is.' Ruth on the other hand, would only return home to find misery. Remarkably, the cycle ends with a monologue by Orpah at the point when the roads separate.

> Beyond the clouds there lies my home,
> And just because it's beautiful,
> And just because it's familiar and mine,
> That's where I want to go.

There Pan Jesus blesses my father's field
And my mother's bowed head.

Then follows a description of how wonderful that country is. It is clear where this Moab is located: in the Polish countryside.

The cycle ends thus with Orpah's parting words. Naomi still has a long way to go. According to Hellerstein (pp. 108–9), these words reflect Manger's own wistful longing for the country he was forced to leave and Naomi's uncertainty at this point is the same as his uncertainty then. In his case, it would take many years before he would find his destiny in Israel.

## Context and transformation

We started out from a book in the Bible, a text from which believers assume that God in some way speaks (even though God does not play an active role in the story!). Automatically all sorts of associations followed – events in our world, all kinds of cultural expressions – which shed more light on the issues discussed in the Bible text. Then we went back to the text and looked more closely at what exactly it wants to convey, to then once again come to another association. This pattern of nourishment is thought-provoking and could even change someone's point of view.

Thus a person who meets a refugee can get a different view on the refugee issue. It is even possible that people who nourish themselves with texts and consequential associations, come to the conclusion that something needs to be 'done' and take steps in that direction.

In this way, reading the Bible can lead to 'transformation', which is a widely used concept in publications that favour context-oriented Bible reading. Reading the Bible changes the reader(s). If reading and reflecting is carried out in a group, there is a chance that this transformation will not only have an individual character, but that joint action will lead to changes on a larger scale. In one of our chapters, Sietske Blok, who worked for a Brazilian organization for contextual Bible reading (CEBI) said: 'CEBI studies the Bible with the purpose of transformation and liberation in mind. The Bible is seen as a "medium" to talk about the important things in life and society.'

Paulo Ueti, authoritative CEBI theologian says:

Popular reading of the Bible is a purposeful reading. The person who claims neutrality stands by default with the dominant power. We read both life and the Bible in order to attain, in Christian terms, transformation and conversion. It is important to realize that even the sacred text has an agenda. The challenge is to get involved in it.[18]

He speaks of 'the loving, transgressive dynamism of the Kingdom of God, the dream of transformation and of happiness'. In Brazil, this way of reading the Bible is strongly associated with a social movement that defends the poor and fights injustice. Here, the intended transformation has a distinct socio-economic character.

Although the Scottish equivalent of this approach, partly inspired by the Brazilian (and South African) experiences, has a different character and its context leans more towards the northwest European secularization rather than social injustice, it also underlines 'the power of the text to transform' (Riches 2010, pp. 23–34). In both parts of the world they are reading from the bottom up, as a joint process where everyone can be involved regardless of prior knowledge and reading experience ('Theology is for everyone', Riches, pp. 32–4).

Interesting here is the bundle *Bible and Transformation. The Promise of Intercultural Bible Reading* (Hans de Wit and Janet Dyk, 2015), with, for example, articles by Fernando F. Segovia on 'Intercultural Bible Reading as Transformation for Liberation', Hans de Wit on 'Bible and Transformation', John Mansford Prior on 'The Ethics of Transformative Reading' and a host of other articles relevant to this subject. In particular the practice of interculturally reading the Bible – groups from different backgrounds reading together – can be enlightening when reflecting on one's own context and may lead to new insights and change.

But transformation is a central concept for the manual on contextual theology, *Let's Do Theology* by Laurie Green (2009), previously discussed. In the end, for Green it is all about the 'respond' phase in the 'Doing Theology Spiral'.

> I do believe that any theology worthy of the name must be transformative theology. Good Christian theology is editable to change us and change situations. The style of theology which this book proposes is designed to integrate action and reflection. (p. ix)

Biblically speaking, change is an obvious category. Think of the patriarchs who are called to go to the promised land, the people of Israel who are freed from slavery and can leave Egypt, the prophets who demand justice and who keep people moving with threatening or hopeful visions, and Jesus who announces the coming of the kingdom of God. This last notion in particular, the image of the kingdom of God, is the driving force for transformation. Indeed, it constitutes a counter-reality, a 'realm' where other, surprisingly unusual and innovative values apply, that make you look at the actual reality differently and critically. While parables, stories and visions provide alternatives to the current practice, there are opportunities to do it very differently.

In this book, we saw that even ancient laws on debt and interest, or difficult to understand stories of sacrifice, may lead us to look differently at our own situation, and to consider alternatives. Furthermore, it is only a small step from reading biblical texts about nature in an engaging way to a change in awareness when dealing with today's ecological problems. Facing future scenarios – taking the threats seriously, and letting yourself be stimulated by visions as is very common in the Bible, can be helpful for this. The recent increased attention in society for anything vulnerable, where various sides advocate for a more positive appreciation of being vulnerable, is deepened by reflecting on central texts on vulnerability from the Bible.

## Conclusion

In this book too, we wanted to 'contextualize' the Bible, to enter into dialogue with the text, by questioning those texts on their potential significance to the issues of our time, in our society.

We did not hesitate to question the text in a critical way. Conversely, we were open to the fact that the text could very well have something to tell us. Even things that we would not appreciate very much.

We broadened the discussion through the sound of other voices, by listening to what novels, philosophy, poetry and art, and even film, could add to the conversation as a parallel flow of imagination.

We were engaged with the Bible – Re-imagining the Bible for Today.

## *Notes*

1 See the overview in Green (2009), pp. 177–80.

2 A (critical) reflection on the meaning of postmodern thinking for biblical studies: Jasper (2004), pp. 111–17.

3 Jasper (2004), pp. 122–5. Compare Lawrence (2009), pp. 13–15.

4 Cf. Gestrich (2001). 'What we call God is also that "virtual doppelganger" of the individual human *Wesen* who holds his place … without taking it over and who at the same time represents in anticipation the true *Wesen* of the human being (the so-called self) for as long as it has "not yet appeared"' (2001, p. 318).

5 *For God and His Glory Alone* (1988), as discussed in the same chapter and in which central gospel texts were reread in the context of the Troubles in Northern Ireland, is a clear example of context-oriented Bible reading.

6 www.ruthineenanderlicht.nl/, accessed 8 December 2016. See www.gofoto.nl/ruth-in-een-ander-licht-bij-033fotostad/.

7 www.033fotostad.com/locaties/#5, accessed 6 December 2016.

8 www.033fotostad.com/locaties/#6 see, www.onzelievevrouwetoren.nl, accessed 6 December 2016.

9 www.stefbos.nl/page/Liedteksten/detail/1827/Lied_van_Ruth, CD In een ander licht (2009), DVD In een ander licht (2010), accessed 8 December 2016. Our translation.

10 http://academievoorlevenskunst.nl/deverplaatsing/, accessed 11 December 2016.

11 Compare for a similar approach with great emphasis on the importance of local, social context: Sedmak (2002). His book is called: *Doing Local Theology. A Guide for Artisans of a New Humanity*. Apart from 'local theologies', he also speaks of 'little theologies'.

12 Compare Jasper (2004), pp. 123–9, on the importance of intertextuality for contemporary biblical hermeneutics, and especially the importance of visual culture, including movies because, after all, our culture shows a strong shift from the verbal to the visual.

13 The largest part of this film review appeared in *AdRem* magazine.

14 *Integratie in zicht. De integratie van migranten in Nederland op acht terreinen nader bekeken* (2016), p. 19, accessed at www.scp.nl/Publicaties/Alle_publicaties/ Publicaties_2016/Integratie_in_zicht, 16 December 2016.

15 Cf. LaCocque (2007).

16 See in Genesis the daughters of Lot, who get their father drunk and seduce him, out of fear of remaining childless – Gen. 19.30–38. The NRSV titles it: 'The Shameful Origin of Moab and Ammon'. As indicated in the previous chapter, the two become in this way the matriarch of the nations of Moab and Ammon.

17 According to Hellerstein (2006), p. 90; according to the online Holocaust Encyclopedia she died in the ghetto of Warsaw, in 1942, www.ushmm.org/wlc/en/ article.php?ModuleId=10007033, accessed 26 December 2016.

18 Contemplation on https://kairoscenter.org/contextual-bible-study/, accessed 21 December 2016.

# Bibliography

Alter, Robert, 2011 (1981), *The Art of Biblical Narrative*, New York: Basic Books.

Anbeek, Christa and Ada de Jong, 2013, *De berg van de ziel: een persoonlijk essay over kwetsbaar leven*, Utrecht: VBK Media.

Anbeek, Christa, 2013, *Aan de heidenen overgeleverd: Hoe theologie de 21ste eeuw kan overleven*, Utrecht: Ten Have (English translation *Delivered unto the Heathens: How theology can survive the 21st century*, accessible online at www.arminiusinstituut.nl/files/Rem_Christa_Anbeek_Engels.pdf).

Armstrong, Karen, 2015, interview, *Trouw* newspaper, 8 December 2015.

Arndt, Emily K., Yvonne Sherwood, and Jean Porter, 2011, *Demanding Our Attention: The Hebrew Bible as a Source for Christian Ethics*, Grand Rapids, Michigan: William B. Eerdmans Publishing.

Atwood, Margaret, 2003, *Oryx and Crake*, London: Bloomsbury.

———, 2009, *The Year of the Flood*, London, Berlin and New York: Bloomsbury.

———, 2013, *Maddaddam*, London, Berlin and New York: Bloomsbury.

Baart, Andries and Christa Carbo, 2013, *De zorgval*, Amsterdam: Life Line.

Balabanski, Vicky and Norman C. Habel, 2002, *The Earth Story in the New Testament*, The Earth Bible, Vol. 5, London, New York and Cleveland: Sheffield Academic Press.

Bauckham, Richard, 2010, *Bible and Ecology: Rediscovering the Community of Creation*, London: Darton, Longman & Todd Ltd.

Bekkenkamp, Jonneke, 1993, *Canon en keuze: Het bijbelse Hooglied en de Twenty-One Love Poems van Adrienne Rich als bronnen van theologie*, Kampen: Kok Agora.

Berryman, Jerome, 1995, *Godly Play: An Imaginative Approach to Religious Education*, Minneapolis: Augsburg Books.

Berryman, Jerome W., 2009, *Teaching Godly Play: How to Mentor the Spiritual Development of Children* (Revised, Expanded), Denver: Morehouse Education Resources.

Bodoff, Lippman, 2005, *The Binding of Isaac: Religious Murders, and Kabbalah: Seeds of Jewish Extremism and Alienation?*, Jerusalem, NY: Devora Publishing Company.

Bonhoeffer, Dietrich, 2010, *Letters and Papers from Prison*, Minneapolis, Minnesota: Fortress Press.

Bourland Huizenga, Annette, 2016, *1–2 Timothy, Titus*, Collegeville, Minnesota: Liturgical Press.

Brandt, Ria van den and Rob Plum (ed.), 1999, *De Theologie Uitgedaagd: Spreken over God binnen het wetenschapsbedrijf*, Zoetermeer: Meinema.

Brown, Brené, 2012, *Daring Greatly: How the Courage to Be Vulnerable Transforms the Way We Live, Love, Parent and Lead*, New York: Penguin Books.

Brown Taylor, Barbara, 2014, *Learning to Walk in the Dark*, New York: HarperOne.

Brueggemann, Walter, 2016, *Money and Possessions. Interpretation Resources for the Use of Scripture in the Church*, Louisville, Kentucky: Westminster John Knox Press.

Cady Stanton, Elisabeth, 1895–1898, *The Woman's Bible*, New York, online edition, www.sacred-texts.com/wmn/wb/, accessed 14 December 2016.

Carley, Keith, 2000, 'Psalm 8. An Apology for Domination', in Norman C. Habel (ed.), *Readings from the Perspective of Earth*, The Earth Bible, Vol. 1, Cleveland and Sheffield: Sheffield Academic Press, pp. 111–24.

Carter Heyward, Isabel, 1982, *The Redemption of God. A Theology of Mutual Relation*, Eugene, Oregon: Wipf and Stock.

Charles, J. B., 1987, *De groene zee is mijn vriendin: Gedichten 1944–1982*, Amsterdam: Uitgeverij De Bezige Bij.

Claiborne, Shane and Jim Wallis, 2006, *The Irresistible Revolution: Living as an Ordinary Radical*, Grand Rapids, Michigan: Zondervan.

Claiborne, Shane, Jonathan Wilson-Hartgrove and Enuma Okoro, 2010, *Common Prayer: A Liturgy for Ordinary Radicals*, Grand Rapids, Michigan: Zondervan.

Coenradie, Sigrid, 2016a, 'Animal Substitution as a Reversed Sacrifice: An Intertextual Reading of Genesis 22 and the Animal Stories of Shūsaku Endō', in Joachim Duyndam, Anne-Marie Korte and Marcel Poorthuis (eds), *Sacrifice in Modernity: Community, Ritual, Identity: From Nationalism and Nonviolence to Health Care and Harry Potter*, Leiden: Brill, pp. 288–308.

———, 2016b, 'Towards a Grown-up Faith: Love as the Basis for Harry Potter's Self-Sacrifice', in Joachim Duyndam, Anne-Marie Korte and Marcel Poorthuis (eds), *Sacrifice in Modernity: Community, Ritual, Identity: From Nationalism and Nonviolence to Health Care and Harry Potter*, Leiden: Brill, pp. 164–80.

———, 2016c, *Vicarious Substitution in the Literary Work of Shūsaku Endō: On Fools, Animals, Objects and Doubles*, Utrecht: Utrecht University.
Coenradie, Sigrid, Bert Dicou and Anne-Claar Thomasson-Rosingh, 2017, *Weg met de Bijbel. Gids voor vrijzinnig bijbellezen*, Utrecht: Meinema.

Dalferth, I. U., 2010, 'Self-sacrifice: From the act of violence to the passion of love', in *International Journal for Philosophy of Religion* 68, pp. 77–94.
Daly, Mary, 1973, *Beyond God the Father: Toward a Philosophy of Women's Liberation*, Boston: Beacon Press.
Doherty, Sean and Jeremy Kidwell, 2015, *Theology and Economics: A Christian Vision of the Common Good*, New York: Palgrave Macmillan.
Doorn, Neelke, Bas van Stokkom and Paul van Tongeren (eds), 2012, *Public Forgiveness in Post-Conflict Contexts*, Series on Transitional Justice, Cambridge: Intersentia Ltd.
Douglas, Mary, 1999, *Leviticus As Literature*, Oxford: Oxford University Press
———, 2004, *Jacob's Tears: The Priestly Work of Reconciliation*, Oxford: Oxford University Press.
Duncan, Celena M., 2000, 'The Book of Ruth: On Boundaries, Love and Truth', in Robert Goss and Mona West (eds), *Take Back the Word: A Queer Reading of the Bible*, Cleveland, Ohio: Pilgrim Press, pp. 92–102.

Endō, Shūsaku, 1973, *A Life of Jesus*, New York/Mahwah: Paulist Press.
———, 1980 (1966), *Silence*, New York: Taplinger Publishing Company.
———, 1996, *Deep River*, translated by Van C. Gessel (Reprint), New York: New Directions.

Feeley-Harnik, Gillian, 1990, 'Naomi and Ruth: Building Up the House of David', in Susan Niditch (ed.), *Text and Tradition: The Hebrew Bible and Folklore*, Semeia studies, Atlanta: Scholars Press, pp. 163–84.
*For God and His Glory Alone: Contribution Relating Some Biblical Principles to the Situation in Northern Ireland*, 1988, Belfast: ECONI.
*For God and His Glory Alone: A Contribution Relating Some Biblical Principles to the Situation in Northern Ireland*, 2013, 3rd edition, Belfast: Contemporary Christianity.

Gafney, Wil, 2009, 'Mother Knows Best. Messianic Surrogacy and Sexploitation in Ruth', in C. A. Kirk-Duggan and T. Pippin (eds), *Mother Goose, Mother Jones, Mommie Dearest. Biblical Mothers and Their Children*, Atlanta: Society of Biblical Literature, pp. 23–36.
Ganiel, Gladys, 2008, *Evangelicalism and Conflict in Northern Ireland*, New York: Palgrave MacMillan.

Gestrich, Christof, 2001, 'God Takes Our Place: A Religious-Philosophical Approach to the Concept of Stellvertretung', in *Modern Theology* 17:3 (July), pp. 313–34.

Girard, René, 1986, *The Scapegoat*, translated by Yvonne Freccero, Baltimore: Johns Hopkins University Press.

Goodman, James, 2013, *Abraham and his Son*, Dingwall, Scotland: Sandstone Press.

Green, Laurie, 2009, *Let's Do Theology: Resources for Contextual Theology*, London and New York: Mowbray.

———, 2015, *Blessed Are the Poor? Urban Poverty and the Church*, London: SCM Press.

*Green Bible (NRSV)*, 2007, New York: HarperCollins.

Guest, Deryn, Robert Goss and Mona West, 2006, *The Queer Bible Commentary*, London: SCM Press.

Habel, Norman C. (ed.), 2000, *Readings from the Perspective of Earth*, The Earth Bible, Vol. 1, Cleveland and Sheffield: Sheffield Academic Press.

———, 2001, *Earth Story in the Psalms and the Prophets*, The Earth Bible, Vol. 4, Cleveland and Sheffield: Sheffield Academic Press.

Habel, Norman C. and Shirley Wurst (eds), 2000, *The Earth Story in Genesis*, The Earth Bible, Vol. 2, Sheffield: Sheffield Academic Press.

———, 2001, *Earth Story in Wisdom Traditions*, The Earth Bible, Vol. 3, Cleveland and Sheffield: Sheffield Academic Press.

Hagdom, Michiel, 1991, 'Connie Palmen onder theologen', in *De Bazuin*, 14 June.

Hampson, Daphne, 1997, *After Christianity*, Valley Forge, Pennsylvania: Trinity Press International.

Harrill, J. Albert, 2006, *Slaves in the New Testament: Literary, Social, and Moral Dimensions*, Minneapolis: Augsburg Fortress.

Harris, Maria, 1996, *Proclaim Jubilee!: A Spirituality for the Twenty-First Century*, Louisville, Kentucky: Westminster Press.

Heijst, Annelies van, 1992, *Verlangen naar de val. Zelfverlies en autonomie in hermeneutiek en ethiek*, Kampen: Kok Agora.

Hellerstein, Kathryn, 2006, 'Ruth Speaks in Yiddish: The Poetry of Rosa Yakubovitsh and Itsik Manger', in Peter S. Hawkins and Lesleigh Cushing Stahlberg (eds), *Scrolls of Love: Ruth and the Song of Songs*, New York: Fordham University Press, pp. 89–109.

Hessel, Ruth and André Mulder, 2014, *Gewoon of beperkt? Hoe jodendom, christendom en islam omgaan met mensen met een handicap*, Zoetermeer: Boekencentrum B.V.

Heyward, Isabel Carter, *see* Carter.

Hillesum, Etty, 1996, *An Interrupted Life: The Diaries, 1941–1943 and Letters from Westerbork*, New York: Henry Holt and Company, Inc.

Hurkmans, Rini, 2003, *Dear Son*, video-installation, 6 minutes, 2003. (Exhibited in the Catharijneconvent Utrecht in 2007.)

Jansen, Tjitske, 2007, *Koerikoeloem*, Amsterdam: Podium B.V. Uitgeverij.
Jasper, David, 1992, *The Study of Literature and Religion: An Introduction*, London: Palgrave Macmillan.
——, 2004, *Short Introduction to Hermeneutics*, Louisville, Kentucky: Westminster John Knox Press.
Jefferson, Thomas, 2016, *De Jefferson bijbel*. Dutch translation and introduction by Sadije Bunjaku and Thomas Heij, Leusden: ISVW Uitgevers.
Jens, Walter and Hans Küng, 1991, *Literature & Religion: Pascal, Gryphius, Lessing, Hölderlin, Novalis, Kierkegaard, Dostoevsky, Kafka*, St Paul, Minnesota: Paragon House Publishers.

Kidwell, Jeremy and Sean Doherty (eds), 2015, *Theology and Economics*, New York: Palgrave Macmillan.
Kwok, Pui-lan, 2003, *Discovering the Bible in the Non-Biblical World*, Eugene, Oregon: Wipf and Stock.

LaCocque, André, 2006, 'Subverting the Biblical World: Sociology and Politics in the Book of Ruth', in Peter S. Hawkins and Lesleigh Cushing Stahlberg (eds), *Scrolls of Love: Ruth and the Song of Songs*, New York: Fordham University Press, pp. 20–30.
Lawrence, Louise J., 2009, *The Word in Place: Reading the New Testament in Contemporary Contexts*, London: SPCK Publishing.
Levine, Amy-Jill and Maria Mayo Robbins (eds), 2006, *A Feminist Companion to the New Testament Apocrypha*, London and New York: Bloomsbury; T&T Clark.
Löwisch, Ingeborg, 2013, *Genealogy Composition in Response to Trauma. Gender and Memory in 1 Chronicles 1–9 and the Documentary Film My Life*, PhD dissertation, Utrecht 2013.
*Liedboek. Zingen en bidden in huis en kerk*, 2013, edited by Interkerkelijke Stichting voor het Kerklied, Den Haag, Zoetermeer: BV Liedboek.
Luyendijk, Joris, 2015, *Dit kan niet waar zijn: onder bankiers*, Amsterdam: Atlas Contact Uitgeverij.
——, 2016, *Swimming with Sharks: Inside the World of the Bankers*, Norwich: Guardian Faber Publishing.

Marion, Jean-Luc, 2002, *Being Given: Towards a Phenomenology of Givenness*, Stanford University Press, translated by Jeffrey L. Kosky.
Marsman, H., 1940, *Tempel en Kruis*, Amsterdam: Em. Querido.
McFadyen, Alistair and Marcel Sarot (eds), 2001, *Forgiveness and Truth, Explorations in Contemporary Theology*, Edinburgh and New York: Bloomsbury; T&T Clark.

McFague, Sallie, 2001, *Life Abundant (Searching for a New Framework): Rethinking Theology and Economy for a Planet in Peril*, Minneapolis, Minnesota: Fortress Press.

———, 2008, *A New Climate for Theology: God, the World, and Global Warming*, Minneapolis, Minnesota: Fortress Press.

Mtshiselwa, V. Ndikhokele N., 2016, 'Reading Ruth 4 and Leviticus 25:8–55 in the light of the landless and poor women in South Africa: A conversation with Fernando F. Segovia and Ernesto 'Che' Guevara', in HTS Teologiese Studies / Theological Studies 72 (1), online edition, http://www.hts.org.za/index.php/HTS/article/view/3140, accessed 14 December 2016.

Multatuli, 1987 (1860), *Max Havelaar: Or the Coffee Auctions of a Dutch Trading Company*, translated by Roy Edwards, London: Penguin Books Ltd.

Newsom, Carol A., Sharon H. Ringe and Jacqueline E. Lapsley (eds), 2012, *Women's Bible Commentary*. Third edition: revised and updated, Louisville, Kentucky: Westminster John Knox.

Nissen, P., 2016, '"In alles zit een barst." Een spiritualiteit van de kwetsbaarheid', *Speling* 2016-3, pp. 13–20.

Nouwen, Henri J. M., Donald P. McNeill and Douglas A. Morrison, 1983, *Compassion: A Reflection on the Christian Life*, New York: Image Books/Doubleday.

Nouwen, Henri J. M., 1997, *Adam: God's Beloved*, Maryknoll, NY: Orbis Books.

Nussbaum, M. C., 1986, *The Fragility of Goodness: Luck and Ethics in Greek Tragedy and Philosophy*, Cambridge: Cambridge University Press.

Pettit, Alice, 2015, *Jubilee Spirituality, Seeking a Free and Equal Society*, Cambridge: Grove Books Ltd.

Pope Francis, 2015, *Laudato Si'. On Care for Our Common Home*, London: Catholic Truth Society.

Primavesi, Anne, 1991, *From Apocalypse to Genesis: Ecology, Feminism and Christianity*, Minneapolis: Fortress Press.

Riches, John, 2010, *What Is Contextual Bible Study?: A Practical Guide with Group Studies for Advent and Lent*, London: SPCK.

Ricœur, Paul, 1984, *Time and Narrative*, Vol. 1, translated by Kathleen McLaughlin and David Pellauer, Chicago: University of Chicago Press.

———, 1991, *Oneself as Another*, translated by Kathleen Blamey, Chicago: University of Chicago Press.

Rieger, Joerg, 2011, 'Alternative Images of God in the Global Economy' in Jione Havea and Clive Pearson (eds), *Out of Place: Doing Theology on the Crosscultural Brink*, London and Oakville, CT: Routledge, pp. 26–41.

Sarot, Marcel, 1995, 'Divine compassion and the meaning of life', *Scottish Journal of Theology*, pp. 155–68.

Schottroff, Luise, Marie-Theres Wacker and Martin Rumscheidt, 2012, *Feminist Biblical Interpretation: A Compendium of Critical Commentary on the Books of the Bible and Related Literature*, Grand Rapids, Michigan: William B. Eerdmans Publishing.

Schussler Fiorenza, Elisabeth, 1984, *In Memory of Her: A Feminist Theological Reconstruction of Christian Origins*, New York: Crossroads.

——, 2001, *Wisdom Ways: Introducing Feminist Biblical Interpretation*, Maryknoll, NY: Orbis Books.

Sedmak, Clemens, 2002, *Doing Local Theology: A Guide for Artisans of a New Humanity*, Faith & Cultures Series, Maryknoll, NY: Orbis Books.

Sherwood, Yvonne, 2012, *Biblical Blaspheming: Trials Of The Sacred For A Secular Age*, New York: Cambridge University Press.


*The Poverty and Justice Bible. Contemporary English Version*, 2008, Swindon: Bible Society.

*The Queer Bible Commentary*, 2006, edited by Deryn Guest, Robert Goss and Mona West, London: SCM Press.

Thomasson-Rosingh, Anne-Claar, 2015, *Searching for the Holy Spirit: Feminist Theology and Traditional Doctrine*, London: Routledge.

Trible, Phyllis, 1984, *Texts of Terror: Literary Feminist Readings of Biblical Narratives*, Overtures to Biblical Theology, Philadelphia: Fortress Press.

——, and Letty M. Russell (eds), 2006, *Hagar, Sarah, and Their Children: Jewish, Christian, and Muslim Perspectives*, Louisville, Kentucky: Westminster John Knox Press.


Urbrock, William J., 2001, 'The Earth Song in Psalms 90–92', in Norman C. Habel (ed.), *The Earth Story in the Psalms and the Prophets*, The Earth Bible, Vol. 4, Cleveland and Sheffield: Sheffield Academic Press, pp. 65–83.


Van Nistelrooij, Inge, 2014, *Sacrifice: A Care-Ethical Reappraisal of Sacrifice and Self-sacrifice*, Vianen: BOXPress.

Verbin, N., 2006, 'Faith and Fiction', in Lieve Boeven, Joeri Schrijvers, Wessel Stoker and Hendrik Vroom (eds), *Faith in the Enlightenment?: The Critique of the Enlightenment Revisited*, Amsterdam, NY: Rodopi, pp. 182–94.


Wells, Samuel, 2004, *Improvisation: The Drama of Christian Ethics*, Grand Rapids, Michigan: Brazos Press.

Wiesenthal, Simon, 1997, *The Sunflower: On the Possibilities and Limits of Forgiveness* (original edition 1969, extended edition 1997), New York: Schocken.

Williams, Rowan, 1996, 'The body's grace', in C. Hefling (ed.), *Our Selves, Our Souls, & Bodies: Sexuality and the Household of God*, Cambridge, Massachusetts: Cowley Publications, pp. 58–68.

———, 2012, *Faith in the Public Square*, London and New York: Bloomsbury.

Wiman, Christian, 2013, *My Bright Abyss: Meditation of a Modern Believer*, New York: Farrar, Straus and Giroux.

Wit, Hans de and Janet Dyk, 2015, *Bible and Transformation: The Promise of Intercultural Bible Reading*, Atlanta: SBL Press.

Wright, T. R., 1988, *Theology and Literature*, Oxford: Basil Blackwell.

# Acknowledgements

Chapters 1–3 and 4–5 were originally published in Sigrid Coenradie, Bert Dicou and Anna-Claar Thomasson-Rosingh, *Weg met de Bijbel*, Copyright © 2017, Uitgeverij Meinema, www.uitgeverijmeinema.nl. Used by permission.

The 'Blessing of the Land or a Garden' on p. 123 is taken from *Common Prayer: A Liturgy for Ordinary Radicals* by Shane Claiborne, Jonathan Wilson-Hartgrove and Enuma Okoro. Copyright © 2010 by The Simple Way and School for Conversion. Use by permission of Zondervan, www.zondervan.com.

The fragments from *The Year of the Flood*, by Margaret Atwood, Copyright © 2009, on pp. 120 and 127 are used by permission by Bloomsbury Publishing

The fragments from Pope Francis' Encyclical *Laudato Si'*, Copyright © 2015, on pp. 113 and 116 are used by permission by Libreria Editrice Vaticana

The lines from the song 'Lied van Ruth' by Stef Bos on pp. 205 and 218 are taken from the webpage www.stefbos.nl/page/Liedteksten/detail/1827/Lied_van_Ruth. Copyright © 2008 Stef Bos. Used by permission of Stef Bos, www.stefbos.nl.